God's Own Language

God's Own Language
Architectural Drawing in the Twelfth Century

Karl Kinsella

THE MIT PRESS
Cambridge, Massachusetts . London, England

1 Noah's Ark in Twelfth-Century Paris

One morning, sometime in the early twelfth century, the theologian and teacher Hugh of Saint Victor left his cell inside the abbey of Saint Victor in Paris and went for a walk. His stroll soon took him along the banks of the Seine, and as he gazed across the assorted vessels his curious and energetic mind, perhaps naturally, turned to the tricky problem of Noah and his ark. What especially caught Hugh's attention was that the barges and sailing boats in front of him could stay afloat only by employing a keel—something that could cut through the water and prevent the vessel from toppling over.[1] But such a simple observation made a fundamental historical problem abundantly clear, for as Hugh knew only too well, the Bible recounts how Noah built his boat—the first-ever structure, on land or water—according to instructions relayed directly from God. These instructions must have been precise since the ark floats with Noah, his family, and the animals inside it, but for those wanting to picture the ark, the account in the book of Genesis is not very clear. The general dimensions are outlined but not whether it should have a window, what type of roof it should have, or even the shape of its hull; there were many questions unanswered. Earlier writers, such as Saint Augustine and Origen, stated that the ark had no keel, and that issues such as whether it would float or not did not really matter since it was, after all, created by God, who was all-powerful.

Seeing the boats in front of him on the Seine and especially their keels, Hugh realized that the ark's design, as conceived by these earlier authors, would immediately fail, and with it the salvation of humanity.[2] His observation, in this sense, disagreed with what he had been taught to be true, and to disagree with people such as Saint Augustine was, frankly, no small matter.

This book is not about Noah's ark or even, for the most part, about Hugh's description of it. Instead, it is about the visual language of architecture; Hugh, his protégé Richard, and their home of Saint Victor in Paris during the twelfth century are an insufficiently studied part of that history and of architectural drawing more widely. This language of architecture was both visual and textual, and applied to structures such as Noah's ark because it could make sense of the strangeness inherent in biblical descriptions. Hugh no doubt would have agreed with the modern statement that "the ark is a symbol of artificial order which floats on natural disorder."[3] From the perspective of Hugh, as a man embedded within a culture of religious and intellectual elitism, the past was defined by the Old Testament and the walking, talking, and communicative God that inhabited it, and the ark was both a historical structure and a platform for better understanding a strange world. Despite the ark's obvious importance, Hugh had no way to visualize it or to represent a historically correct version of it for his intended readers, since in the twelfth century there was little in the way of a recognized formal language of architectural drawing, and plans and elevations were rare. If Hugh did make a drawing, no matter how rudimentary, none has been found. All that is left is a detailed written description of how one could draw it, a text as opaque and convoluted as the complex system of allegory Hugh hoisted onto the ark as a platform for his theology. The difficulty in understanding Hugh's vision for the ark and other buildings could be ameliorated only by drawing it.

In the Old Testament, God gave Noah plans for the ark, and its form was thought to retain the primordial divine spark of its heavenly origins. In this sense, the language of architecture is the language through which God speaks to humanity and his creation. The ark is just one structure among the many described in the Bible, and all are important because they tell something of the mind of God. The architectural nature of God's creation was recognized in the Middle Ages and beyond. Indeed, from the twelfth century, God is sometimes depicted holding a compass,

Fig. 1.1 God creating the universe and holding a compass. Vienna, National Library of Austria, MS 2554, f. 1v.

the tool of the medieval architect and geometers. In this guise, the profession of architect, a profession barely in existence as we might recognize it today, is propelled to the highest status. Concurrently, God becomes an architect, the builder and intellectual driving force behind the universe. We see God, larger than life, at work during the act of creation, not clicking his fingers and transforming nothing into something, but hunched over his work in the guise of both artist and artisan.

And the ark was his first construction. Its physical, material, and historical reality for someone such as Hugh was important to know and to understand, because in doing so it would be possible to know God better. Because of the ark's importance to the history of humanity, medieval authors felt an urgency to understand that language and to comprehend even the simplest elements of the ark and biblical architecture more generally. How else to explain the various and many representations of the ark that exist today?

Many people before and after Hugh searched for the true form of the ark, believing in its key importance as a structure that marked the beginning of humanity's compulsion to build things bigger than themselves. The results of these searches usually say more about the concerns of the present than about the past. The problem was that the ark's appearance cannot be easily understood based on the biblical description alone. Although there were two main Christian theories about the ark's appearance—that it was a long-tapered pyramid or a long flat-bottomed vessel of the kind Hugh rejected—representations of the ark could vary quite dramatically.[4] For example, a third-century fresco portrays it as a simple box from which Noah emerges to greet the returning dove that told him there was dry land near (fig. 1.2). The form reflects the Hebrew term for the ark, which simply means "chest" or "box."[5] In this sense, the ark is a literal melding of word and image, a pictorial pun in which structure or space play no part in the ark's realization to Christian audiences. From the very earliest representations of the ark and other biblical structures, language played a key part in how the past could be visualized, in this case providing a like-for-like indication of Noah's ark without any suggestion that it should be embellished. From a Christian point of view, it is the word of God made manifest in the plainest way possible.

This linguistic focus is one of many ways in which the ark is made real for medieval audiences. In other examples, the ark's physicality and status as, first and foremost, a vessel on the water comes into focus. For example, in the half-page image of the ark in the Old English Hexateuch—a collection of the first six books of the Bible—the ark has both architectonic and naval elements that speak to the experiences of a contemporary audience (fig. 1.3).[6] Its form is like that of a longboat seen on the seas of early medieval England, a vision of the present projected back into the

Fig. 1.2 Noah emerging from the ark. Rome, Catacombs of Saints Marcellinus and Peter.

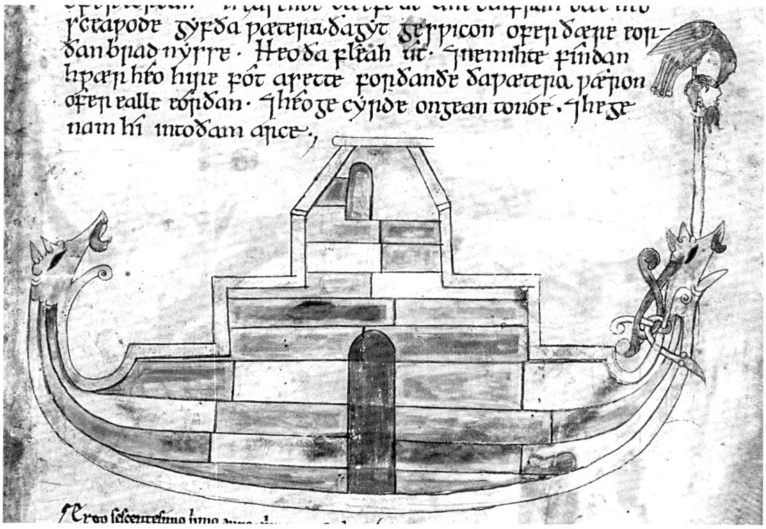

Fig. 1.3 The ark as an early medieval longship. London, British Library, Cotton MS Claudius B IV, f. 15r.

past. It is an anachronism that prioritizes a recognizable visual language over any attempt at historical accuracy, but in the process gives status to all such vessels as having something like the original form of God's creation. It sanctifies the contemporary present through its anachronism, creating a link between the present and the past.

The language of dimensions and precise cubit measurements in the biblical account offered a suggestion to some authors that mathematics and geometry could clarify matters. This gave rise to representations in a tidy and schematic style that convey the structure's overall appearance, enhanced by using geometrical instruments such as a compass. For example, an early twelfth-century copy of the Apocalypse contains an elevation of Noah's ark, where the animals appear in pairs and in separate compartments, giving the image a distinct suggestion of order amid what would no doubt have been chaotic scenes of animals living so close to one another (fig. 1.4). In this case, the artist has taken care to use a straight edge to construct the square compartments, and even the diagonal lines at the intersections suggest how the timbers were joined to each other by Noah according to God's instructions. At the top, Noah welcomes back the dove carrying proof that the flood waters have receded and that the world is safe again.

Fig. 1.4 The ark with individual rooms for the animals. Manchester, The John Rylands Library, MS 8, f. 15r.

The compartmentalization of this structure parallels Massimo Scolari's observation that the ark is the embodiment of order,[7] where both the ark's clear internal layout and the importance of geometry in interpretations of it are significant. In the twelfth century, the point was not to detail to the reader exactly how the ark floated or the arrangement of the animals, but simply to imply a sense of order. In later examples, artists leveraged the significant technological development of the sciences to create rational and hence believable interpretations of Noah's floating menagerie. This iconography of order, like a visual list, begins to address questions of realism in a much more comprehensive way than Hugh's simple observation that an ark should float in the same way as all vessels. This sense of order is foregrounded in Athanasius Kircher's late seventeenth-century series of plans, elevations, and dramatic scenes of the ark on the waters of chaos. These pictures and the mathematical preciseness of their form contain a rhetorical power, their clarity testifying to the truth of Kircher's recreation and giving them a "reality effect" (fig. 1.5). The ark, like so many biblical images, reflects Kircher's historical methodology, a testimony to the Enlightenment, where the methods and ideas of a changing present are applied to the past, each iteration taking the viewer and reader a step closer to the "real ark." But there is no real ark, only an object that reappears over and over again in our conversations about the past and how we can understand it. For Hugh of Saint Victor, God gave drawings to humanity to turn his imagination into something material: the ark, the tabernacle, Solomon's temple—all of these buildings were first conceived of in two dimensions, given as instructions to humanity before being realized in fact. The drawings are God-given instructions, God's voice written in stone and on parchment, and so architectural drawings are a language God uses to talk to his people. An interrogation of biblical architectural representations always indicates something about the historical present, whether it is the seventh or seventeenth century, but in doing so, that investigation can also be a platform for examining the history of drawing.

When looking through the history of architectural drawing in particular, however, the twelfth century is nothing more than an empty space. There are so few examples that if these drawings are the language of God, it is a time of silence. Underlining this absence is the complete lack of architectural treatises written between Vitruvius in the first century BCE and Alberti in the fifteenth century. The fact that no author directly discussed the subject during the intervening period, however, should not be taken as apathy toward its practice and processes; instead, the underlying interest in architecture remained hidden within the cloisters of medieval Europe, kept there by monks and canons who had a highly developed sense of spatial representation both in their imaginations and on the surface of the page. Within these cloisters, there is a protohistory of architectural drawing, but it has never played a significant role in studies of the subject and its origins in the central Middle Ages. There is, however, an overlooked set of medieval manuscripts originally made in Hugh's abbey of Saint Victor and copied widely across Europe. The drawings in these manuscripts testify to both the importance of architectural drawing and their significant development during the twelfth century.

In the middle of the twelfth century, Hugh's protégé Richard of Saint Victor (d. 1173) wrote a biblical commentary—known by its Latin title *In visionem Ezechielis* (On Ezekiel's vision)—which considered the series of buildings that the prophet Ezekiel described in a vision of a temple the Israelites were prophesied to build.[8] The title is modern, but it reflects the contents accurately with its emphasis on the importance of seeing what the prophet saw, and also the importance of the reader seeing the drawings in the commentary. It is then a vision in two ways, one belonging to the prophet and a second for the contemporary reader who has visions of Ezekiel's experiences. There are over a dozen plans and elevations to help readers visualize the buildings Ezekiel saw, making Richard's interpretation of this biblical past plain for all to see. The drawings are the earliest to employ a combination of plans and elevations to illustrate several buildings and their relationship with one another. As a result, Richard's commentary took a leap forward in comparison to Hugh's solely textual description of the ark. Just like the biblical description of the ark, the words and phrases Ezekiel uses can be difficult to follow and even, at times, contradictory, leaving the reader unsure of what the prophet saw. In presenting the biblical past as a series of drawings, Richard was forced to be crystal-clear in his commentary; there could be no fudging of or disregard for inconvenient dimensions. Such clarity in visual form embodies a significant rhetorical power, since, in this case, seeing is believing.

The drawings for *In visionem Ezechielis* demonstrate an extraordinary capacity to communicate a clear vision of the past, and the fact that they were conceived and drawn in a cloister should not stop them from being incorporated into the wider history of architecture. Even today, the images in *In visionem Ezechielis* are easily legible as architectural drawings despite being 850 years old; they still communicate the most important parts of Richard's peculiar interpretation of the prophet's vision. In this sense, the drawings' legibility transcends language and time, as clearly now as on the day they were made. They are a language unaffected by

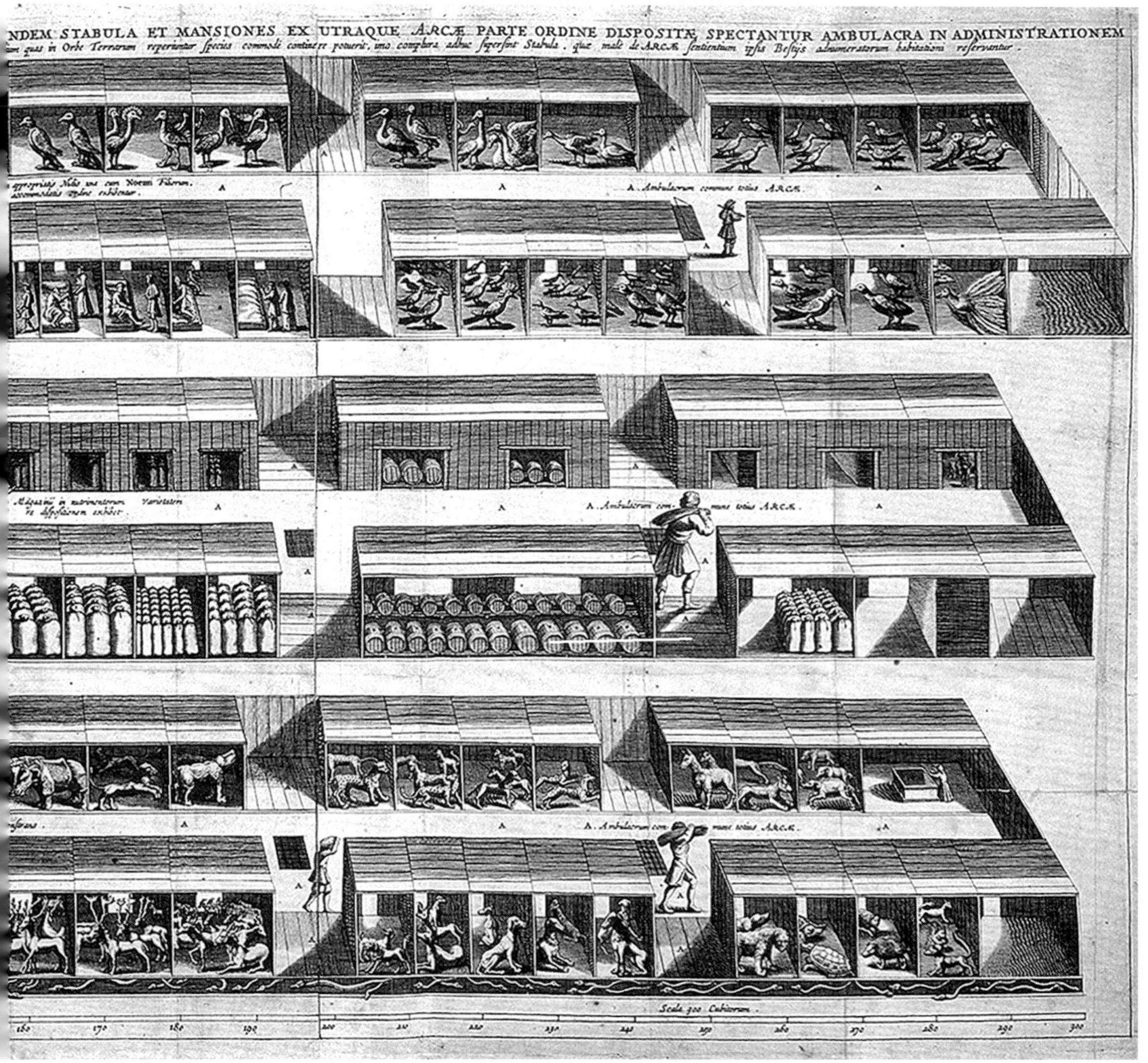

Fig. 1.5 A detailed study of the ark and its parts. Athanasius Kircher, *Arca Noë*. Amsterdam, 1675, fp. 46/47.

time and space that can still speak to a modern audience with only a little exposition. *In visionem Ezechielis* is not without errors, but the visual strategies brought to bear are decades, if not centuries, ahead of their time.

The purpose of Richard's commentary is straightforward: to give readers a sense of what Ezekiel saw by rendering the heavenly buildings in both text and image. This simple aim is a direct result of Hugh's approach to history, which was to bring the past closer to the present, to draw a line between the twelfth-century world and the biblical one. By having one foot firmly placed in the present, Hugh and Richard were able to bring the past to life in a much more vivid way than many other contemporary authors. And by including drawings in *In visionem Ezechielis*, Richard made these links between past and present explicit.

The innovations in Richard's drawings include at least two sectional elevations, the first of their kind, each illustrating the relationship between the interior and exterior appearance of two buildings. Richard is also the first to use the term "plan" in reference to an architectural drawing, paving the way for the language of architecture used today. *In visionem Ezechielis* is the first work to contain these recognizable methods and language for representing the world. While this biblical commentary is the product of one abbey's cloister, their presence speaks to a coherent and nascent literacy in the interpretation of plans and elevations. Such visual literacy no doubt existed to a degree in contemporary masons' yards, but the lack of sources detailing the use of such drawings means evidence for readers' engagement with plans and elevations is lost. Instead, twelfth- and thirteenth-century readers engaged with and copied Richard's drawings in a consistent fashion, suggesting that there was a sizable pool of people who could interpret the drawings along the lines Richard intended. The order in which Richard presents the drawings demonstrates a strategy to lead his readers carefully through the material, illustrating Ezekiel's vision one step at a time.

Of all the buildings described in the Bible, Richard chose to focus on Ezekiel's temple complex. There were no earlier drawings and no substantial commentaries on the temple's appearance, meaning his decision to write about it was an original choice. The details of the temple complex are unclear from the prophet's description, but the general structures are apparent. They are introduced as a visionary experience, something not yet real but a promise of the future. When Ezekiel first saw the complex, he was met by a man with a "brazen complexion" who escorted him around the buildings and took measurements of the different parts. The complex was situated on a mountainside, and the temple was located near the center, on a plateau at the top. Around the temple were three concentric square atria, which were set aside for different people and for certain liturgical functions. The largest atrium, which encompassed the whole temple complex, was 600 cubits square; the middle atrium was 500 cubits; and the smallest one, on a flat surface, was 100 cubits square.[9]

There were gatehouses on three sides connecting each atrium to the other, allowing Ezekiel to move between all the inner parts. The gatehouses are described in detail, painstakingly so. Ezekiel tells his readers that Israelite priests made sacrifices in them, so they also had kitchens. At the very center of everything was an altar on which sacrifices were to be made, and just to the west of it was the temple itself. The temple had two rooms on the ground floor, a larger one called the *sanctum* and a smaller one at the end called the *sanctum sanctorum* (Holy of Holies).

Ezekiel's eight chapters on his architectural vision contain some of the most detailed architectural descriptions in the Old and New Testaments, but they are difficult to follow because Ezekiel moves from building to building and atrium to atrium in a very confusing manner. For example, the breadth of the threshold for the gatehouse is described as one reed (i.e., six cubits), but then the "threshold of the gate by the porch of the gate within, was one reed," then later "he measured the breadth of the threshold of the gate, ten cubits."[10] The passage does not make clear what part of the building is being measured or how one part relates to another. Unlike all earlier commentaries, Richard's *In visionem Ezechielis* explains the appearance of these buildings, as if the prophet's writings described physical structures through which one could really move and not imaginary buildings that existed only in the vision God granted to his prophet.

There was an appetite for understanding Ezekiel's account, even long after the twelfth century. Twenty-two copies of *In visionem Ezechielis* are currently known, suggesting that the work was popular in its own time and for approximately three-quarters of a century after Richard's death.[11] Importantly, the commentary was not confined to a single manuscript witness, written by Richard and never reproduced in significant numbers. Its dispersal suggests a rich and varied audience, despite or perhaps even because of how original it seemed, especially to a twelfth-century audience. At the end of the century, Peter the Chanter—an important theologian at Notre Dame cathedral, itself only a short walk from Saint Victor—complained about *In visionem Ezechielis* and the wasted effort in making "mechanical drawings for the buildings and for the lineaments of an imaginary Temple."[12] Peter's words show that Richard's drawings represented a significant undertaking in paying for and taking the time to reproduce the images. The fact that *In visionem Ezechielis* was never completed is perhaps a consequence of this expense of time and money, as Richard was unable to continue to create figures for every building that Ezekiel described.[13] Peter's complaint also demonstrates that the drawings stood out to contemporary readers, and while Peter was skeptical about their worth, the almost two dozen surviving copies suggest many other readers disagreed.

To many, the phrase "architectural drawing" will conjure images of blueprints and technical drawings created in an architect's office. One definition describes them as a "representation in graphic form of a building or part of a building, either as a stage in the planned construction of an actual edifice or as an imaginative act in its own right."[14] This gives an inclusive and open-ended meaning to the term, encompassing all pictures of buildings derived from a creator's imagination. It is, perhaps, too open-ended. Following this definition, the historiography of the subject would look very different, not least because most of the scholarship focuses on the early modern period. Indeed, even the numerous buildings, crenellations, city walls, and other architectural elements that frequently appear in medieval manuscripts fit into this semantic field, but no one describes these as "architectural drawings." Where those early drawings are evocative, devices that merely set the scene for biblical or hagiographical narratives, the phrase "architectural drawing" should at least partly define the drawings' form or the maker's intentions.[15]

There is no medieval definition of architectural drawing, no reflection on its purpose or appearance; yet this lacuna is not surprising, considering the lack of treatises or even examples from the period. Writing on architecture itself did exist, however, and it is possible to get a sense of what people such as Richard thought about the buildings around them. Again, Hugh offers some insight into the twelfth century, writing: "In every building there are three things which ought chiefly to be considered: order, layout, and precise measurement, having determined the beginning and end."[16] "Order" calls for architecture to be conceived and executed along a rationalized system; "layout" prioritizes a building's footprint on the earth, such as in a plan; and "precise measurement" dictates that a good building should have an internal consistency and a meticulous approach to the bounding of space. Hugh's criteria accurately characterize the purpose of Richard's drawings, suggesting that they are to be interpreted as architectural objects that "determined the beginning" of Ezekiel's vision for the medieval reader. Accordingly, they are not scientific figures, although, as shown later, they have some affinity with such figures; instead, they are rooted in contemporary practices of geometry.

The critical reflection on architecture suited the intellectualized worldview of Hugh and Richard, but their writing on the subject is found deep within biblical commentaries and not within treatises specifically on architecture. For that reason, it is often Alberti's definition of architectural drawing that dictates discussions. Alberti writes:

> The difference between the drawings of the painter and those of the architect is this: the former takes pains to emphasize the relief of objects in paintings with shading and diminishing lines and angles; the architect rejects shading, but takes his projections from the ground plan and, without altering the lines and by maintaining the true angles, reveals the extent and shape of each elevation and side—he is one who desires his work to be judged not by deceptive appearances but according to certain calculated standards.[17]

Alberti's definition describes a series of representational techniques, a way of creating a two-dimensional world that is fundamentally different from illustrations or even doodles of buildings. Alberti also sees this way of representing the world as intrinsically connected to the needs of architects, who require a specific mode of communication to channel their imagination to the viewer.

If Alberti's definition of architectural drawing relies on its belonging to the architect's domain, then architectural drawing cannot be easily identified in the twelfth century. The word "architect" and its meanings were ambiguous until the role became better defined toward the end of the thirteenth century.[18] Discussions of its medieval meanings focus on terminology as distinct from any architectural images or practices, and do not investigate a possible relationship between language and practice. Instead of the architect of a building, there is a focus on the individual roles of workers in a medieval building site. On the other hand, the growing number of extant architectural drawings from the beginning of the thirteenth century suggests a strong association with the expansion of the Gothic style in western Europe, and the linear forms of the style may be a result of the inherent linearity of drawing.[19] Attempts to link architect, architecture, and drawing tacitly assume that the only reason one would make a drawing such as the one Alberti describes is for a building project: it is something an architect makes to convey a building's form. There need not be such an exclusive association for picturing the world in the way Alberti envisions. Hugh's three criteria describe a process whereby architecture is made, not by a certain profession but by anyone, including the biblical commentator. While making architectural drawings is an act of communication that embodies a visual mode, it is not intrinsically tied to the profession of architecture.

Conceiving a design begins within the imagination before it can take shape on the surface of a page, but the two spaces—imagination and page—are linked. The dialectical nature of conception and realization is an inherent part of architectural drawing, as is the impossibility of perfectly modeling a building on the surface of a page.[20] Any architectural image is a "representation of something in that it is not the thing in itself," and relies on geometry as the medium facilitating a transposition from two dimensions into a third.[21] It has a "distinctiveness from and unlikeness to the things that it represented."[22] The drawing represents the original statement of purpose but is a performance in itself, a melody from which music draws energy and inspiration, a hint of it still present, but only if you listen closely sometimes. By recognizing the impossibility of a complete representation, drawings must have another definition besides one dominated by their inherent limitations. They can instead be an "explanatory device," an explanation or argument rendered visually for an audience capable of interpreting the lines, dots, and colors accurately.[23] Such drawings are the original movement of architecture, and the physical rendering of the building is, to a greater or lesser degree, contingent on the existence of the drawing. In this sense, architectural drawings echo God's own language to his people, formed as architectural instructions and completed by them and not by the architect. Ezekiel's buildings, however, were never constructed, failing to come down from heaven once the Israelites returned to their homeland; indeed, the first time they came into any form of physical existence is in Richard's mind, in his commentary and on the very corporeal pages of the medieval manuscripts that contain them. The *In visionem Ezechielis* drawings are truly original in many ways, then, both for their precociously modern way of thinking through architectural space and its representations, but also as the first time, so far as is known, that Ezekiel's vision became real. This link between imagination and material form is key to the making of architectural representations both today and in the twelfth century. In this way, that phrase "architectural drawing" can move through time to encompass more than mere technical drawings. At the same time, for Hugh and Richard, the bread held up at the climax of the mass is the body of God, not a symbol and certainly not a metaphor, but one and the same with God. Similarly, God's architecture defines how he communicated with his people, and the drawing is the visual manifestation of his voice and his intentions.

Since the fifteenth century, there has been a tendency to remove the Middle Ages from the discourse of architectural drawings, due to their supposed lack of sophistication in comparison to the early modern period's examples. Alberti's *De re aedificatoria* was influenced by Vitruvius's first-century BCE *De architectura*, leaving the twelfth century devoid of influence.[24] There is, however, no reason for Alberti to have known Richard's writings; indeed, many late medieval and early modern writers deliberately avoided the scholastic musings of the twelfth and thirteenth century. But Richard fills the gap between antiquity and the Renaissance in many ways, including his delineation of architectural drawing into types. While there are few drawings from Vitruvius's time, he describes and names three types: *ichnographia*, *orthographia*, and *scaenographia*, which correspond respectively to plans, elevations, and drawings that possibly incorporate perspective.[25] His clear and concise description of the drawings' form and purpose indicates that they were recognized by the Roman architect and that making them was an important skill in one's education.[26] Vitruvius's clear process, as has been argued, was "forgotten in the Middle Ages" and had to be redeveloped alongside the spread of the Gothic style, attaining the modern modes of representing only at the start of the sixteenth century.[27] Such a teleological understanding of drawing's history, oriented toward what it can say about the present and not the past, skips people like Richard who did not work with the same aims as architects such as Brunelleschi and his professional colleagues. The bypassing of the Middle Ages was the aim of Renaissance humanists who sought to tie their own intellectual achievements to antiquity, extolling the fact that civilization had been rebooted after a "dark age." For example, Poggio Bracciolini was said to have "rediscovered" the *De architectura* in Saint Gall in 1416 and used it to revive the language of antiquity during the Italian Renaissance, which is why fifteenth-century architectural drawings often used the same language for drawings, calling them *ichnographia* and *orthographia*.[28] Like many discoveries of so-called lost works, *De architectura* was there all along in the libraries of Europe, read and digested by people for centuries, but as its content was not widely dispersed among architects, the early modern humanist deemed it newly discovered in their time, with little acknowledgment that Vitruvius's work was read throughout the Middle Ages.[29]

Although a long literature exists about medieval architectural drawings, it is usually found in studies whose focus is on something else and never exclusively on the development of the genre. For now, it is helpful to track what some people have written about the subject by taking the fall of Rome as the beginning of the Middle Ages—an arbitrary starting point, but useful in that it led to the deterioration of Roman architectural education. Architectural education degenerated because of the decline of the Western Roman Empire starting in the fifth century, resulting in buildings that were less complex than those built during the Roman Empire's heyday. While the decline was felt less in the eastern part of the empire, Byzantine architects were still not likely to use plans beyond the seventh century; instead, experience and rules of thumb were passed on from master to apprentice.[30] However, training for architects continued and a profession called "architecture" still existed, standing in contrast to the situation in Western Europe's early Middle Ages. Within this context, there is a useful distinction between architectural drawings and drawings of architecture, where the latter are illustrative only and not carried out by trained people to solve problems of construction.[31] No drawings, however, were used along the lines that Alberti would have expected.

Building on Alberti's definition, a question looms over any history of architectural drawing: How could there be architectural drawings without an architect to make them? Any answer must acknowledge that classical approaches to architectural drawing continued to exist outside of what was left of the profession after the decline of Roman influences. Drawings were studied by authors who communicated visually by using the representational language of antiquity, derived from their eagerness to devour the legacy of Greece and Rome. These intellectuals were not builders, but they were architects. Such a distinction had already been established at the beginning of the Middle Ages. Saint Paul, the convert to Christianity whose life and letters make up much of the New Testament, refers to himself as the "wise architect" who has "laid the foundation" for the Church according to Christ's instructions (1 Cor. 3:10). In this sense, Paul uses the term figuratively, as one who is responsible for building Christian communities around the Mediterranean world. Even in Pevsner's discussion of the term "architect" in the Middle Ages, he never touches on this type of significance, but it is exactly what people such as Richard of Saint Victor understood "architect" to mean.

It should not be surprising that a twelfth-century cleric such as Richard was interested in the writing of antiquity. Paris, at this time, was alive with the same intellectual curiosity that led to Hugh observing boats on the Seine. The twin platforms of Vitruvius's *De architectura*, with its strange Greek terms for architectural drawings, and Saint Paul's self-identified status as a figurative Christian architect provided an important context for Richard to write *In visionem Ezechielis*. It has long been known that *De architectura* was read from the beginning of the Middle Ages onward, appearing in dozens of manuscripts from the period.[32] Even if Vitruvius's text may not have been known directly, there were abridged versions circulating that would have been quicker for copyists to make. In the third century, an author known as M. Cetius Faventinus wrote a book on architecture called *De diversis fabricis architectonicae* which relied heavily on Vitruvius's *De architectura*, and it is possible that copies of Vitruvius's text that appear in medieval libraries derive from this shorter version.[33] Faventinus decided that Vitruvius's description of architectural drawings was important enough to include in his own work and, more importantly, they were read by medieval audiences. One ninth-century person, for example, questioned the meaning of the Vitruvian term *scaenographia*, which suggests that they knew a version of *De architectura* and had read the section on types of architectural drawings. That this writer did not ask the meaning of *ichnographia* and *orthographia* suggests they believed they already knew the meaning of these terms.[34] Antiquity was a presence in the writings of medieval scholars, especially the highly educated Victorine scholars.

When turning the pages of *In visionem Ezechielis*, one is tempted to think that Richard had seen examples of plans and elevations, and thought them a useful addition to his commentary. As prior of Saint Victor, he would have been responsible for overseeing the constant building projects in the abbey, and so he would have spoken to one or more master masons over the years. Such a conjecture is ultimately unprovable, not least because there were social and cultural barriers that should be acknowledged first. Part of Vitruvius's aim in writing *De architectura* was to elevate the profession of architect to the liberal arts, the subjects studied by free men of intelligence in antiquity and the Middle Ages.[35] By the twelfth century, architecture had begun to settle into contemporary intellectual systems. To help them navigate those systems, Hugh helpfully outlines a curriculum for Victorine students, one structured around the seven liberal arts. The seven subjects are divided into two parts, called the *trivium* and the *quadrivium*. The *trivium* are the subjects based on language—grammar, rhetoric, and logic—and were the first stage of a twelfth-century education. The *quadrivium* is made up of mathematical-based subjects: arithmetic, geometry, music, and astronomy. Hugh adds an extra level, however, extending the disciplines of human interest to include what he called the "mechanical arts."

Hugh is relatively clear about what he means by the "mechanical arts" (*mechanice*), dividing them into seven branches: fabric making, weapon making, commerce, agriculture, hunting, medicine, and theater.[36] The number seven, in this instance, is most likely a rhetorical choice echoing the seven liberal arts; indeed, Hugh divided the mechanical arts into three and four parts in the same way as the liberal arts were divided. Whereas three are concerned with one's interior life, the rest are concerned with exterior things and intellectual matters. Hugh's broader definition of the mechanical arts fits architectural practice rather well, as he writes that artisans (those who work in the mechanical arts) take inspiration from nature and use it to make objects and things. Because the mechanical arts are one step away from nature, Hugh calls them adulterated or bastardized branches of knowledge when compared to the liberal arts, which are the subjects that focus on nature itself. The mechanical arts may not have been studied in detail at Saint Victor, but there is clear evidence that twelfth-century monks did practice such things as metalwork and the making of stained glass.[37]

Despite some overlap, by the early twelfth century there were distinctions drawn between Richard's work on architectural drawings for the high-minded purpose of biblical commentary and the labor of builders working in Saint Victor. The division is topographical, between the cloister and the workshops. The two cultures were marked by different backgrounds, education, outlooks, the tools with which they worked, and even where they could be found in the relatively small campus of a Parisian abbey. Such division makes it difficult to draw meaningful connections between the outputs of these two places. To paraphrase a modern question and apply it to the twelfth century, what does a biblical commentary have to do with a building? The answer lies in the language of architecture, which is necessarily visual but relies on the practice of geometry too. Plans and elevations communicate better than even the most finely wrought piece of text, as we will see, a fact acknowledged even at the beginning of the Middle Ages. In this sense, the key word in Richard's title is *visionem*. The act of seeing is a powerful catalyst to belief, for the prophet, for Richard, and for Richard's readers. By visualizing the past in the manner Richard has done, he in turn gives us a glimpse of a rapidly developing set of visual strategies for three-dimensional objects.

Modern speculation on the relationship between medieval architecture and the flourishing of scholarship from the twelfth century onward reflects this concern for the two cultures. For example, in his controversial and somewhat misguided study of the links between the highly structured textual forms of theological scholasticism and Gothic architecture, Erwin Panofsky argued that the clear-minded and highly legible Gothic emphasis on linearity was born in the strict logic that forms the basis of scholastic literature, which used highly formalized methods for systemized analysis.[38] The argument is an extension of his work on iconology, but the details of relationships between intellectuals and builders is too unclear to make any arguments definitive, with one critic laconically pointing out that patrons—readers and authors of scholastic works—did not create forms and that Panofsky was being "silly."[39] Yet the seemingly parallel innovations in architecture and intellectual culture during the twelfth century still seem too much of a coincidence to suggest that there was no connection between them. These are two realms with a gulf between them, but it is possible that the methods for solving problems, such as the representation of physical objects, share some commonalities that stretch back to antiquity.[40] The twelfth century has been called a renaissance for authors and artists who used antiquity as a starting point to understand and represent the world with better methods.[41]

These visual strategies are difficult to map before the thirteenth century because there are so few examples of plans and elevations, and those that have survived usually come from very different times and places to one another. The primary identity of *In visionem Ezechielis* as a work of exegesis makes its inclusion in the history of architectural drawing suspect, but after examining the drawings, it will become clear that the images within it belong in the historiography that embraces people such as Vitruvius and Alberti. It has been suggested that there are so few surviving architectural drawings from western Europe before the thirteenth century because they were not used in any significant numbers.[42] This suggestion assumes a strictly Albertian definition for architectural drawings—namely, that they are made by architects and look a certain way. However, it was not just architects who devised convenient ways of representing the world in two dimensions. Albertian frameworks implicitly locate the making of drawings in the building site, a location associated exclusively with a master mason or architect, but they can just as easily be made by clerics in a cloister. In resorting to drawing, there is an implicit sense of text's inadequacy in describing architectural forms, so much so that architecture is a visual medium unsuited to conventional linguistic platforms, requiring authors to draw and paint from their imagination.[43]

If drawing is the language of architecture, there must be a community of "speakers" able to interpret the lines, strokes, and colors on the page as representations of three-dimensional objects. After all, in making his drawing, Richard assumes there is already an audience competent in looking at plans and elevations. Despite the relatively few examples of architectural drawings prior to his writing *In visionem Ezechielis*, such drawings must have existed within the monastic community to a greater or lesser degree. Such an assumption—not an unreasonable one—is in tension with many histories of the subject, which begin with Villard de Honnecourt's portfolio.[44] Villard looms over this discussion because he was originally thought to be an architect, and his portfolio was nothing less than a collection of his ideas and drawings, a prototype notebook for later centuries.[45] This introduction cannot discuss every architectural drawing up to the thirteenth century, even to contextualize Richard's work, but it is informative to briefly examine where most medieval histories begin and to question why that starting point might have been chosen.

Villard started his portfolio at some point in the early thirteenth century, creating hundreds of drawings, with a diverse range of subjects including buildings, machines, masonry templates, and many other objects. There is evidence of later hands in the portfolio, suggesting that it was continually used and referenced long after the thirteenth century. Overall, the collection points to a person interested in the architecture of his own day, but the suggestion that Villard was an architect is no longer accepted. Some parts of the portfolio contain a number of structural inaccuracies that an experienced mason would not have made. Villard's identity and occupation remain unknown and will probably remain that way, at least without any additional discoveries.[46] The text accompanying the drawings is not in clerical Latin like Richard's commentary, but in the Old Picardish and Old French vernacular of the period. The linguistic differences between Richard and Villard are a key signifier for the different spaces they occupied and the different audiences for their visions. Where Villard's vernacular suggests that he discussed the portfolio's content with masons and builders, possibly in contemporary lodges and building sites, Richard's Latin is the language of an intellectual elite, of patrons, and of the quiet heart of an abbey or monastery, the cloister, which seems a world away from the building site.[47] *In visionem Ezechielis* contains a more substantial architectural vision than anything in Villard's portfolio; it is the result of a hard-won reflection on the limits and processes of representing the world. Villard, on the other hand, takes these methods of representation and sees them as a tool for building, and nothing more.

Villard's drawings certainly have the character of early architectural drawings. Among the many other drawings, for example, there are two plans on a single page (fig. 1.6). The drawings are stark and diagrammatic in style, with clear outlines that depict the chevet of two churches. The wall widths of the building are proportional with the rest of the building, indicating that Villard considered the relationship between the drawing and physical structures; that is, there is a sense that the building would remain standing if built in the real world. There is a specific and legible visual language as well, one that Villard assumed his readers would know, such as the single lines that indicate the location of the rib vaults and not, for example, the foundations. Overall, there is an emphasis on clarity of design with a well-defined sense of a formal visual language of architecture. Villard includes small pieces of text to clarify ideas or to contextualize what is happening in the drawing, emphasizing the importance of both text and image in a joint enterprise. But that is all there is; there is no reflection on the nature or limitations of architectural drawing, little analysis of the drawings' purpose or the intellectual framework that could have elicited something like this portfolio. It is an uncontextualized oasis that creates more problems than it solves for the architectural historian.

Despite its apparent complexity, *In visionem Ezechielis* is an accessible work. The commentary's structure, for example, is defined by Ezekiel's account as he is led around the complex's buildings and spaces. Richard hovers over the prophet's shoulder, allowing himself to be led by Ezekiel as he explains what exactly was on the side of the holy mountain. In turn, this book walks in Ezekiel's and Richard's footsteps, following them and trusting in the fact that the biblical account provides a solid structure for both a vision of a temple and for a book about that vision. There is a clear strategy to the order in which Richard presents the drawings, moving from those that show the entire complex in only the most general terms, to those that focus on small elements within individual buildings before suddenly zooming out again to give a sense of the entire land of Israel. By presenting the drawings in this order, Richard gives his readers an opportunity to fully come to terms with not only what he intends to illustrate but also the techniques he uses to do so. This strategy works brilliantly, and so is paralleled here. *God's Own Language* begins with the reality of *In visionem Ezechielis*—who Richard was, the founding of Saint Victor, and the types of architectural drawings that had been made up to the middle of the twelfth century—before focusing on the commentary itself. For the most part, each drawing is considered in the order in which it appears in the manuscripts, but the drawings are grouped together for convenience's sake and as a means to examine their wider implications. First, there are the plans for

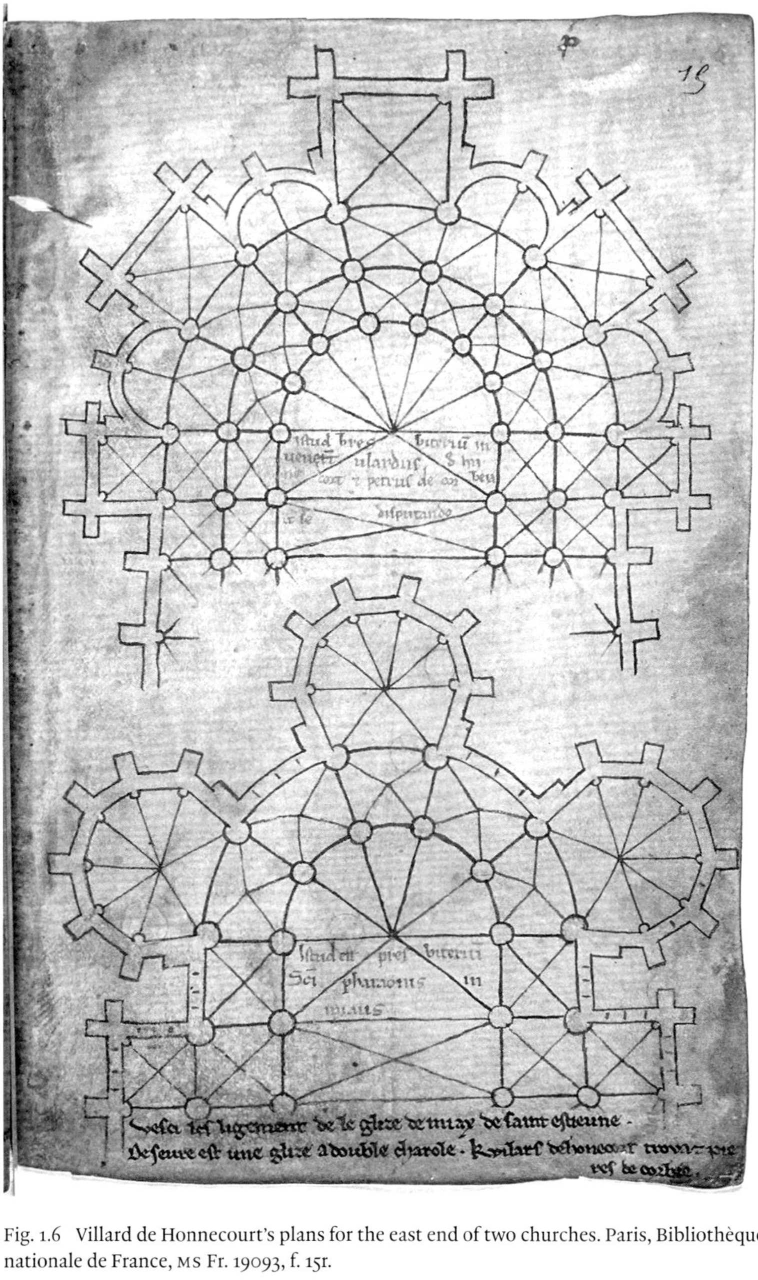

Fig. 1.6 Villard de Honnecourt's plans for the east end of two churches. Paris, Bibliothèque nationale de France, MS Fr. 19093, f. 15r.

Ezekiel's entire temple complex, showing the general layout of the scheme; following this, there are the plans and elevations for the gatehouses that join the different parts together. Then there are the buildings and the altar in and around the temple which lay in the heart of the entire complex; finally, there is the map of the Promised Land which appears in about half of the extant copies and shows remarkable similarities to contemporary Jewish maps of the same type. As a result, the structure of the book is led by Richard and Ezekiel, following not only their structure but also the many topics that the drawings force a modern reader to consider in light of their context and place in the history of architectural drawing.

There is one exception to this structural outline. In a chapter longer than the rest, the central part of this book focuses on the only nonarchitectural image in the commentary: a seemingly innocuous diagram of a circle with a right-angled triangle set into it. But embedded within that diagram is the beating heart of *In visionem Ezechielis*, relying, as it does, on the practice of geometry which defines the drawings' appearance and the lexicon Richard uses to make sense of the prophet's difficult vision. Only an in-depth analysis of its implications can show why, for example, Richard refers to his plans as "plans" and also why the drawings in *In visionem Ezechielis* are not a fluke, stumbled upon by a cloistered canon in Paris, that just happen to look like modern types, but were in fact a conscious creation founded on a strong theoretical understanding of what geometry offers the student of architecture. Geometry and its practice in twelfth-century Europe are the key to understanding the purpose of the drawings in *In visionem Ezechielis*; as a result, their discussion is figuratively and literally at the center of this book.

Overall, the aim of *God's Own Language* is to help modern readers understand Richard's intent and visual vocabulary for *In visionem Ezechielis*. Part of reaching this comprehension is to understand why the drawings appeared at Saint Victor when they did; thus, it will be important to look back at earlier examples of drawings. Fewer examples are drawn from the thirteenth century and later, but there is plenty of excellent scholarship on that subject already.[48] More importantly, my aim is to show that architectural drawing is a genre that can and should be studied outside of the exclusive realm of architects who make pictures of buildings.

An entire class of architectural drawing exists in the realms of theological texts, the authors of which faced the same problem as any architect: how to best represent a three-dimensional structure on a two-dimensional surface. We will see that the drawings' intentions are rarely made explicit, but their content is unmistakable, filled as they are with representations of the world and unique visions for and of it. In the process, architectural drawing becomes more than the sum of its parts and comes to embody the principle of order and imagination on which they rely and which medieval canons such as Richard fully accepted were part of their underlying significance.

In visionem Ezechielis is a prototype for a language of architecture that sees the value in creating a true vision of the past, one that prioritizes drawing over text. Richard's cloistered life has obscured him from the gaze of architectural historians, and his theologically oriented objectives seem to place him outside the silo of our discipline. But interpreting Richard's work as part of the development of a technique in the representation of a historical fantasy situates him where his work might tell us something about how we came to have architectural drawings, as well as the linguistic and visual strategies that term encompasses. Hugh's ark is made of two parts: the first is the historical imagination, the conjuring of a structure that never existed into his mind and his reader's mind; the second part is rooted in reality, his riverside reverie that provided a platform for a believable vision of the past. Richard's buildings comprise the same two parts, imagination and reality, two sides of the same coin that defines any piece of architecture and the process of its birth into this world.

The simple act of drawing a picture of a building seems a natural way of showing other people what it looks or looked like, much more effectively than words ever can. Such drawings should be expected throughout much of human history, drawn on ephemeral media such as sand, wax tablets, and scrap material. That we no longer have these images is only evidence that the drawings were not as valued as parchments containing important texts such as the writings of Saint Augustine or, indeed, the Gospels themselves. Fortunately, for our purposes we are not looking for lost lines in the sand, but for ink in a biblical commentary by a Scottish man in twelfth-century Paris. And that is where and when we start.

2 Richard and the Abbey of Saint Victor

Hugh of Saint Victor insisted that history was the foundation of all knowledge and the first step one must take on the road to wisdom. Hugh's system of biblical commentary centered on history and the people, objects, and places that inhabit it, the literal *things* of Scripture. That is exactly where our discussion begins, in twelfth-century Paris and Saint Victor's cloister. This focus gives a strong sense of Richard of Saint Victor, the author of *In visionem Ezechielis*, and addresses what made the abbey so special. The comparatively well-documented foundation of Saint Victor offers context to the intellectual framework of twelfth-century Paris within which its people worked. While Villard de Honnecourt remains a mystery, Richard's life and aims are better sketched against a rich historical backdrop. Saint Victor's position on the outskirts of the city, along with its clear educational focus, offer an avenue to understand *In visionem Ezechielis* in nuanced ways, something that is, at the moment, difficult to do in the case of other architectural drawings from the early and central Middle Ages. Finally, the drawings are the commentary's central feature, both for us and for medieval audiences; and so, following Richard's approach to the writing of history, this chapter gives an overall sense of their appearance and placement in various versions of *In visionem Ezechielis*.

Richard of Saint Victor

Dante included Richard in his *Paradiso*, describing him as standing alongside Saints Isidore and Bede because he was "in contemplation, more than human."[1] The sentence captures the essence of Richard's ability to transform an idea into the more concrete forms of text and image, his humanity surpassing itself through his writing, which embodied the past and the people within it, such as Ezekiel and his God-given vision. Richard was born at the beginning of the twelfth century in Scotland, giving him a national identity that was strong enough for contemporary and later copyists to refer to him as "Scottus."[2] Nothing is known about his early life before he joined the canons regular of Saint Victor in Paris at some point between 1130 and 1145. He most likely received an education before he traveled southward or at least showed a talent for learning. It is possible that Richard's early life followed a similar trajectory to that of the later Scottish Victorine author, Adam of Dryburgh (d. 1212), who was educated in Scotland before moving to Paris to further his studies at Saint Victor. Either way, Richard must have been relatively young when he traveled to France, because he lived and worked at the abbey until his death in 1173.[3] He was made subprior in 1159, and prior—a position just below that of abbot, the abbey's leader—in 1162. As prior, Richard would have been responsible for teaching the novices and others.[4] While he never became abbot, his status as prior was a prestigious one, a reputation reinforced by his prolific activity as a theologian.

Richard arrived at Saint Victor in the first half of the twelfth century, only a few short decades after the establishment of the abbey and during the height of its influence and power. The school within the abbey had a growing reputation and possessed a burgeoning and royally endowed library, which must have been attractive to a prospective student such as Richard. Probably more important, however, was the presence of Hugh of Saint Victor, the man who stood on the banks of the Seine and imagined Noah's ark.[5] Hugh died in 1141, and it is impossible to be certain whether Richard met him in person; this uncertainty has led to some debate as to exactly when Richard joined the Victorine community.[6] Hugh's work made Saint Victor famous during the first half of the twelfth century, creating a legacy that continues to this day.[7] Whether or not they met in person, Hugh exerted a strong influence over Richard in many areas of his life, and the close intellectual connection between the two men certainly suggests that they knew each other personally, even if only for a short time. Despite never traveling outside of Paris once Richard reached the abbey, he remained in contact with the Augustinian houses in England and would have been an important figure for foundations connected with Saint Victor when he became prior.[8] He then had an international reputation, and was known across Europe as an important man in an important place.

The exact dates during which Richard wrote *In visionem Ezechielis* are unknown. Stylistic evidence suggests that the earliest copy was completed at the beginning of the 1170s in Saint Victor, and so just before his death in 1173.[9] That copy, like all others, remains incomplete. The commentary ends with nothing more than notes for what Richard would probably have written for the last section, just quotations from the Bible and Richard's thoughts above them.[10] Despite the sketchiness of the final section, later copyists thought it important enough to include, perhaps thinking something is better than nothing when it came to finishing the commentary. If Richard was alive when the earliest copy was made in Saint Victor, it is likely that he made some effort to make sure it did not contain mistakes. The incomplete state of *In visionem Ezechielis* suggests that it belongs to Richard's later works, possibly made after he became prior in 1162. He started other works in this later period, such as an allegorical reading of the entire New Testament, collected now in a work known as the *Liber exceptionum*. So it is possible that Richard was too busy to complete *In visionem Ezechielis* and chose to move on to greener pastures. As will become clear, the drawings were conceived as an integral part of *In visionem Ezechielis* but were likely difficult to conceive and make, and perhaps Richard simply ran out of energy or inspiration to finish the work.

Despite the little that is known about Richard's life, he was a prolific author and his works demonstrate the wide variety of his interests.[11] For the most part, he has always been recognized for his focus on mystical theology and his sustained connection to the intellectual program at Saint Victor, a program that, in the words of one modern critic, "closely align[ed] the historical narratives, things, and signs of the Scriptures with rationally ordered bodies of theological, moral, and contemplative doctrine."[12] He was, in some ways, a twelfth-century Renaissance man, with one foot in the spiritual world and another firmly rooted in our own.

The themes in Richard's work reflect the duality of his interests, encompassing the exploration of the divine and the way one might approach it. While an overview of his work indicates an emphasis on mystical theology and allegorical interpretations of Scripture, history was at the heart of Richard's approach to Scripture and its teaching. In this vein, *In visionem Ezechielis* is rooted in this care for an in-depth knowledge of historical events; the work is, first and foremost, a historical commentary and a means for the reader to understand the literal events of the past. In the commentary, Richard's only concern is for the historical circumstances and objects associated with Ezekiel's vision. By taking this focus, Richard followed Hugh's advice that "just as you see that every building lacking a foundation cannot stand firm, so also is it in learning. The foundation and principle of sacred learning, however, is history."[13] Richard's utter focus on a historical reading was unusual enough to frustrate later commentators who wanted something more from him.[14] The study of history was a part of the blood that ran through Saint Victor's veins, the basis of everything produced there, and so it must take center stage as a formative part of Richard's intellectual life.

The Abbey of Saint Victor

Despite its later success, Saint Victor did not have an auspicious beginning. It was founded by William of Champeaux (d. 1120), who was previously the head of the Cathedral School at Notre Dame and one of the most important intellectual figures of early twelfth-century Paris. The great logician and self-promoter Abelard gave a vivid picture of William as a teacher and ambitious intellectual. Abelard was at one time William's student, but they fell out because of the teacher's supposed jealousy of his student's abilities. Abelard believed that William suffered from an ambition that led him to vacate his position as head of the Cathedral School and to establish Saint Victor as a mark of his piety. If so, the strategy worked, because only a few years after he founded Saint Victor, William became bishop of Châlon and left the institution he had established.[15] More importantly, in 1113 the abbey received royal money to create a large library that became one of the most celebrated in France.

Paris in the twelfth century was undergoing nothing less than an intellectual renaissance, as new writings by ancient scholars such as Aristotle and Euclid were translated into Latin and distributed throughout the city. Against this backdrop, William had founded Saint Victor as an Augustinian abbey. As such, Saint Victor had an abbot as its leader, and under him a prior—Richard, from 1162—who acted as second in command. Like any abbey, Saint Victor contained a group of men who lived together under a rule that defined the rhythm of their days and nights, ordering their lives so they could live, work, and worship God. Saint Victor was one of many Augustinian houses in which people across Europe lived through similar daily routines, but Saint Victor was particularly successful. When it grew too big to contain people in Paris, it spawned daughter houses throughout Europe, from England to Italy, and in doing so some of its practices spread as well.[16] These other abbeys remained connected to Saint Victor in Paris, following its liturgy and emphasis on education.

Saint Victor was very much a Parisian institution and was founded on the left bank and just outside the city's walls (fig. 2.1). The location is liminal, being outside the city walls but looking inward at the events and people within those walls. One seventeenth-century view of the buildings shows its setting was then still somewhat rural, surrounded by trees and grass, giving a sense that this was a retreat away from the growing urbanization of Paris (fig. 2.2). Indeed, it was used for exactly that purpose by a variety of people, including Thomas Becket during his exile from Britain later in the twelfth century, and others who wanted to escape the high-stakes philosophical disputes taking place in the city and elsewhere. By being no more than a thirty-minute walk to Notre Dame cathedral, but still gaining and retaining a reputation as a peaceful and contemplative place, Saint Victor was consistently a key institution in medieval France. Despite being outside the walls, its presence could be felt by those on the left bank, as the road through the gate and heading southeast was named after the abbey, thus memorializing it even within the city's boundaries. The relationship of Saint Victor and other abbeys to urban areas somewhat defines their character, marking them out as different from, for example, the Cistercian monasteries set within secluded valleys.[17] Saint Victor was an urban intellectual center that was famous for its most important component, the school.

The abbey's school was indeed at the core of its identity, and within the walls of the school the pedagogical principles encouraged students to connect the contemporary and biblical worlds.

Fig. 2.1 Nicholas de la Mare, map of Paris in the thirteenth century.

It is no coincidence that the nascent University of Paris (established at the end of the twelfth century) was located near Saint Victor on the city's left bank, filled as the area already was with eager students. Victorine education took on particular pedagogical stances designed to facilitate efficient learning, including a recognition that images could form an important part of a complete education. Take, for example, the *rota* diagram from the late twelfth or early thirteenth century now in the Bodleian Library (fig. 2.3).[18] *Rota* diagrams were composed of circles to generate links between different concepts and were a common means of drawing connections, especially in the early Middle Ages.[19] The

Fig. 2.2 Saint Victor Abbey, Paris, by Matthäus Merian, 1661.

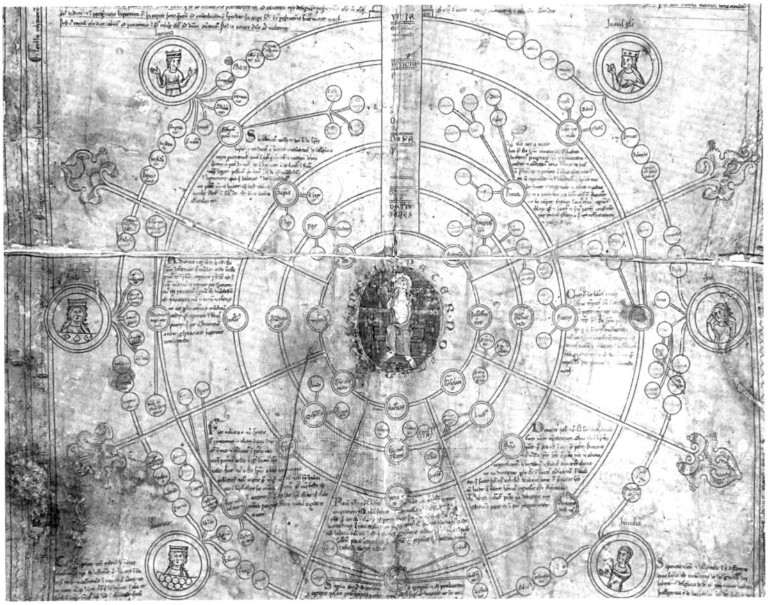

Fig. 2.3 A thirteenth-century teaching diagram. Oxford, Bodleian Library, MS Lyell 62.

scroll of parchment shows Christ enthroned in the center—added later to replace the original image that was cut out—set against a background of vibrant blue. Christ is surrounded by five concentric circles: the outermost contains representations of the seven deadly sins, with "pride" placed at the top as the worst of all and shown holding a mirror up as an act of vanity. The next circle represents the seven petitions of the Lord's Prayer; the third circle shows the seven gifts of the Holy Spirit; the fourth contains the seven virtues; and the final and smallest circle lists the seven beatitudes. The parchment was probably intended as a wall hanging; it was not made at Saint Victor but for the University of Paris, a sort of quick guide to prayer for students. The text on the bottom half is taken from Hugh's *De quinque septenis* (The five sevens), which outlines the relationship between the sins, beatitudes, and the rest of the diagram's content. A thirteenth-century teacher at the university wanted to visualize the associations between the seven sins and the means to combat them through the petitions, gifts, virtues, and the beatitudes, and he believed that creating a diagram such as this was the best means to do so. Creating visual relationships between abstract concepts was an important part of how learning could take place from the twelfth century on, and especially, as seen in this example, with Victorine content. With complex ideas grounded in the concrete lines and images of parchment, the student could recall the information more readily, but more importantly the connections between ideas could be recognized and understood at a glance.

These diagrams suggest that Saint Victor was a place where the act of seeing was not just acknowledged for its importance, but was a central part of Victorine communication methods, one embraced by teachers and students alike into the following century. Where contemporary authors such as Bernard of Clairvaux, the charismatic head of the Cistercian order, criticized the presence of outlandish beasts and scenes of war in the images produced within the cloisters of many monasteries, his words could also be taken as a general recognition of the power of images to distract. Hugh and Richard, on the other hand, recognized that pictures could reveal things to the viewer in a way text could not.[20] Richard, as a canon of Saint Victor, was embedded in a world that expected authors to offer readers visual access to the complex theological worlds, and every drawing in *In visionem Ezechielis* embodies this ideal.

The Drawings and the Manuscripts

Richard begins *In visionem Ezechielis* with a general overview of what he is going to do, giving his readers an explicit statement of intent: "First, I want to touch briefly upon the whole, so that more freedom be allowed in the description of the individual parts."[21] By giving a sense of Ezekiel's entire building complex at the very beginning, Richard offers an oasis to his readers, a firm location to which they can return if they get lost in the abyss of detail contained in the rest of the commentary. As a result, sketching the boundaries of Richard's drawings—and thus giving a sense of everything in *In visionem Ezechielis*—will provide some context for the drawings and an overview of what Richard believed to be important in the commentary. It is nothing less than a map to find your way through *In visionem Ezechielis*.

Thirteen plans and elevations were intended for *In visionem Ezechielis*, and in almost half of the copies of the manuscript a map of the Promised Land appears immediately after the end of the text. Of the thirteen drawings, five are plans of the entire complex; three plans and two elevations are of the gatehouses that Ezekiel describes in some detail; one is a plan of the temple; and there are two additional elevations, one of a building adjacent to the temple and one of the altar located in the central atrium. The largest plan of the entire complex, to which Richard refers in chapter twelve, appears in only two copies.[22] Richard, however, makes an explicit reference to this plan, writing, "Regarding all these things of which we have most recently spoken, here, in a large figure, it is able to be seen, as we show the form and general shape," and so it appears that it, or something like the existing versions, was intended to be included from the beginning.[23] The drawings are grouped into certain sections. Initially there are four plans of large areas of the entire complex, and then there are three plans of the gatehouse, followed by two elevations of it. The result is a crystal-clear visualization of the building. Afterward, Richard contextualizes the gatehouse's location with a plan in chapter twelve. His attention then moves to a plan of the temple, which is, spiritually, the most important building and at the center of the entire complex. Following this is an elevation of the building beside the temple, and finally one of the altar that stands in the inner atrium in front of it.

The drawings are of various sizes on the manuscripts' pages, ranging from approximately two inches for the first drawing to two-page spreads of the manuscripts, meaning the reader can see the building's layout in a single glance.[24] The drawing sizes are roughly equivalent across the range of manuscripts, however, suggesting copyists were concerned with consistency. In other versions, the artist reduced the overall size of the elevations to include them on a single folio, perhaps showing some concern for saving space and saving money.[25]

The drawings usually appear after the chapter in which Richard discusses a particular part of the temple complex, so that the reader is armed with the textual description which can then be transposed onto the accompanying drawing. The process defines a way of combining text and image in the wider interpretation of Ezekiel's vision. It all begins from the widest point possible, from a bird's-eye view of everything, and ends with the same and the map of the Promised Land. It is as if the reader stands apart from the complex before walking step by step closer to it, focusing on tiny details and then, having finished the work, walks away and sees it again, only from miles away. That gentle rhythm is what defines the structure of *In visionem Ezechielis*.

There are twenty-two copies of *In visionem Ezechielis* that are more or less complete and two fragments that contain at least one drawing.[26] The copies range from the remarkably early, such as Paris, BnF, MS Lat. 14516, to one made in fourteenth-century Paris (Paris, BnF, MS Lat. 3438). Considering the large amount of manuscript material that has been lost since the twelfth century, these twenty-two copies constitute a relatively high number and suggest that the work spread widely, especially in England and France. The copies appear in a variety of communities, from Augustinian houses—not surprising, since Richard himself belonged to the order—to Cistercian monasteries, and even the personal library of Pope Alexander VII.[27] The relative popularity of the work is important because when we discuss Richard and *In visionem Ezechielis*, we are not referring to an obscure writer working in isolation who produced a single copy of his work; instead, we can speak with some confidence about a text that was relatively widely disseminated, read, copied, and studied, and thus made an impact on the intellectual lives of its readers.

There is a remarkable consistency among the manuscript witnesses, especially those created in the twelfth and thirteenth centuries, with the drawings largely resembling each other.[28] The complicated processes of manufacturing copies could never ensure perfect fidelity between iterations, but the copyists of *In visionem Ezechielis*, despite the complexity and uniqueness of the drawings, did a good job of it. The most significant extant manuscript is the earliest, Paris, BnF, MS Lat. 14516. While the dating remains uncertain (being based on stylistic observations only),[29] partly because the unique appearance of the architectural drawings cannot be compared to anything else from the period, it is generally thought that the manuscript's contents were completed within Richard's lifetime. That being the case, one may assume that Richard took some interest in its making. The manuscript contains two parts: the earlier and longer section (ff. 1–167) consists of Richard's theological works, *Benjamin major*, *Benjamin minor*, *De exterminatione mali et promotione boni*, and *De statu interioris hominis*. A summary of *Benjamin major* was added a little later (ff. 167v–173v). The second part of the manuscript contains *De tabernaculo*, *De fini mundi*, and finally *In visionem Ezechielis*.

For that reason, the Paris manuscript will take center stage in the following pages. As will become clear, however, some of the drawings within the manuscript were left incomplete, making it important to supplement any discussion with other examples. The Paris manuscript will be examined and interrogated as if we, the modern reader, were standing over it looking through its pages and peering at each of the drawings within it. It is important to recognize that *In visionem Ezechielis* is not just a text to be read in a modern edition; it was and still is an object to be studied, existing on the surface of leathery parchment that has suffered scuffs and other damage over time. Richard placed the drawings in particular places and in relation to the text block, creating a mise-en-scène that the reader is supposed to interpret, all of it managing to communicate his vision of the prophet's vision.

3 The First Plans

At Saint Victor, images formed a central part of *how* one learned about the world, the past, and the manner in which one approached God. Images were a component of a clear pedagogy defined and practiced in the abbey's school. *In visionem Ezechielis* aligns with this approach, perhaps more so than anything else produced at Saint Victor. Ultimately, it is a book, a physical object. The drawings are not singular sheets like those produced in an architect's office, arranged and rearranged easily; instead, the commentary enforces a strict order in how the reader engages with them. Page after page is turned to see the drawings embedded within the text block or, sometimes, set out on their own with only few words alongside them. Now that we have some context for these drawings, it is time to start turning the pages of that book. There is no better manuscript to open than the one Richard would have known and taken an interest in when it was being produced.

Most of the drawings covered in this chapter are relatively simple and rather anticlimactic in the face of my claims for their precociousness. But they should be seen as an introduction in themselves, as guiding both Ezekiel and the contemporary reader through the material. As there are so few architectural drawings earlier than those in *In visionem Ezechielis*, it is important not just to show and explain Ezekiel's vision, but also to demonstrate how to read the images in the first place. Despite this uniqueness, Richard's work still functioned within a preexisting visual language of architecture, and there are elements of that language in the drawings. This chapter introduces some earlier examples of drawings to show that Richard was an innovator working with one eye on the past. So, while the focus is on the objects in the Paris manuscript, it will be necessary to introduce other manuscripts into the conversation.

When opening the Parisian manuscript, we need to turn a lot of pages before reaching *In visionem Ezechielis*, as it is the last work to appear in this collection of Richard's writing. Once we get to the right spot, everything starts with a preface that outlines the reasons Richard wants to write a commentary. The first drawing (fig. 3.1) comes in the first chapter, showing everything simultaneously as if we were God himself looking upon a vision of his own creation and able, at a glance, to comprehend everything within the three atria that define the complex's boundaries. Each

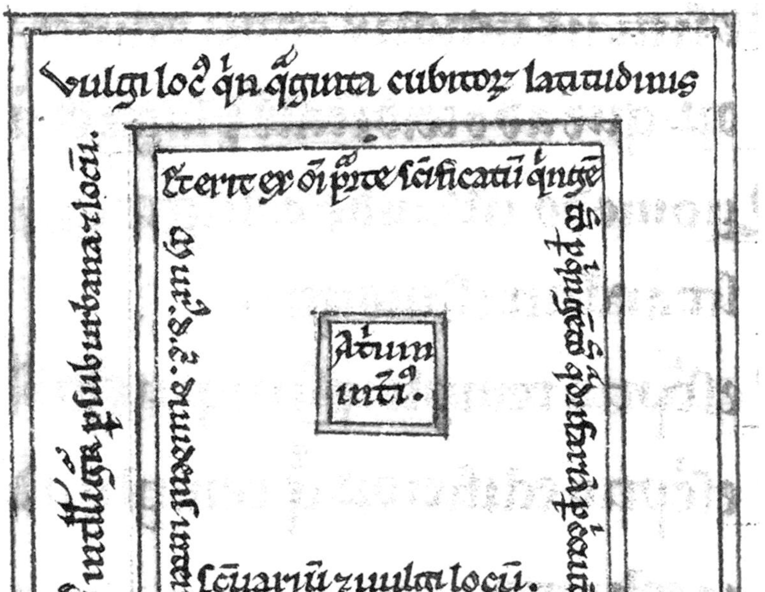

Fig. 3.1 Richard's plan for the entire temple complex. Paris, BnF, MS Lat. 14516, f. 211v.

subsequent drawing brings the viewer closer to the building, offering more detail as we move closer. The commentary begins with only the most general aspects of the temple and the buildings around it. The first four drawings provide an overall image of Ezekiel's vision, setting out the main elements bit by bit with an express concern for clarity above all else.

The first plan is nothing more than three squares one within the other, with a relatively small one located in the center that represents the "inner atrium" (fig. 3.1). Richard calls the entire complex an *aedificium*, suggesting he sees it as one entire object comprising many smaller spaces and buildings.[1] The drawing is small compared to some of the later drawings, only taking up the space of seven lines of text.[2] Richard does not include any buildings in it; instead, he offers only an outline of the walls that separate one atrium from another.

The figure contains inscriptions running around the edges of two walls to indicate the different atria's functions and their sizes in cubits. The text tells the reader that "The complex has three walls. The first is 600 cubits, the second is 500, the third, in the middle of them, is the smallest of them all," and is 100 cubits on each side.[3] The text around the middle atrium is drawn from Scripture, but from two different parts, Ezekiel chapters 42 and 45, which are primarily concerned with the walls' dimensions.[4] The text set within the outer atrium is largely Richard's own words that state the size but also indicate the atrium's purpose. We are told that this atrium is set aside for the "common people," referred to as the *suburbana* in both the diagram and the commentary's first chapter.[5]

In the accompanying text, Richard introduces the plan unremarkably by giving the measurements for the complex, followed by the words "in this way."[6] Both this reference to the drawing and the plan itself set the tone for many of the following drawings, using a combination of Richard's own words and Scripture to explain the complex's different parts. It introduces the reader to the temple complex's entire layout, but also to *how* one should read the drawings: as a combination of text and image and as part of a whole sequence of drawings.

The plan appears after Richard refers to it in the text, interrupting the flow of things and forcing the reader to look carefully at it. Even a quick glance shows the first plan to be so general in nature that it is missing openings in the atrium walls, and so it is unclear how the prophet could walk between the atria—something Richard has deliberately chosen to ignore at this early stage. As a result, the drawing is, in all practicality, incorrect. In the following section, Richard spends much time and effort describing the gatehouses placed around three of the atria walls, but these are ignored completely at this point. Their absence suggests he has a strategy for presenting the drawings in a particular order, one that values accessibility over pedantic exactitude. From Richard's perspective, there is no point overburdening the reader with an abundance of detail so early in the commentary; indeed, it would be detrimental to the overall purpose of the drawings, which was to explain the buildings as clearly as possible to all readers.

The second figure (fig. 3.2) follows the first on the next page. Richard refers to it at the end of the first chapter: "About these

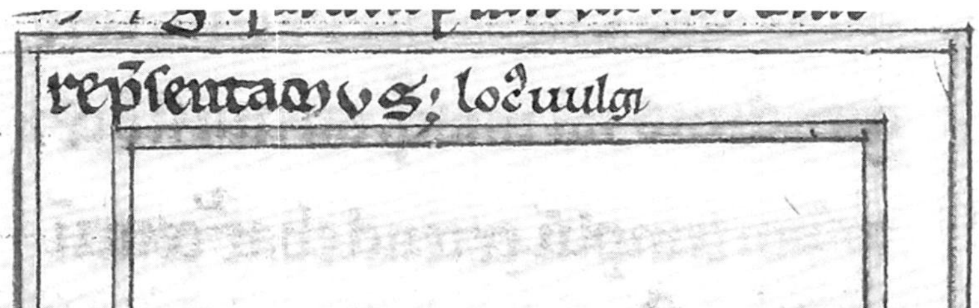

Fig. 3.2 Richard's plan for the temple complex with the gatehouse locations indicated. Paris, BnF, MS Lat. 14516, f. 212r.

things, which I described, I represent the form in this way."[7] Having illustrated the general appearance of the entire complex in the first drawing, Richard provides a little more detail in the second. The outer atrium in this drawing (the middle atrium in the overall plan) remains empty and far too small to reflect its actual size, as if the plan has collapsed that section to make room for the inner part of the complex, which is this drawing's focus. Here much more information is given than in the previous drawing, including the locations of specific buildings along with the spaces between them. These green passageways are what Ezekiel calls *gazophylacia*, which are porticos running westward and facing outward.[8] There are six gateways marking the passage between the different atria from three sides and access to the inner atrium right at the center of the plan. There is no indication that the colors and lines represent buildings, only abstract indications of how much space they take up and their location within the atrium.

This figure's scale has changed compared to that of the previous drawing. While it is approximately the same size on the page as the first, it shows only the middle and central atria, not the outermost. The shift in scale demonstrates Richard's flexible approach to representing the entire complex; he is not bound by a strict sense of proportion.[9] Despite changes to the drawing's scale, the orientation is the same as in the first plan, with west placed at the top. Given that medieval maps frequently, although not always, placed east at the top, Richard seems to have deliberately chosen for the plan to be oriented in this way.[10] As a result, the reader—placed at the east—faces the temple's entrance; it is as if one could simply walk forward and enter the building, almost as an echo of Ezekiel's own journey into the complex. The inscriptions are much simpler than those in the first plan; there are no extended quotations from Richard's commentary or Scripture, only short descriptive words to indicate what the spaces represent. But there are important elements present; for example, it is only at this point that Richard shows the viewer the means by which the prophet moved between the different parts, with gatehouses (*portici*) on three sides, colored in a pale yellow wash. From this drawing onward, the drawings become more like plans for historical spaces that Ezekiel moved through, and readers can use their imaginations to do so as well.

The third figure (fig. 3.3) contains similar information to the second, but with some important differences. Richard introduces

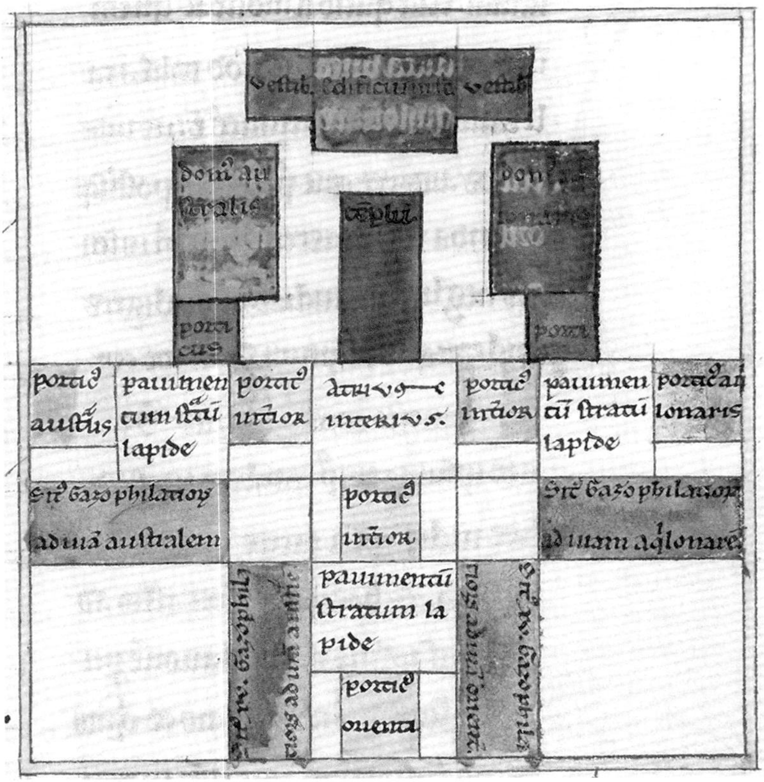

Fig. 3.3 Richard's plan for the middle and inner atria indicating the temple's location. Paris, BnF, MS Lat. 14516, f. 213r.

the drawing by writing, "concerning these things we described, we represent the form in this manner."[11] The plan is slightly larger in size than the previous one, which gives Richard more space for the buildings and inscriptions. The western section (that is, the top) is now filled with four buildings, including the temple, and others alongside it to the south, west, and north. These are represented in a different color from the buildings shown in the previous plan, emphasizing the differences between the two plans. The northern and southern buildings on the west side of the complex are accessed via gatehouses on the northern and southern pavements (that is, right and left). The temple, on the other hand, can be accessed only via the inner atrium. Just as in the second plan, there is little sense that the colored rectangles are buildings; they are just spaces whose function is indicated by the names attached to them. Since the drawing is slightly larger than the previous two, the proportions have also changed: the *gazophylacia* are wider and their *tituli* (identifying notes) contain more information. Where the second drawing only says that there are fifteen (xv) on each side, the third plan gives their direction, thus making the plan's orientation immediately obvious. Also, the outer gatehouses follow this emphasis on the direction of the complex's parts by including their locations and original positions. The consistency in the color and the inscriptions demonstrates to the reader that the plan shows the same space as the previous figures. After viewing three drawings, we have the sense that Richard chose to give readers higher resolution as they progressed into the commentary, zooming in on certain sections while disregarding others for the moment.

The fourth drawing (fig. 3.4) requires us to turn more pages than before, since Richard treats his readers to a lengthy

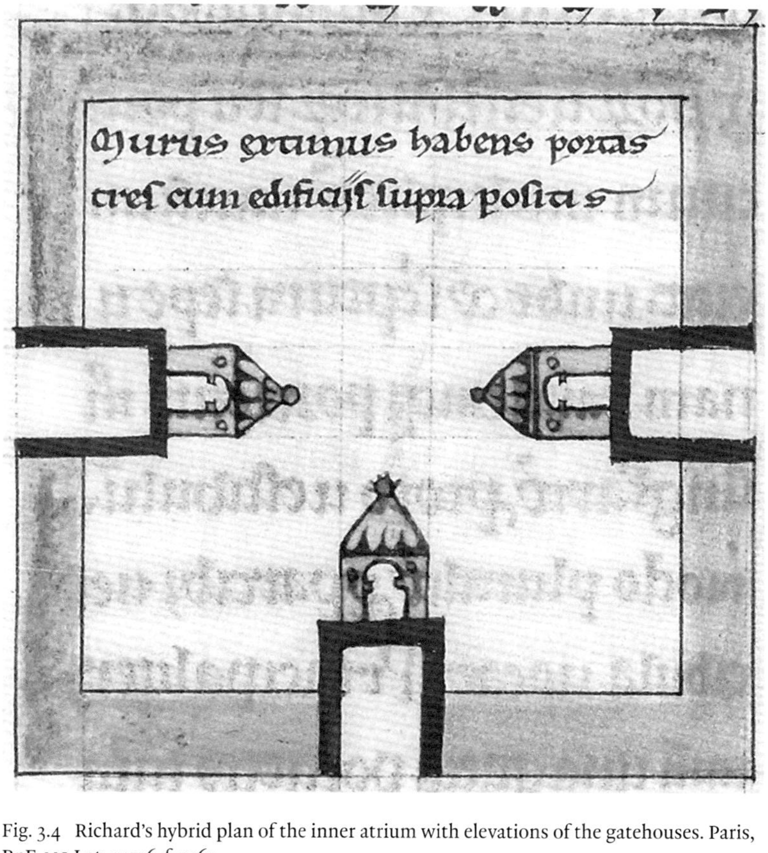

Fig. 3.4 Richard's hybrid plan of the inner atrium with elevations of the gatehouses. Paris, BnF, MS Lat. 14516, f. 216r.

explanation of the measurements and their significance. This plan shows the atrium with the gatehouses to the north, south, and east (right, left, and bottom, respectively). The wall is colored in a light pink, and the gatehouses in brown and the upper levels in yellow. The brown lower half of each gatehouse is a plain rectangular shape, giving only the merest hint that an entrance is represented. In comparison, the upper half of each gatehouse is relatively elaborate, with capitals on either side of the door jamb, and a gabled roof with a circular pinnacle. The bottom, or east, superstructure is left unfinished, lacking one of the curvilinear decorations that appears on the other roofs; also, the right capital is not as neatly drawn as the others.

It is only when we see this plan, the smallest in the entire commentary, that we are certain the drawings represent buildings at all. Each drawing up to this point has shown colored squares and rectangles to indicate the buildings and their relationship to one another. By turning the page from the third to the fourth drawing, however, we get a clear sense of continuity between them; we are, after all, looking at a simple square, a wall seen from above, and one of the simplest plans it is possible to make. The elevations that are set within the wall change the drawing's identity; it is a hybrid combination of plan and elevation, giving a sense both of the layout and of the buildings' appearance. The simplicity of the elevations aligns with Richard's approach to the order of the drawings up to this point, where he gently takes the reader by the hand to lead them through the building. He does not assume that any reader is proficient in the visual language that drives his commentary; instead, he shows and teaches them that language simultaneously.

Overall, the first four plans give a sense of Richard's assumptions about how best to represent spaces of different sizes. He begins very simply, with the plan of the entire complex, showing all three walls without any recognizable features such as gatehouses, individual buildings, or anything else. Indeed, it is so simple that it is difficult to call it an architectural drawing at all; no doubt the plan is a disappointment for those expecting something a little more complex, but its simplicity is part of a wider strategy. From that beginning, Richard starts to build in an iterative way. The first plan lacks any detail, but the second contains much more, with all the structures (pavement, *gazophylacia*, etc.) placed in the eastern end, but nothing shown in the western part. The third is largely the same drawing, but with the location of the temple and three other buildings included. The fourth and final drawing is not entirely necessary because the placement of the gatehouses is already indicated in the previous two figures, although only in the most cursory way. Richard may have wanted to make the subject explicit, that these abstract rectangles were in fact real buildings with features that were familiar to a twelfth-century reader.

There is an extraordinary flexibility of scale shown in the drawings. In the first drawing (fig. 3.1), Richard shows all three atria walls, which are accompanied by text describing what exactly the individual spaces represent. The following drawing (fig. 3.2), of approximately the same size in each of the manuscripts, shows only the two inner atria. We can assume that the reader was expected to know that certain elements of the second diagram appeared in the first, only now they are represented differently, with new information embedded within the drawing. Moreover, the artist expanded the space between the inner and middle atria (i.e., where the buildings are shown in the second and third drawings) to accommodate the temple and three adjacent buildings that now appear within it (fig. 3.3). Such jumps from one drawing to another may seem natural to modern eyes that are accustomed to interpreting architectural plans and are able to make sense of the shifting representations of space, but to an unpracticed eye, they may have been more difficult. The relative consistency between the extant versions suggests that Richard's readers did not find such shifts in scale incomprehensible (and therefore he did not attempt other solutions). Although very few architectural drawings survive from this period, contemporary readers could still interpret rather complicated representations of space, scale, and proportion, and also identify significant changes to those characteristics from one drawing to the next.

The Fifth Plan

Another drawing belongs to Richard's attempt to provide an overview of Ezekiel's vision (fig. 3.5).[12] It appears in only three copies, but the text at this point refers to a drawing, which suggests Richard intended for it or something like it to be included.[13] It does not appear in the early Paris manuscript, which suggests that it may be a later addition either overlooked by Richard or not available to the first manuscript's copyists.[14] Every drawing looked at

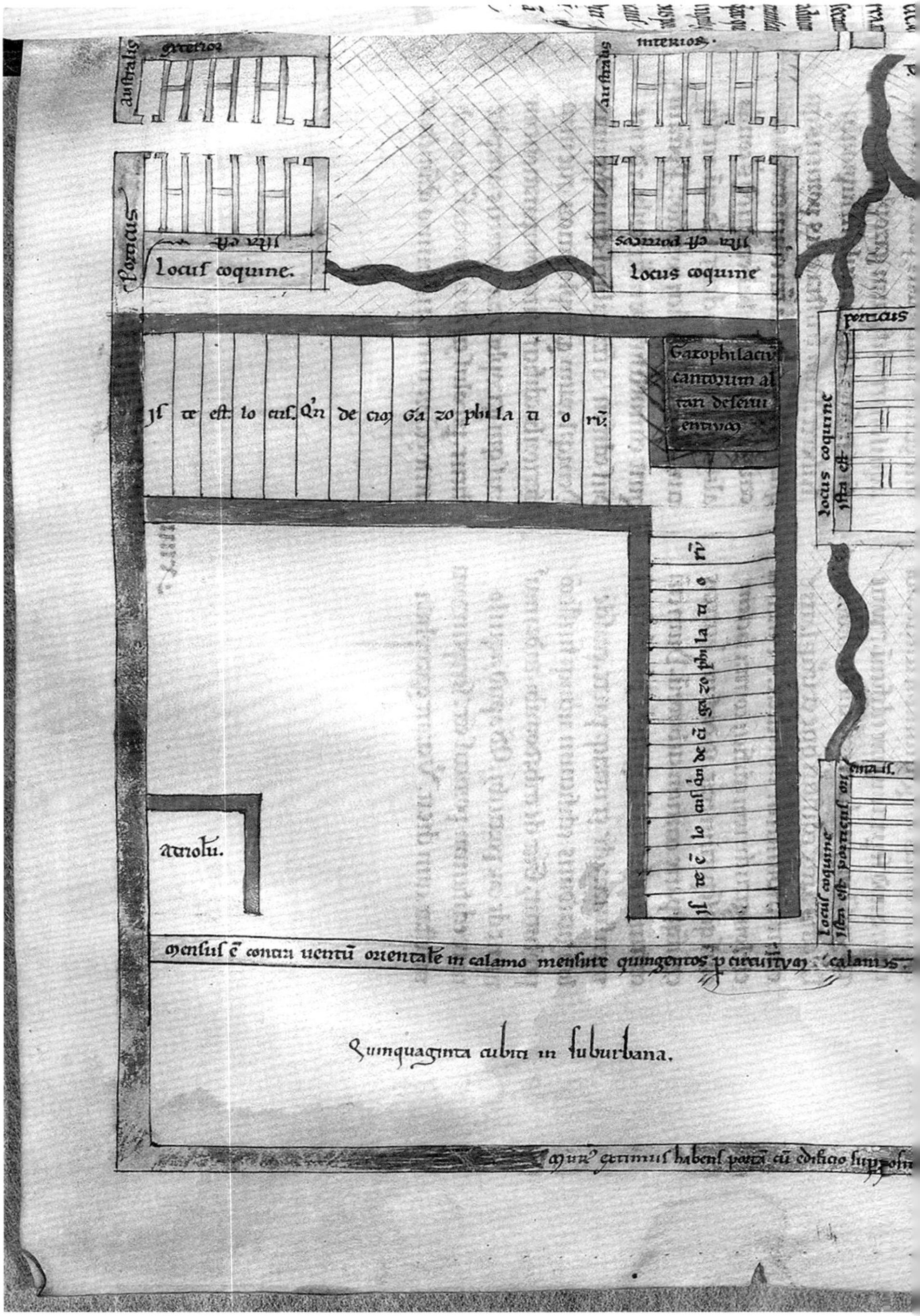

Fig. 3.5 Richard's detailed plan showing the gatehouses and *gazophylacia*. Paris, BnF, MS 2165, f. 56r.

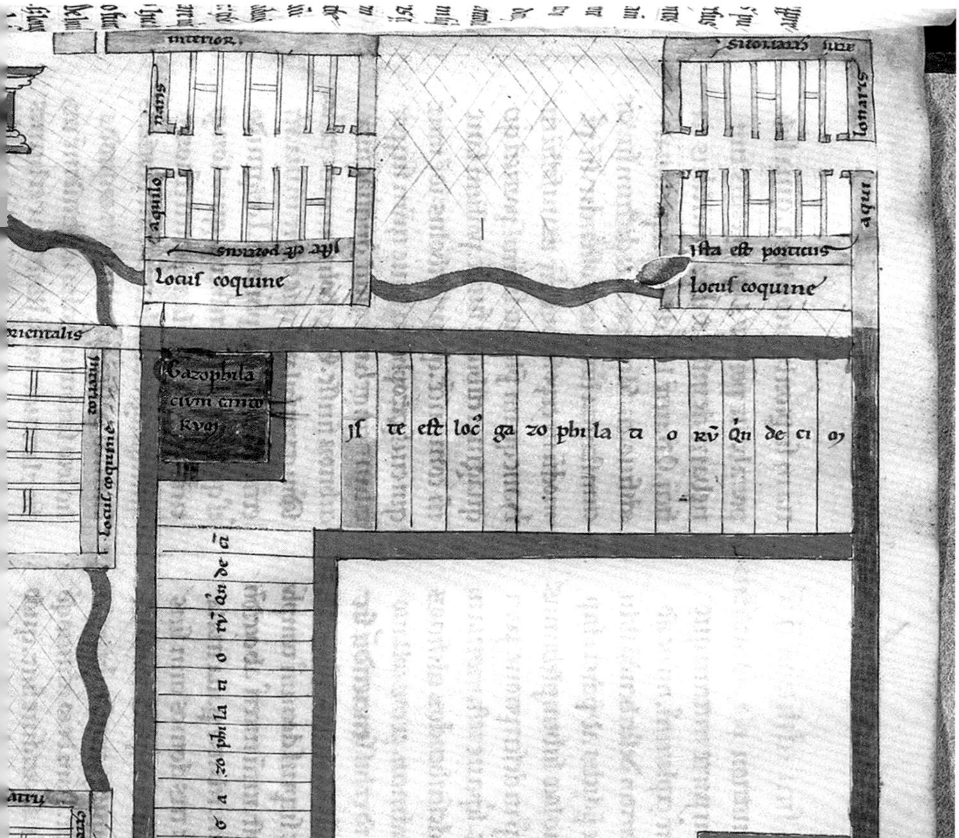

interior.
locus coquine
ista est porticus
locus coquine
Gazophila cium
Is te est loc' ga zo phi la ci o rum Qn de ci m
Iste e lo cus ga zo phi la ci o rum qn de ci
atriolum.
murus dividens inter sanctuarium et vulgi locum.
Vulgi locus. quinquaginta cubitorum. latitudinis
unius cubiti. latitudinis et altitudinis.
56

so far has fit into the text block, inserted into it as if it could be part of the text, but this fifth plan is monumental in comparison, taking up an entire page. Every image would have been a major undertaking for Richard, as implied in Peter the Chanter's criticism of *In visionem Ezechielis*'s pointless drawings, and perhaps the fifth plan was originally planned but not completed until much later, leaving certain manuscripts without it. In the manuscripts that include it, this drawing appears after the gatehouse plans, but before the large and impressive elevations for the gatehouses, which are discussed in the next chapter. As a result, we are forced to flick through a large number of pages, bypassing some important drawings, but the fifth plan is the culmination of Richard's order for the first four plans. It contains an immense amount of information compared to the others, and draws to a close some of the questions brought up by the simplicity of the first few pages of the manuscript.

The plan's monumental size implies it must have been a large endeavor to conceive and create. The drawing shifts the view slightly to the east (downward) so that the temple does not appear, leaving the focus on the area in the bottom part of the second plan. The full gatehouse plan is replicated throughout the atria, and the viewer is finally able to see their relationship with the entire temple complex. The map shows the *gazophylacia* in detail for the first time. Richard interprets them to be long rooms running parallel with the pavement, here marked as lightly drawn hatching. The hatching in itself is a useful addition because it gives a sense of the surface on which the prophet walked, as if the lines are squared stones neatly put together, a comparative rarity for the roads of medieval Paris. Perhaps most significant of all is the representation of the kitchens attached to the gatehouses separating each of the atria. These gatehouse plans are discussed in detail below, but their insertion in the large plan shows Richard thought in great detail about the relationship between the different parts and made an effort to be consistent across the entire commentary. The northern and southern gatehouse kitchens are attached to their eastern walls, where the river meets them and flows through them. The eastern gatehouses have kitchens on their northern and southern walls with the river splitting in the inner atriums so it can serve both sides. The strategy of placing this large drawing at the end of a series of increasingly sophisticated plans encourages the reader to learn the visual language at play gradually.

Richard intends the fifth plan and the commentary's twelfth chapter to do several things, the most important of which is to indicate the location of the gatehouse kitchens which were used for the sacrifices; consequently, the stream of water that issues out of the temple and through the entire complex does so in a very specific manner.[15] He explains how the sacrificial offerings were washed before being taken to the altar at the center of the inner atrium, and how the water source—needed to clean the offerings—flows through the entire complex.[16] The biblical text does not do a good job of explaining where the river flows in relation to the buildings, forcing Richard to improvise: he suggests that kitchens are attached to each of the gatehouses and the water runs beneath them. Though not present in most copies, the fifth plan brings to light the complexity of Richard's vision and the care he brought to the project. This is an extraordinarily detailed vision of Ezekiel's complicated and contradictory description, all brought together at a time before there were any detailed architectural drawings that incorporated separate elements.

There is very little to which these five plans compare from the early and central Middle Ages, and the iterative approach by which Richard presents the drawings is especially uncommon for the period. Earlier architectural drawings contain little or no information regarding scale or proportions, and there are no drawings representing the same building or layout over multiple versions. *In visionem Ezechielis*, however, is not completely isolated; it is possible to draw some lines between it and earlier examples, suggesting that there was a visual language of architecture in which Richard fits his work.

The Plan before In Visionem Ezechielis

To the modern eye, Richard's drawings may seem crude compared to later examples from the early modern period, or even Villard's from the thirteenth century, but within them there is an essence of a distinctive visual language that speaks to and asks much from his readers. Many earlier plans and elevations lack consistency in their application of that visual language, presenting a single drawing that attempts to depict an entire building, producing a confusing image.

There is a good reason for not including the twelfth century in studies on architectural drawing, since there are too few examples to build a picture. Also, the implicit Albertian influence on the definition of architectural drawings, which emphasizes the motivations of the architect, means the twelfth century inevitably falls out of focus. Richard, however, still had to use a visual language that others could understand correctly, and so his approach to the drawings had to overlap in some way with earlier examples. This is not to suggest that he had firsthand knowledge of specific drawings, but by the twelfth century there were certain expectations audiences had when interpreting drawings and, despite his remarkable innovations, Richard's drawings largely conformed to these expectations. While there are examples of buildings, monasteries, or entire cities being represented before the twelfth century, there is no synthesis of how artists and readers interpreted such drawings from late antiquity to the twelfth century.[17]

The Saint Gall plan (fig. 3.6) is one of the most well-known examples of architectural drawing from the early Middle Ages, and can demonstrate the sheer variety of ways scholarship has approached the subject. It was completed near the beginning of the ninth century, having been sent from an anonymous source to Bishop Gozbertus in Saint Gall, Switzerland.[18] The plan illustrates a monastery complex with a large church, cloister, and ancillary buildings such as those needed for farming and the housing of guests.[19] It is drawn on a large piece of parchment (112 cm x 77.5 cm) which unfolds to reveal the plan on one side. The cloister is at the center, the church to the left (when the plan is oriented so that the text appears to be right side up), with two towers flanking the west front. There is an extraordinary attention to detail throughout much of the drawing, from the barrels storing wine on the cloister's west side (toward the bottom of the cloister), and the individual beds for the monks in the dormitory. On the reverse side someone wrote the life of Saint Martin during the twelfth century; its presence is likely why the plan survived for so many years and the parchment was not reused or destroyed.

The drawing gives an outline of the many monastic buildings spread throughout a site, using red ink for the walls and a brown/black ink for the notes that identify the different buildings and their parts. In many plans from the period these notes (*tituli*) appear in certain locations to indicate the functions or other properties of a particular space. In the Saint Gall plan, they are

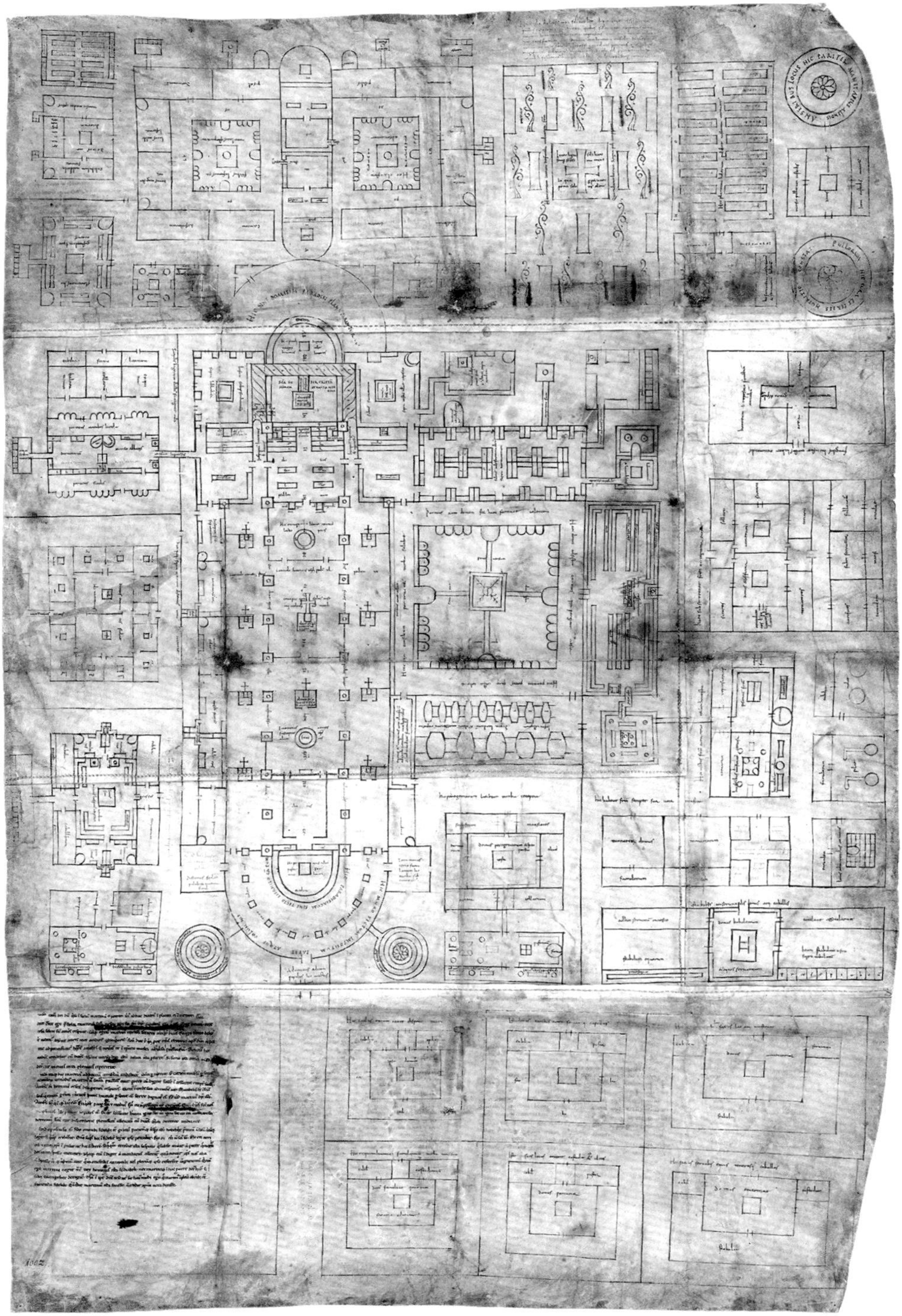

Fig. 3.6 An unrealized plan for a Carolingian monastery. St. Gallen, Stiftsbibliothek Sankt Gallen, Cod. 1092.

used abundantly, with important areas such as the dormitory, the steps (*gradus*) into the church, and even the measurements of the church indicated in Carolingian feet (*pedus*).[20] The overall appearance is similar to a scientific diagram, where the *tituli* draw attention to the important parts to communicate the creator's vision as clearly as possible to the reader. Even the simple red lines that give the outlines of the buildings echo this diagrammatic style. In some parts, such as the space between the church and the cellar, the artist indicates the wall widths, but this detail is not consistently represented. Certain passages are more akin to a sketch than a fully realized representation of the buildings. The artist was aware that he was trying to show three-dimensional objects but struggled to do so in some passages. For example, in the church's two flanking west towers, he included a spiral shape to indicate the presence of a staircase winding around the interior. The size of the stairs, which take up the entire tower, does not relate to how stairs are set into ninth-century towers, and the artist seems to have included them as a shorthand to indicate that circular stairs were there and that it is a three-dimensional object.

The buildings in the plan were never constructed at Saint Gall or anywhere else, and while the church shares some stylistic features with contemporary Carolingian churches, scholarship is divided over the plan's purpose. This question is important since it addresses the possible reasons that architectural drawings such as the Saint Gall plan and Richard's drawings were made in the first place. The earliest argument suggested that the plan was a result of Carolingian monastic reforms in 816 and 817.[21] In this view, "the arrangement of the buildings shown on the Plan of Saint Gall aimed [for] the establishment of guiding rules that could be followed in the physical layout of a monastic settlement."[22] Similarly, the plan has been described as an "exhaustively detailed and comprehensive plan for a monastic building complex," one which responds to the contemporary requirements of Carolingian monasticism, having been "designed by learned Carolingian scholars."[23] According to this view, the Saint Gall plan is a prototype of a perfect monastery, if site and money were to pose no problem. However, there is no suggestion that a plan or series of stringent measurements was decreed for Benedictine foundations during the Carolingian reforms.[24] The reforms were fairly well documented, and such an extraordinary act of standardization would have been sure to appear in instructions to foundations, but there is nothing of the kind. Indeed, in effect, drawings of this type could have been templates, but that does not mean the drawings were conceived along such lines.[25]

The Saint Gall plan has been described as the "most astonishing document of early medieval Benedictine monastic architecture," but one where its religious identity partly defines its purpose, an attempt to achieve perfection (*perfectio*) within the context of contemporary attitudes to "Carolingian spirituality and piety."[26] It is a "type," one that follows the concepts of medieval architectural iconography, where the exact imitation of an exemplar was unnecessary; instead, only a "memento of a venerated site" was required.[27] In this sense, the plan does not represent a specific structure and it does not even show an idealized layout or set of buildings for the ninth-century monastery; it shows a road to salvation, acting as the object of meditative action by the monks of Saint Gall. In this interpretation, it has more in common with a mandala than with a plan used by a mason.[28]

Both Richard and the Saint Gall artist expected their readers to understand their plans as depictions of walls laid down and viewed from above. In essence, they expected their drawings to be legible as representations of three-dimensional objects arranged in a certain pattern.[29] More than this, the visual strategy of the Saint Gall plan overlaps with that of Richard's drawings in the attempt to offer a representation of an entire set of buildings schematically with only a few *tituli* included where essential.[30] Both authors emphasized the legibility of the plans and the relationship between one building and another. In the ninth-century plan, the artist did not represent the spaces between the buildings, since even a quick glance shows that many of those spaces are too small to facilitate movement between the buildings and bear little resemblance to Carolingian monastic plans. Fudging some of these distances is secondary to the overall effect of the plan and its ability to convey the appearance of not just one building but an entire space filled with people and structures. The reader was still required to do some work, however, and to read the walls and buildings as they appeared on the plan, but the distances between the buildings needed to be lengthened in their imagination. In *In visionem Ezechielis*, Richard makes this flexibility explicit by, for example, expanding the space of the inner and middle atria to fit in the temple and other buildings in the third plan, whereas the Saint Gall plan's expectations are much more implicit. In the cases of the five plans in *In visionem Ezechielis* as well as the Saint Gall plan, the image acts only as an imaginary catalyst—nothing more or less than a proposition to the reader who must use their imagination to build a three-dimensional building from the two-dimensional shapes on the parchment.

These comparisons between *In visionem Ezechielis* and the Saint Gall plan suggest a shared visual vocabulary, but Richard's drawings are much more sophisticated in their presentation of space, not least because where the ninth-century artist arranges the lines like a geometrical figure, Richard presents his subject as architectural forms, as seen in the fourth plan (fig. 3.4), which presents the elevations as twelfth-century buildings. The representation of the same buildings and spaces over several separate drawings illustrates a generosity to the reader that the Saint Gall artist does not offer. The Saint Gall plan was intended for a particular person who was expecting something like a monumental plan, but Richard did not have that luxury. Instead, his audiences were educated clerics interested in the past, but certainly not expert in the visual language Richard used.

The purpose of another ninth-century plan is much more obvious. It appears in the Irish manuscript called the Book of Armagh and it shows the Celestial Jerusalem (fig. 3.7). The manuscript was written for the bishop of Armagh and contains material from the New Testament and, by coincidence, a life of Saint Martin, such as appeared on the Saint Gall plan. The drawing appears at the end of the book of Revelation and depicts the heavenly city of Jerusalem described in chapter 21. The biblical chapter describes the city in some detail—although not in as much detail as in Ezekiel's vision—with particular attention paid to the twelve gateways that surround the city. The Book of Armagh plan appears as a square with three openings on each side and with the walls filled with knotted decoration. Within the walls, at the top of the city, there are two rectangular shapes, one set within the other, and text that indicates it is "Our Lord Jesus Christ." *Tituli* also appear between each of the openings, each one indicating an angel associated with the gate, the name of an apostle, one of the Israelite tribes, and finally a gemstone. Scripture lists the different stones which served as the foundations to each of the gates; it also states that there were angels at each gate, that the names of the twelve tribes of Israel were written on the gates, and that the names of the apostles were written on the wall of the city. The

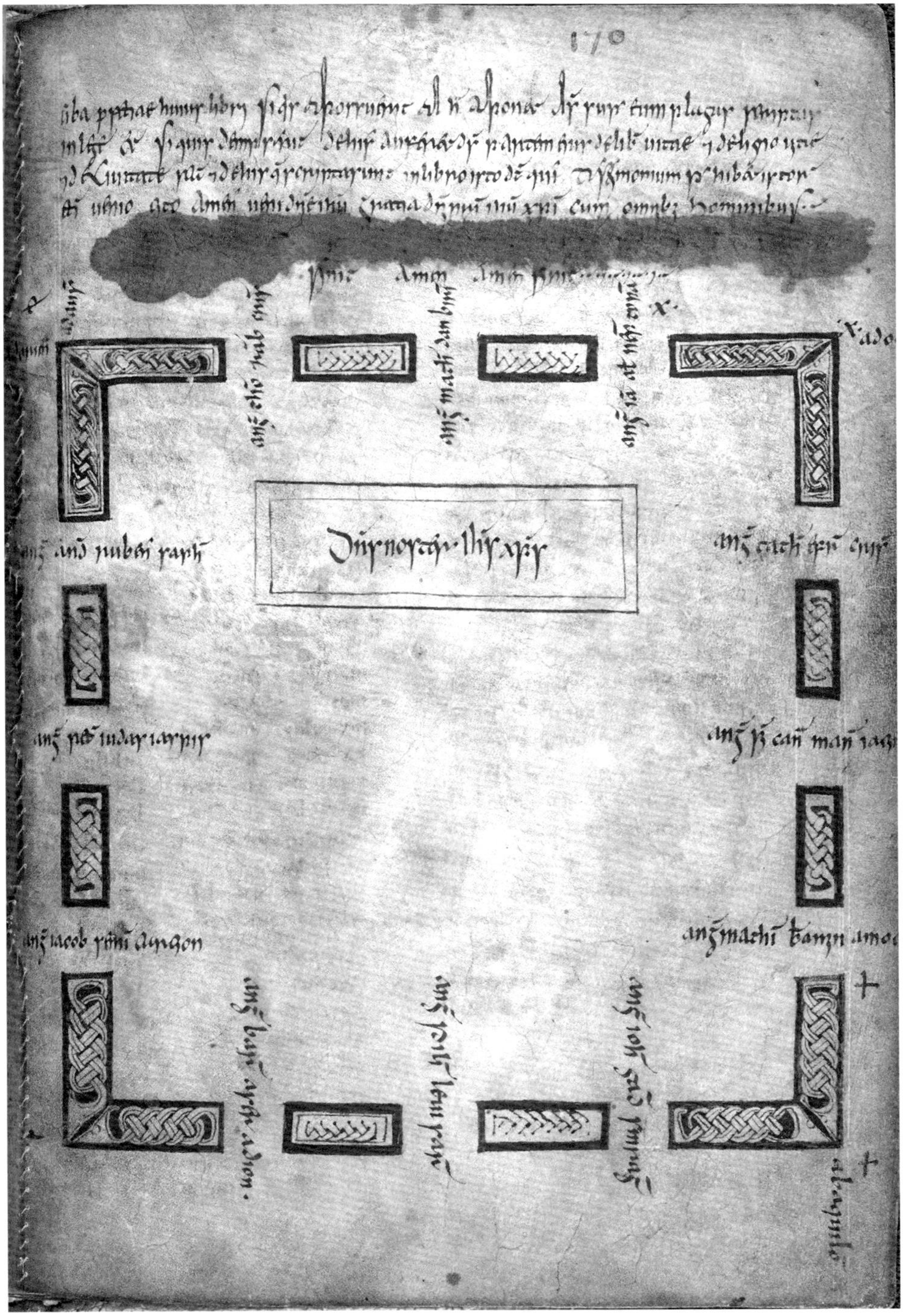

Fig. 3.7 A plan of the celestial Jerusalem. Dublin, Trinity College, MS 61, f. 170r.

drawing's presence and size suggest that it was more "than a decorative tail-piece" added to Scripture; and since it draws on other parts of the Bible (for example, for the list of the Israelite tribes), it is a form of visual exegesis, and thus the drawing "served a practical purpose."[31]

Similarly to the way Ezekiel is escorted around the temple complex by the man with a brazen complexion who takes measurements of the building, the author of Revelation gives the measurements for the Celestial Jerusalem; in this instance, a "golden reed" is used to measure the entire circumference of the city. The information appears slightly jumbled in Revelation, with the stones set within the foundation listed at the end, and the other information appearing elsewhere in the short description. By presenting the material in different parts of the Old and New Testaments in a single image, the artist has given order to the material. The act of distilling the information, however, is an interpretive action, where the artist has simplified Scripture in some regards. For example, the names of the Israelite tribes were not written on an opening, as shown in the drawing, but on the walls flanking the entrances. This would have been difficult to represent without also showing an elevation of the city walls, so the artist has chosen instead to include all of the information on the gates, even if Scripture did not indicate which apostle should be associated with which gate, among other things. The plan is a form of visual exegesis, and if so, is an early example of the type. Indeed, it is possible that the plan is a copy of an earlier drawing, indicating that it could be a lost type that was associated with some copies of Revelation from before the ninth century.[32] The concerns of exegetes such as Richard when representing biblical architecture was to organize information for the convenience of the reader, much as Hugh did in the case of the ark, which acted as an organizational platform that encompassed a visual system. Even if a physical picture never existed, Hugh hoped that with his commentary anchored in an image, the student would both understand and remember the content better. While there is no suggestion that Richard ever saw the Book of Armagh's Celestial Jerusalem, the motivations that underlie it echoed throughout Saint Victor. Put simply, Scripture describes the plan of a building, in a way that is not always easy to follow, but the artist simplified certain elements to help the reader make sense of the historical significance of the prophet's words. The inclusion of *tituli*, small pieces of text that explain what the viewer can see but also communicate the artist's interpretive act, certainly aligns the plan with Richard's more fully realized series of architectural drawings; and, as we have seen, *tituli* were also used in the roughly contemporary Plan of Saint Gall.

While there is little to which we can compare Richard's five plans, we can thus see some overlap in approaches to earlier architectural drawings. The plans in *In visionem Ezechielis* are intended to be read in order, and rely on the viewers' ability to recognize the same structures in different drawings and with slightly different proportions and sizes. The specific colors Richard uses to represent the space helps in this; also, the first three plans appear close to one another, just one page turn apart. The juxtaposition of the plans in this way inevitably leads to connections made between them and the search for consistencies between them, which Richard makes easy by including the *tituli* and the enumeration of the various spaces. The drawings' changing sizes and the plans' disregard of the outer atrium suggest a flexibility in the interpretation of the visual language at play through the five plans. The ordering of the material is key; it gives the drawings a syntax without which the careless reader could easily get lost, but the vocabulary is identical throughout, with the colored spaces providing an imprint of the buildings' footprint on Ezekiel's mountain. Comparisons between the five plans and earlier examples should not be taken as an attempt to find the expression of this language long before Richard started his commentary; instead, they should make Richard's innovations obvious. Something very important is happening in the pages of his manuscript: the first suggestion that architectural drawing was present long after Vitruvius, but long before Villard and Alberti.

By the time the reader finishes examining the third plan, there is a comfort in knowing the complex's overall appearance. It would have been easy for Richard to stop there, but instead he zooms into his and Ezekiel's vision in a lot more detail, and in so doing creates the first sectional elevation.

4 The Gatehouse

The Gatehouse Plans

The fifth plan, one of the most complex drawings in the entire commentary, ends Richard's overview, and after this point he provides much more detailed drawings of individual structures. From the fourth plan, we only need to turn the page twice to get to the first plan of the gatehouse. There are three gatehouse plans and two elevations, one from the front and the other from the side. The large number of drawings devoted to the gatehouse reflects the number of times it appears in Ezekiel's vision. As seen in the fifth plan, identical gatehouses are the transition points between the atria; between the inner and middle atria, there are six gatehouses in total. That five drawings are devoted to describing a single structure is remarkable, even in a precocious work such as *In visionem Ezechielis*. The result is almost a complete vision for the building, the like of which would not be seen for centuries afterward. The presence of these brilliant drawings raises the question of what exactly their purpose is, especially in the context of Victorine education. The last part of this chapter takes a step back from the plans and elevations to consider how figures were used in the Middle Ages in the context of theological texts.

As seen in the drawing for chapter twelve of *In visionem Ezechielis*, the gatehouse acts as a transition on three sides of the atria, and thus is the most common building in the entire complex. Richard focuses his and his readers' attention on it, since by describing one gatehouse, he describes them all. Like that of the ark, the biblical description is difficult to follow and gives little detail about the gatehouses' appearance or layout. Most of this description runs from Ezekiel 40:6 to 40:16. In the vision, Ezekiel's companion first measures the threshold as six cubits and the building's inner chambers as the same width, with chambers of five cubits between them.[1] The porch is eight cubits and the "front" (*frontem*) is two cubits. The companion then numbers the inner rooms, giving three on each side, all equal in width. Ezekiel then contradicts himself in verse eleven when he writes that the width of the gate was ten cubits, not six as stated earlier (Ez 40:6). The prophet then describes the "borders" (*marginem*) between the *thalami* and the rest of the inner room as one cubit. Finally, he gives the larger measurements: the height of the room is twenty-five cubits, the front is sixty, and the entire length is fifty cubits. The last part of the description treats the windows. The description gives some sense of how complicated Ezekiel's vision was, but it is clear from an examination of the Scriptural text that part of the issue is with the architectural vocabulary—namely, the exact meaning of the words "gate," "border," and "portico." The five drawings for the gatehouse (three plans and two elevations) echo this concern with the language of Scripture, spelling out the different parts and making sense of what can be read.

The first plan for the gatehouse is simple, with two rectangular spaces placed on either side of a vestibule that runs between them and with *tituli* that repeat on opposite sides of the rectangle (fig. 4.1). The short side gives the width of the wall as twenty-five cubits, and the long side gives the length of the structure as fifty cubits, as Ezekiel gives it. In doing so, Richard is selective about how he introduces information into the drawings. The width of the short walls is twenty-five cubits, as indicated, but the total size, including the width of the central passage, is sixty cubits.[2] So the reader must add the total length together since it is not explicitly done in the drawings (25 + 10 + 25). For the most part, the drawing is very similar to the earlier plans of the entire complex; while they were square and the gatehouse is a rectangle, the actual drawing makes it difficult to be sure of this shape. The key

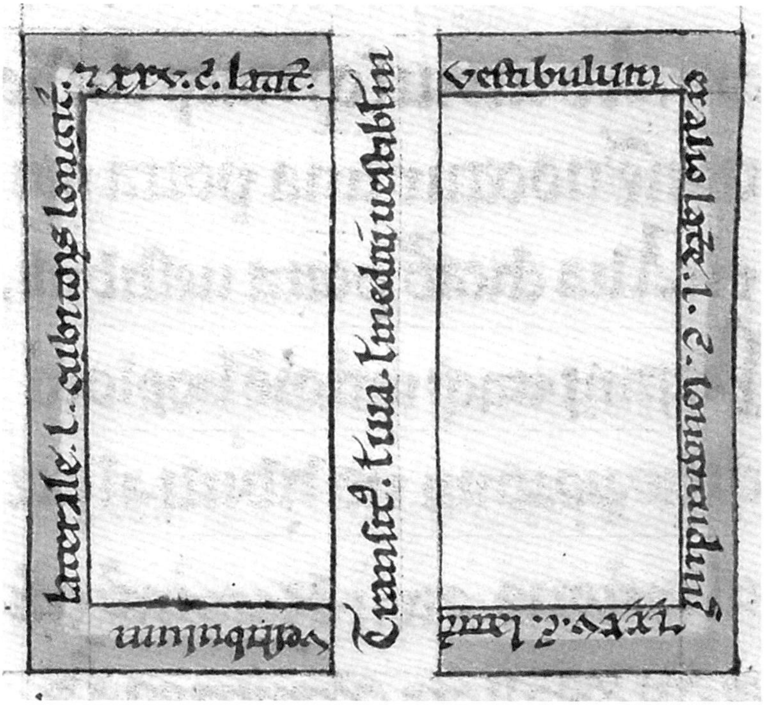

Fig. 4.1 Richard's plan for a gatehouse. Paris, BnF, MS Lat 14516, f. 217v.

identifiable element here and in the rest of the gatehouse drawings is the vestibule running through it, which distinguishes this building from the earlier plans.

In the Paris manuscript, the second gatehouse plan follows one page turn later; as he did with the first three plans, Richard placed related plans together, encouraging the reader to make connections between them. This plan offers much more detail about the building's internal structure (fig. 4.2). It shows one half of the gatehouse, detailing the divisions between the rooms that make up the building. At a right angle to the middle passage are seven long rooms, which Richard calls vestibules. There are also three inner rooms, called *thalami*, placed at the end of alternate vestibules, with the thresholds marked. The long rooms at either end of the passage are slightly wider than those set between them, including those enclosing *thalami*. There is little indication of the building's context, or that it is only one part of a larger structure. Richard must rely on the reader's ability to connect the sequence of plans to make sense of how they relate to one another.

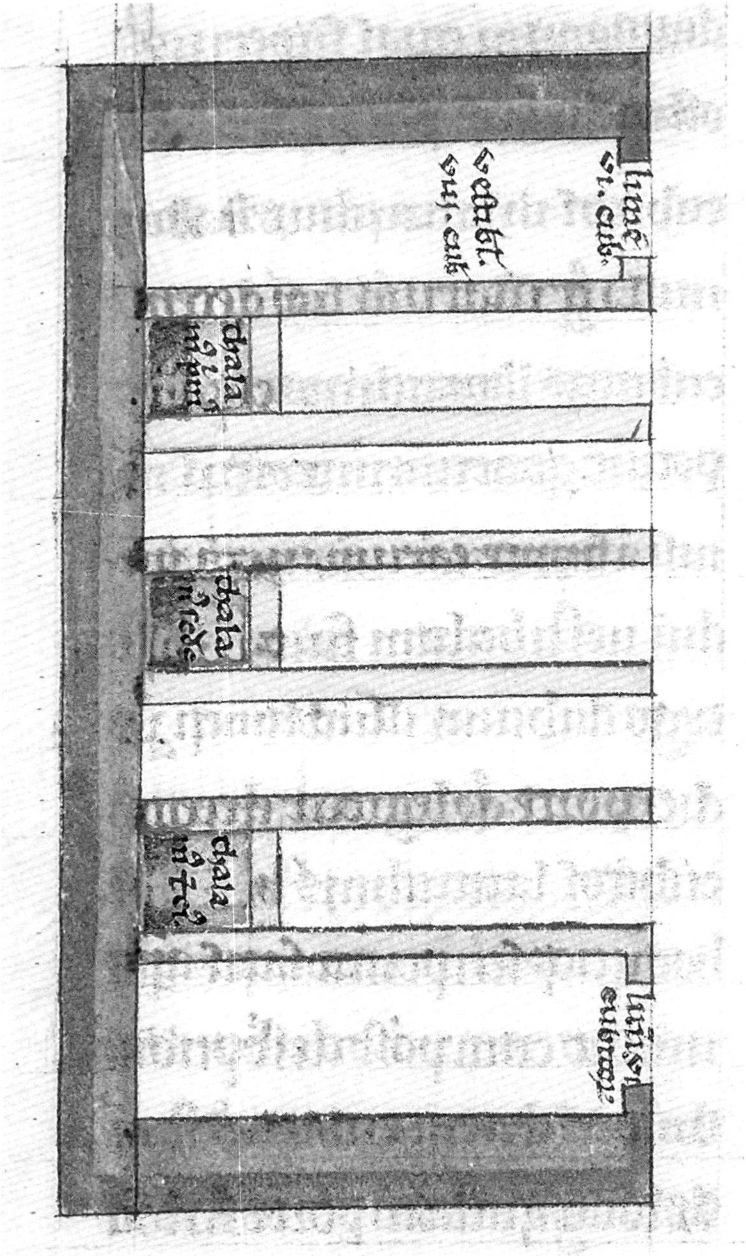

Fig. 4.2 Richard's plan for half a gatehouse. Paris, BnF, MS Lat. 14516, f. 219r.

The Victorine manuscript uses two green tones for the external walls, two red tones for the *thalami*, and yellow for the internal dividing walls. The construction of the plan was relatively simple, with a vertical construction line on the inner (that is, right) side, which marks the limit of the interior and the jamb of the entrance at the top and bottoms ends. A similar construction line appears on the inner side of the wall on the left side that marks the end of the inner chambers. This line extends into the green of the upper and lower short walls, which makes little structural sense and seems to be a vestigial construction mark made during the artist's process; for example, it is possible that the line was one of the first drawn by the artist to establish the length for the inner chambers and was never removed.

The *tituli* give the measurements for the threshold of the wide outer vestibules (six cubits), and the width of the vestibule itself is given on the top side (eight cubits). The vestibules containing the *thalami* are six cubits wide. Knowing that the building's total length is fifty cubits, as indicated in the previous drawing, it is possible to know the remaining measurements. If we do not include the thickness of the exterior walls, the remaining two vestibules are five cubits in width, because the thickness of the internal divisions is one cubit. Many of these measurements appear in Scripture, but Richard's innovation is to combine them into a sensible and consistent structure. But still, *In visionem Ezechielis* expects the reader to do a certain amount of imaginative and mathematical work to fully understand the appearance of the buildings it describes. It is a platform for understanding the past, not a complete description of it.

The third and final plan requires us to turn the page twice, but the connection between it and the second plan are very clear; indeed, it simply combines the two previous drawings to illustrate the entire structure of the gatehouse as if from above (fig. 4.3). The plan comprises the two parts of the previous plan but gives a much better impression of the passage that runs through the middle of the structure and its contextual relationship with the building. The colors in MS 14516 are the main difference between this plan and the previous one. The external walls change from green to yellow and bare parchment, and the internal walls are rendered in green instead. The drawing has an unfinished appearance because there are no *tituli*, unlike in every previous drawing. If the viewer references the previous plan, some of the spaces are

Fig. 4.3 Richard's detailed plan for a gatehouse. Paris, BnF, MS Lat 14516, f. 220v.

clear, such as the measurements of the two outer vestibules and the width of their thresholds. There is, however, a tendency for redundancy by the Victorine artist in the *tituli*, such as in the first plan of the gatehouse, where the measurements of the external walls are included on both sides, where only one would have been necessary. All of this suggests that the diagram in this manuscript is unfinished. If it is unfinished, it is necessary to draw on some later examples of the plan.

The large number of *tituli* in other manuscripts demonstrate their usefulness regarding this particular plan. For example, a thirteenth-century Cambridge manuscript (fig. 4.4) gives a strong idea of the gatehouse's measurements and the relationships

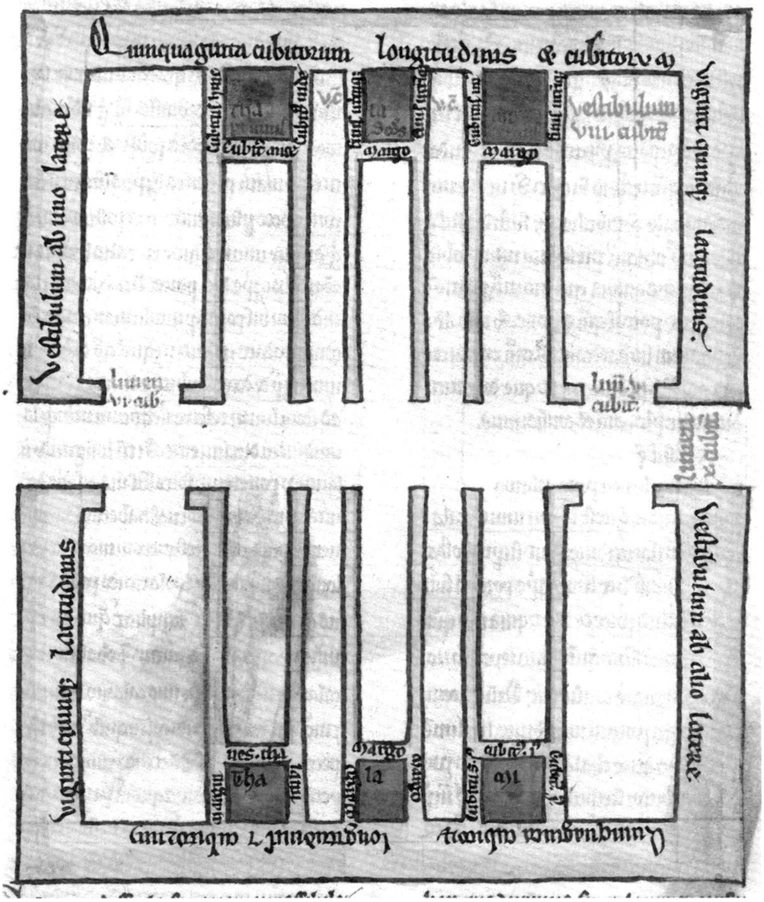

Fig. 4.4 Full plan of a gatehouse. Cambridge, Corpus Christi College, MS 315, f. 87r.

among its different parts.[3] As in the first plan, the dimensions of the entire structure are given within the external walls, and the length of the long side is intended to be read additively. Richard gives one side a length of twenty-five cubits, followed by the width of the threshold as ten cubits, and finally the other side of the external wall as twenty-five cubits, giving a total of sixty cubits. As in the previous drawing of half the structure, the threshold width and the width of the flanking vestibules are given as six and eight cubits, respectively. Richard identifies the individual rooms by numbered *tituli*. On the upper side, the word *thalami* is split between the three rooms, with the first, second, and third identified; however, there is no identification on the opposite side, where "thalami" is simply repeated. This leaves a question hanging over the formulation of the rooms' identification: should the unnumbered three rooms be numbers four, five, and six, or should they retain the same numbering as their counterparts on the other side of the vestibule? The numbering and placement of the rooms is consistent across the plans and elevations, discussed below. Further information is given in the plan on the top side, where the width of the rectangular rooms between the *thalami* is given as five cubits, which confirms the result of adding the measurements together shown above. So the measurements are not strictly needed in this case. Finally, the internal thresholds for the *thalami* are called "margins" (*margine*), and measured as one cubit, which corresponds to the jamb width on the flanking vestibules, suggesting consistency in the measurements.

The plans begin to offer an important glimpse into Richard's processes for making the drawings and show that they were highly integrated into conventional methods of manuscript construction during the twelfth century. When making a manuscript, the scribe would write the text before the codex was bound, so the parchment would be laid out flat in front of him. To ensure that the text would be perfectly straight, guides were used—light vertical and horizontal lines made with drypoint or lead, their lightness being important so that the reader would not be distracted from the text. These guidelines usually form about two dozen horizontal lines on the surface of each folio, and vertical lines on either side created a grid on which the copyist and the artist could work. The construction of architectural diagrams and drawings is suited to the gridlike pattern formed by these rulings. They are made with a straight edge and have regular intervals separating the horizontal lines, thus giving a set measurement defined by the tool used to make the ruling. In this sense, the actual measurements between the parts are not an issue; all that matters is that they are consistently followed. Some evidence exists to suggest that earlier architectural plans used the advantages gained from using the rulings in this way. For example, a ninth-century plan illustrating the alphabet written on the church's pavement during the consecration rite uses the vertical margin to frame the diagram, and the text within it aligns with the regular rulings.[4] The gridlike pattern resulting from the lines suits any architectural forms, especially those in the context of visual exegesis, where issues of scale and exact measurements were not important. The result is something like modern graph paper.

This grid may explain how later artists were able to copy Richard's plans so accurately. For example, in the second gatehouse plan in our Paris manuscript (fig. 4.2)—showing half the building—the top line, representing the external wall, is drawn along the top horizontal guideline. The width of the wall is defined by the column width of the horizontal guidelines. Two green tones mark the wall, split in half, but the darker shade of green bends round to fill the outer jamb. In this instance, the artist simply used the textual guidelines as a somewhat arbitrary thickness and constructed the diagram around it. Not all the latitudinal walls coincide with a textual guideline, because the presence of the jambs makes them irregular and the long rooms on each flank are supposed to be two or three cubits broader than the inner rooms. Due to this irregularity, while the textual guidelines mark the top, they do not align with the bottom external wall. This suggests that the drawing was begun from the top, using the premade drypoint marks as a convenient straight line to illustrate the external line. The concern, however, for an inner consistency between the internal measurements means that Richard did not end on a drypoint line.

The horizontal textual guidelines were not the only ones followed by the artists who copied the plan. In a late twelfth-century manuscript, Oxford, MS Bodl. 494, the plan appears on folio 137v in the lower left corner (fig. 4.5). Here it is reversed compared to the previous examples, showing the mirror image and hence the other side of the building (both sides are identical, so the diagram's content is not affected). The artist has clearly decided to use the outermost vertical guideline to define the inner side of the door jambs. The inner vertical line is then used to orient the *tituli* that indicate the width of the doorframe. The same *tituli* at the bottom of the diagram are slightly different where the outermost line is used for the same reason. The horizontal guidelines are slightly less consistent, although they do demonstrate a relationship between the plan and the textual grid. Unlike in the Paris example, the upper external wall is not perfectly in line with a horizontal; it is placed partially above it. This seems an unusual choice, because if, like the Paris example, the figure was drawn from top to bottom, the most natural way to start would be to place the external wall along an existing line. However, the artist

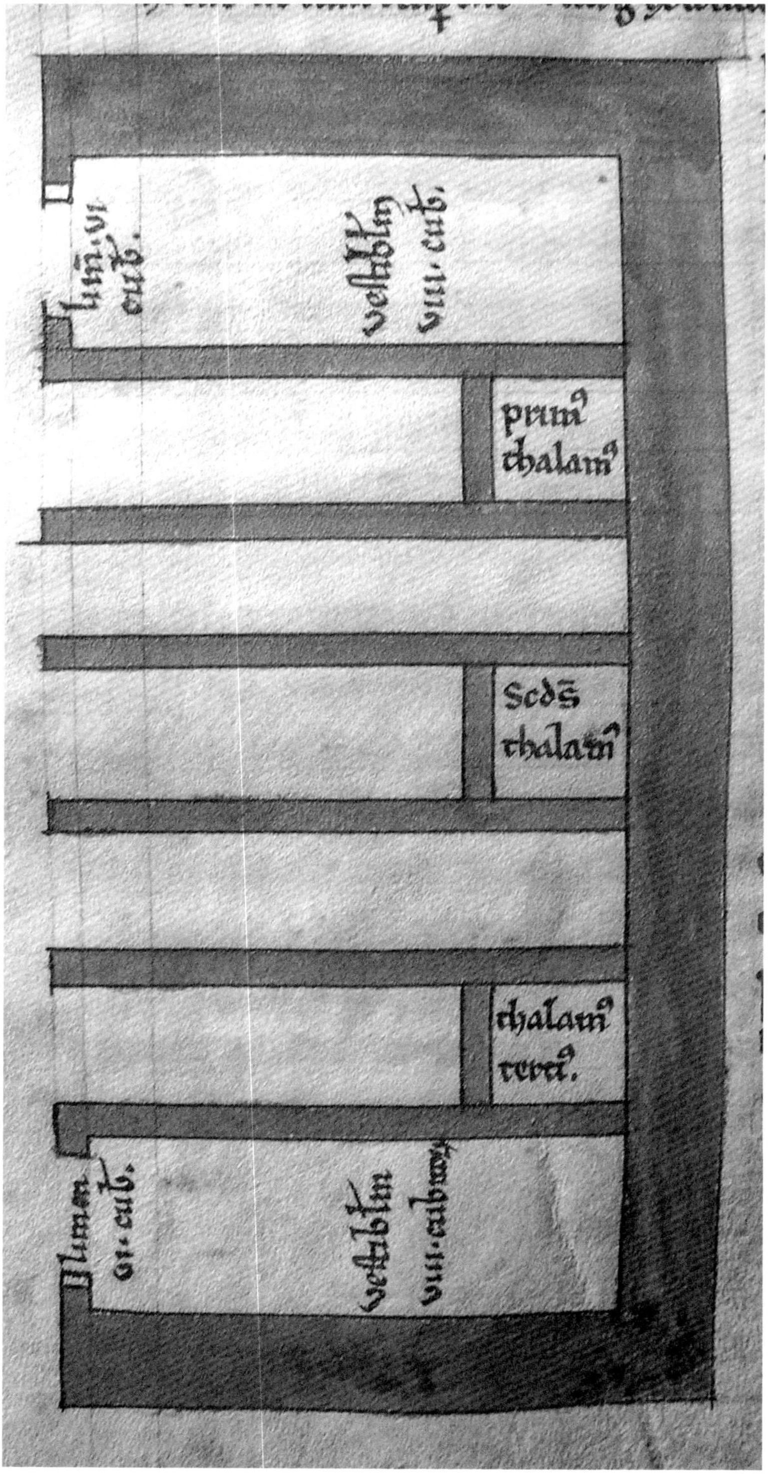

Fig. 4.5 Richard's plan for half a gatehouse. Oxford, Bodleian Library, MS Bodl. 494, f. 137v.

in Bodl. 494 may have begun the drawing from the outer jamb at the top, and not necessarily the external wall. This is one of the only parts of the drawing to coincide with a textual guideline, doing so on the horizontal and vertical axes. The artist appears to have misjudged the relative size of the cubit-length jamb, as implied by the brown paint's not completely filling the space.

This grid is not just a by-product of the manufacture of the manuscript but represents an important part of Victorine education. The grid integrates both the practice and theory of historical methodologies at the abbey's school, and is inherent in how Hugh, Richard, and many others were ble to create architectural structures in their imaginations. To understand this, it is necessary to return to Hugh, who created the legacy of historical practice at Saint Victor.

Grids were an important part of the conceptual underpinnings of the way Victorine students set out ideas, and formed an integral part of a complex and popular mnemonic system described by Hugh of Saint Victor in his *De tribus maximus circumstantiis gestorum*. Their use in the transmission of *In visionem Ezechielis* partly accounts for the consistency between the different copies, and ensured that the commentary could be situated within a recognizable intellectual context. Hugh's *De tribus* is not associated with an architectural drawing but uses a diagrammatic figure to organize information within a grid. As a result, the reader's engagement with the past is highly structured, with text and image combining and becoming fixed in the reader's mind.[5] The *De tribus* is "a schoolbook of history" addressed explicitly to a student.[6] It would have been read or at least known by students passing through Saint Victor's school, as it was not an obscure work of history but an integral part of the abbey's educational system, which placed history as the basis for all knowledge.[7] Near the beginning of *De tribus*, Hugh discusses the utility of a grid system as a basis from which the student can memorize and come to a fuller understanding of the people and events of the past.[8]

Hugh describes three methods through which memory functions: number, location, and occasion.[9] On "number," Hugh writes, "Learn to construct in your mind a line [of numbers] numbered from one on ..., become accustomed to quickly turning your mind there where its sum is enclosed. ... For example, when you hear ten, think of the tenth place."[10] After readers have memorized and become comfortable with this number line, Hugh explains how it may be used to learn the psalms. "I learn them [the psalms] all in order so that I know which is the first, which the second, which the third, and so on. I then place them all by order in my heart along my numerical line, and one at a time I designate them to the seats where they are disposed in the grid."[11] When the student has assigned the beginning of each psalm its appropriate number, they should turn their attention to the individual psalms. "I then devise the same sort of scheme for each separate psalm, starting with the words of the verses just as I did for the whole Psalter starting with the first words of the psalms, and I can thereafter easily retain in my heart the whole series one verse at a time. ... I have reduced a large amount of material to such conciseness and brevity."[12] As a result, the grid is the basis for all other work, a *tabula rasa* on which the student can build knowledge and creativity.

Importantly, for our purposes, Hugh's envisioned "gridlike" structure reflects the two-dimensional nature of the architectural representation in *In visionem Ezechielis*: the architectural drawings are formed with lines, and the information is given order by envisioning a grid. As a result, this geometrical construction comprising "plane figures" (two-dimensional objects) is a key component not only in architectural representation, but even in the conceptual models trained into Victorine students. Richard's drawings rely on the conceptual models given by geometry to the text and images in *In visionem Ezechielis*, while the manuscripts themselves, filled with the sort of grids that Hugh describes, offer a foundation on which to build Ezekiel's temple complex.

Hugh's *De tribus maximus circumstantiis gestorum* contains a series of tables (fig. 4.6).[13] The tables begin with an outline of the stages of creation ordered along the vertical axis, indicated by the term "creation" set within an arch at the top of the second column. The six days of creation and what occurs on those days are then listed; these are grouped into six overlapping stages, also indicated by arches set within the first and fourth columns.[14] This outline of creation is then separated from the information set below it, which Hugh indicates to display "years since creation," "patriarch," "became father, aged," and "years lived." The centrality of memory in Hugh's discussion of the table comes to the fore, especially where he mentions the importance of organizing the material in a way which would aid its recall, writing, "it is necessary to retain it [the 'good foundation the table provides'] in

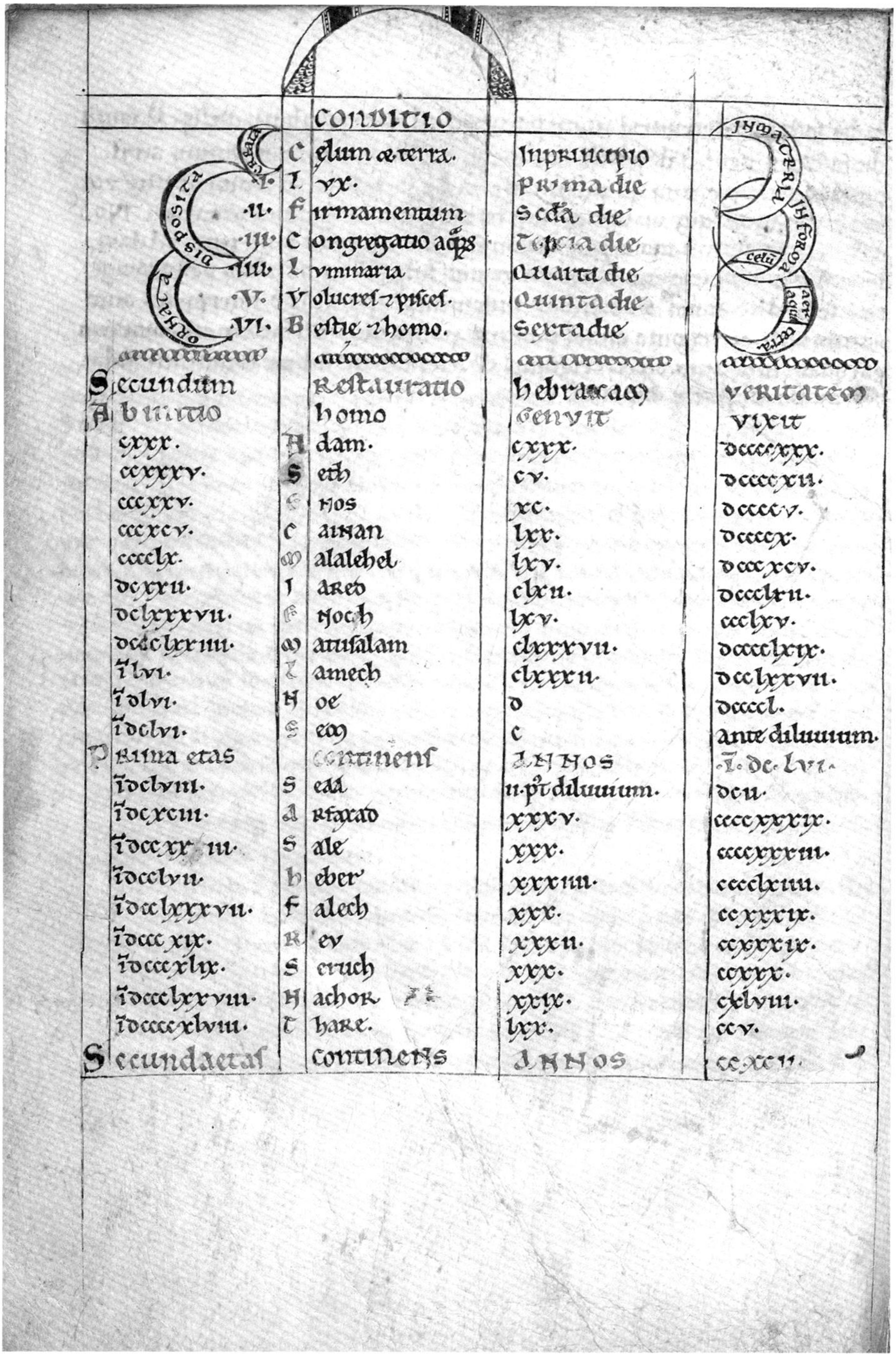

Fig. 4.6 Hugh of Saint Victor's historical table. Paris, BnF, MS Lat. 15009, ff. 3v–4r.

memory and by diligent retracing to have it customary and well known ... by a suitable distribution according to its place, date, and person."[15] For Hugh, the act of ordering the material at hand is an important step in the process of remembering.

Hugh's words suggest a strong correlation between architecture and memory at Saint Victor, where images do not just act as storehouses for thoughts but help arrange those thoughts, and more importantly, give the reader an image on which to meditate. The imaginative structure underpinning both architecture and memory is similar to a modern gridded notebook, except it is a structure through which one can travel, depositing and reclaiming memories depending on what is needed. Despite the relative rarity of architectural representation in the early and central Middle Ages, certain authors were accustomed to thinking about architecture and using this framework to order their thoughts and memories. When it comes to architecture, the richness of the medieval imagination stands in stark contrast to the dearth of physical pictures. Yet the relatively few extant images do not mean that monks, canons, and clerics were not interested in architecture, only that they found another more spiritually oriented function for it.

In the discussion that follows, we will not have strayed far from Richard's commentary in this discussion; indeed, the investment of time and energy manifest in *In visionem Ezechielis* shows an author comfortable envisioning architectural forms in two and three dimensions. The only way to make sense of that is by engaging with the most common use of architectural forms in a monastic context during Middle Ages: their mnemonic application.

In this sense, by the twelfth century, memory was spoken in the language of architecture, visualized and embodied insomuch as the imagination would allow.[16] According to this view, techniques used for improving recall, andfor developing inspiration from remembered items, stem from antiquity, and are transmitted in the pseudo-Ciceronian *Rhetorica ad Herennium*.[17] This text was known during the Middle Ages and provided an outline for rhetorical education, including the memorization of texts and ideas with a view to using them in the creation of new works. Elements from a speech or memorized text were envisioned as an object and placed against an architectural backdrop. This backdrop formed part of a larger structure, which allowed the subject to recall certain memories and, importantly, the order in which the memories were originally placed. When the subject wished to remember the original work, they would imagine themselves walking through the same architectural structure, and be reminded of the work or text based on the images which they had originally placed there in their imagination.[18] Carruthers differentiates between advice given to students in the classical texts and the reality of monastic practice during the Middle Ages. The classical texts encouraged the student to use buildings "such as his own house, which he would revisit frequently," and allowed for a firm recollection of the architectural backdrops.[19] Medieval practice, on the other hand, was "to construct a wholly fictional building," allowing for a variety of structures.[20] And so architecture could retain certain medieval elements, since they would be the most accessible, but organize them into new and varied forms.

The mnemonic techniques of *Rhetorica ad Herennium* involve entire rooms and buildings to hold the objects of memory, but whether they can be applied to architectural history, as opposed to intellectual history, is in doubt, since it was merely "the history of a particular mnemonic technique" and claims of its importance were therefore "far-fetched."[21] The techniques, however, were not confined to their exact description in the Pseudo-Ciceronian work, but were modified for students whose imagination was still being trained. The architectural basis paradoxically comes to the fore once the buildings are removed from the mnemonic system and replaced by a series of grids, as in Hugh's account. When this is done, students have a foundation on which memories could not only be stored but indexed using the same two-dimensional system as Richard uses for *In visionem Ezechielis*. Architecture and memory share in the language of geometry, and it would seem that memory came first, with Richard applying his grid to the representation of Ezekiel's buildings, an approach shared by many of the work's copyists in the twelfth and thirteenth centuries.

Even Hugh's language retains the geometric tone and vocabulary, illustrating a *sui generis* reliance on plane figures. For example, he writes, "For the memory always rejoices in both brevity of length and paucity of number ... so what the mind could not comprehend in a single expanse it can comprehend in a number."[22] In Carruthers's translation, the term *spatio* has been rendered as "length." One possible reason for this translation stems from the infrequent use of the term *spatio* to mean "space," as *locus* is much more commonly used for this. *Spatio*, by contrast, is used almost exclusively with respect to geometric objects, as in a figure or diagram. Hugh uses the language of length (*longitudinem*) and width (*latitudinem*) to describe the diagrams under discussion, using the spatial qualities of plane figures to orient the viewer. Again, these words reflect geometric language used to represent two-dimensional objects, and especially architecture in twelfth-century didactic works. By orienting the reader through references to length and width, the diagrams create a tangible object which the student may interact with and assimilate during the process of learning, aiding their memorization by creating an organizational principle rooted in a physical object. Hugh's tables are certainly less sophisticated than the three-dimensional structures Richard describes, but they are both born of the same concern for order and clarity.

The overwhelming impression given by the structure of Richard's argument echoes his approach in the first four plans; he begins with a very general idea of the entire structure before moving on to any details, such as the measurements of the jambs, vestibules, and thresholds of the *thalami*. It is an important structure because there are six gatehouses in the inner and middle atria; thus, creating a good sense of its appearance helps the reader make overall sense of the atria's composition. There is no need for the second plan because the same information is provided in the third. The drawings' sequence, therefore, is probably derived from the underlying pedagogical role that the plans are intended to carry out. They are not to be read individually, hopping from one to another to understand particular parts of the buildings, but are meant to be examined in their entirety and in the order they appear. This is the syntax of Richard's drawings; to be understood in their entirety, the order of *In visionem Ezechielis* must be kept, otherwise meaning is lost. This gives the plans, and indeed many of the drawings, a rhetorical power that prioritizes simplicity and a sequential narrative that moves from the simple to the complex.

The Gatehouse Elevations

It comes as a surprise that when finished with the third gatehouse plan, the reader must turn quite a few pages before reaching the elevations for the gatehouse. The final plan appears on folio 220v and the frontal elevation is on folio 240r, leaving an immense amount of text between the two drawings. For the

Fig. 4.7 Richard's front elevation for a gatehouse. Paris, BnF, MS Lat 14516, f. 240r.

reader interested in the drawings, the drama is heightened, leaving the vision of the gatehouse only half completed in the plans; the reader knows its footprint but not its two faces. The gap is important, because within it Richard changes perspective from above to beside the building; as the following chapter will show, this change is fundamental to how *In visionem Ezechielis* works.

The elevations are extraordinary. There is nothing like them until half a century later when Villard de Honnecourt compiled his portfolio of architectural drawings. The front elevation (fig. 4.7) shows the taller side of the gatehouse; that is, the end facing outward, away from the inner atrium. As is made clear by the lateral elevation (fig. 4.8), the gatehouse is placed on top of seven steps carved into a mountainside that extend through the

Fig. 4.8 Richard's lateral sectional elevation for a gatehouse. Paris, BnF, MS Lat. 14516, f. 240v.

inner vestibule; since the roof is flat—as indicated—the inner side is shorter than the outer. The frontal elevation is the first that explicitly states what the drawing represents; just below the crenellations, Richard gives a description: "a representation of the gate, as if seen from the front."[23] Before discussing the variety of inscriptions on the frontal elevation, we should consider the type of visual language Richard employs. Elevations were exceptionally rare drawing types in the Middle Ages, and as a result there is little against which to compare Richard's. In the frontal elevation, we are shown a crenellated three-story building divided into three vertical planes: two wide vertical bands on either side, and a slimmer one running from top to bottom in the middle. In the Paris manuscript, the walls are emphasized with a three-tone green band, emphasizing the building's structural parts. The whole edifice is placed on top of the mountain's soil, represented here as three tones of brown and ochre in wavy bands.

The visual language in both elevations can make it difficult to interpret Richard's exact vision for the building, especially when determining how each part relates to the other. Where some have argued for the gatehouse's similarities to contemporary structures, medieval visual strategies are rarely that simple and certainly did not include drawing a building from life. Instead, we must look deeper into both what the drawings represent and how they do it.[24]

In the frontal elevation, crenellations are set within the upper two floors behind the double arches; the first of these floors has a blue background and the second has no coloring but has a sequence of curves that look like clouds on the right side, although it is unclear what these are intended to represent. It is possible that the view extends the entire length of the gatehouse, and Richard intended for crenellations to be placed on the inner side of the two top floors. There is a tendency to show the elevations orthographically (i.e., without perspectival lines), which would support this view. Other drawings do not have crenellations on the middle floor.[25]

Any difficulty in reading the front elevation derives from the slim central section, which shows five narrow windows inserted at regular vertical intervals. The masonry patterns on the bottom part of the section are separate from those on the sides, indicating a boundary between this central part and the rest of the building. The effect is that the central part is somehow separate from the sides, as if it extends forward or backward somehow and we are unable to see it because of the orthographic viewpoint. There are examples of this visual strategy in several places, but especially on seals depicting buildings, where the transepts of a church are seen extending outward from the central section.[26] In these depictions, it is impossible to tell that the transepts are set back from the front of the building. Something else, however, is happening in Richard's front elevation. Instead of attempting to replicate contemporary gatehouses, Richard imprints the interior structure onto the exterior, so that the viewer can see the central passage running through the building in the elevation. This passage has been Richard's main concern up to this point; it is the center of the first plan, the point of division in the second plan, and takes up a large amount of space in the third plan. In the elevation, the central part is not a bay extending from the ground floor to the crenellations; instead, this central "pier" shows the central vestibule running through the middle of the interior. As a result, the elevation is more of a hybrid than a pure elevation, combining elements of plan and elevation for a stronger sense of the building's entire layout. Richard's attempt to combine interior and exterior in a single view takes on another form in the elevation's ground floor.

The same close relationship between interior and exterior is underlined by the *tituli* on the ground floor.[27] In the front elevation, both sides read "lateral vestibule 25 cubits in width" in script running alongside both of the building's flanks (fig. 4.9).[28] Underneath that and running vertically, the text reads, "the location of the inner room."[29] The masonry pattern that takes up much of the drawing, as well as the presence of windows, clearly indicate that we see the building's exterior. The placement of the inscription, however, suggests that the *tituli*'s purpose is to illustrate the building's interior composition and its relationship with the exterior. The ambiguity of whether the viewer sees the interior or exterior is further reinforced by the *titulus* above that refers to the "roof of the *thalami*," which could only refer to the interior spaces since the *thalami* are the inner rooms at the end of three vestibules. This is an important measurement because it is one of the few unambiguous descriptions in the biblical text, where the chamber is given a height of twenty-five cubits (Ez 40:13). The *tituli* reinforce the biblical text without quoting it directly—as in the very first plan—but still explicitly link it with Richard's visual material. A

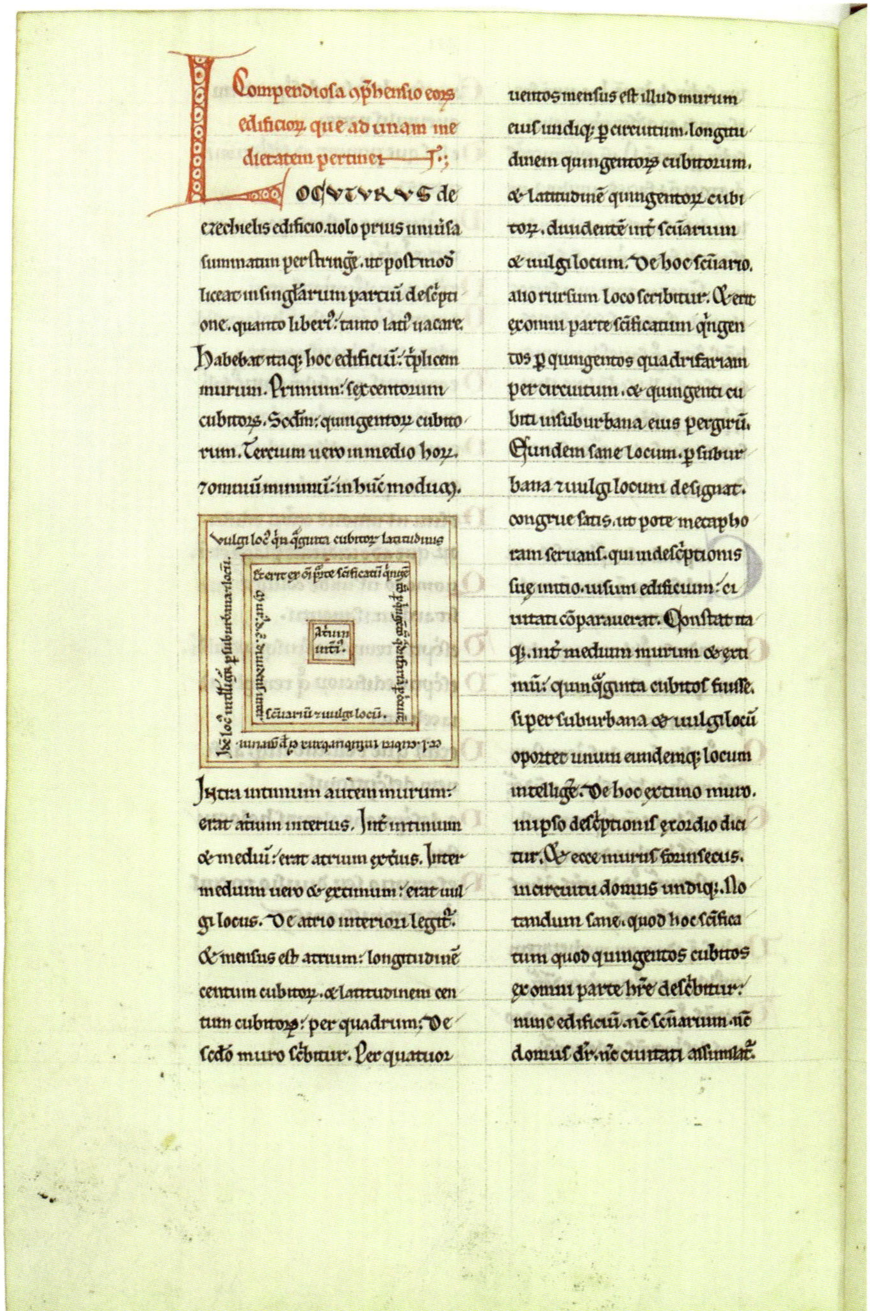

Plate 1 Richard's plan for the entire temple complex. Paris, BnF, MS Lat. 14516, f. 211v.

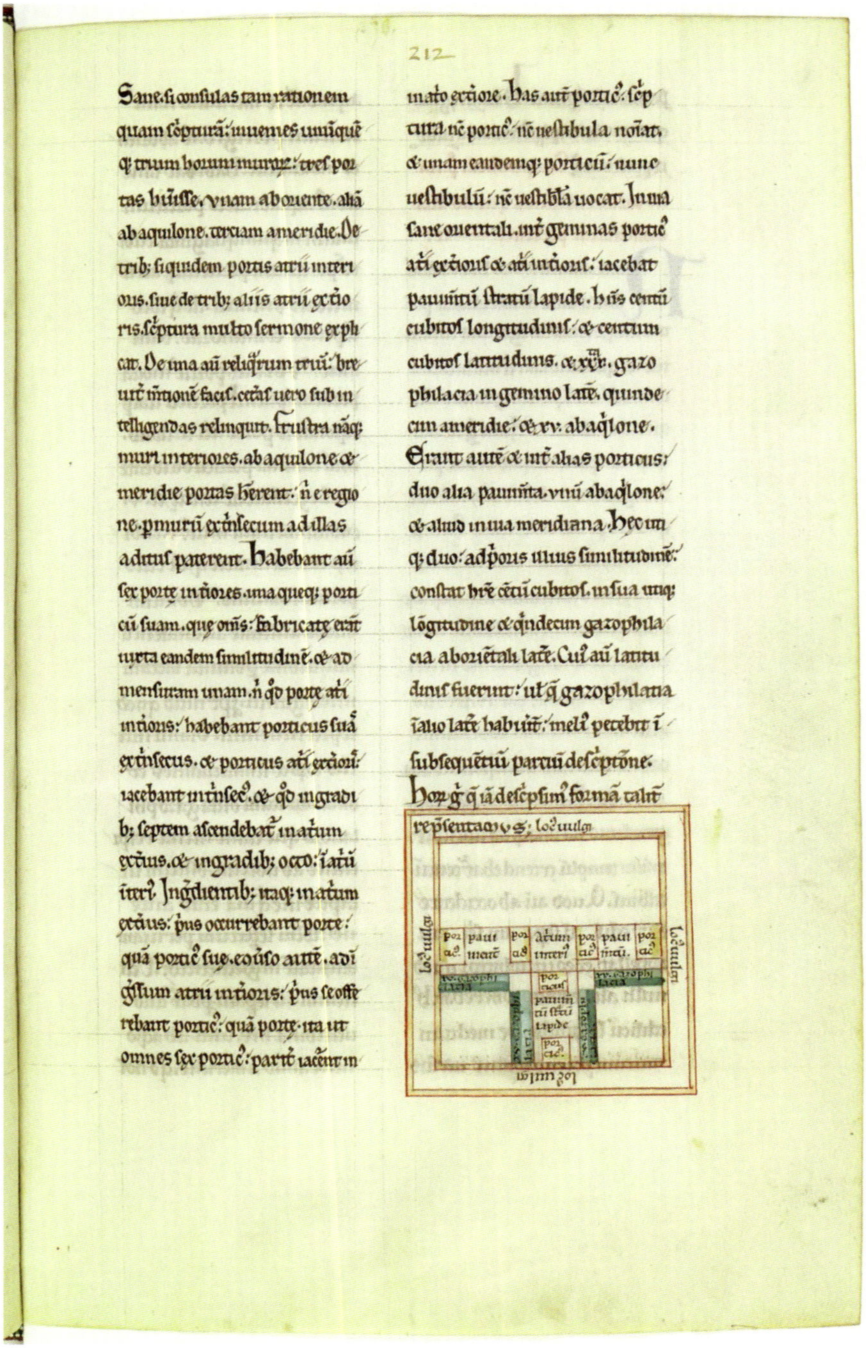

Plate 2 Richard's plan for the temple complex with the gatehouse locations indicated. Paris, BnF, MS Lat. 14516, f. 212r.

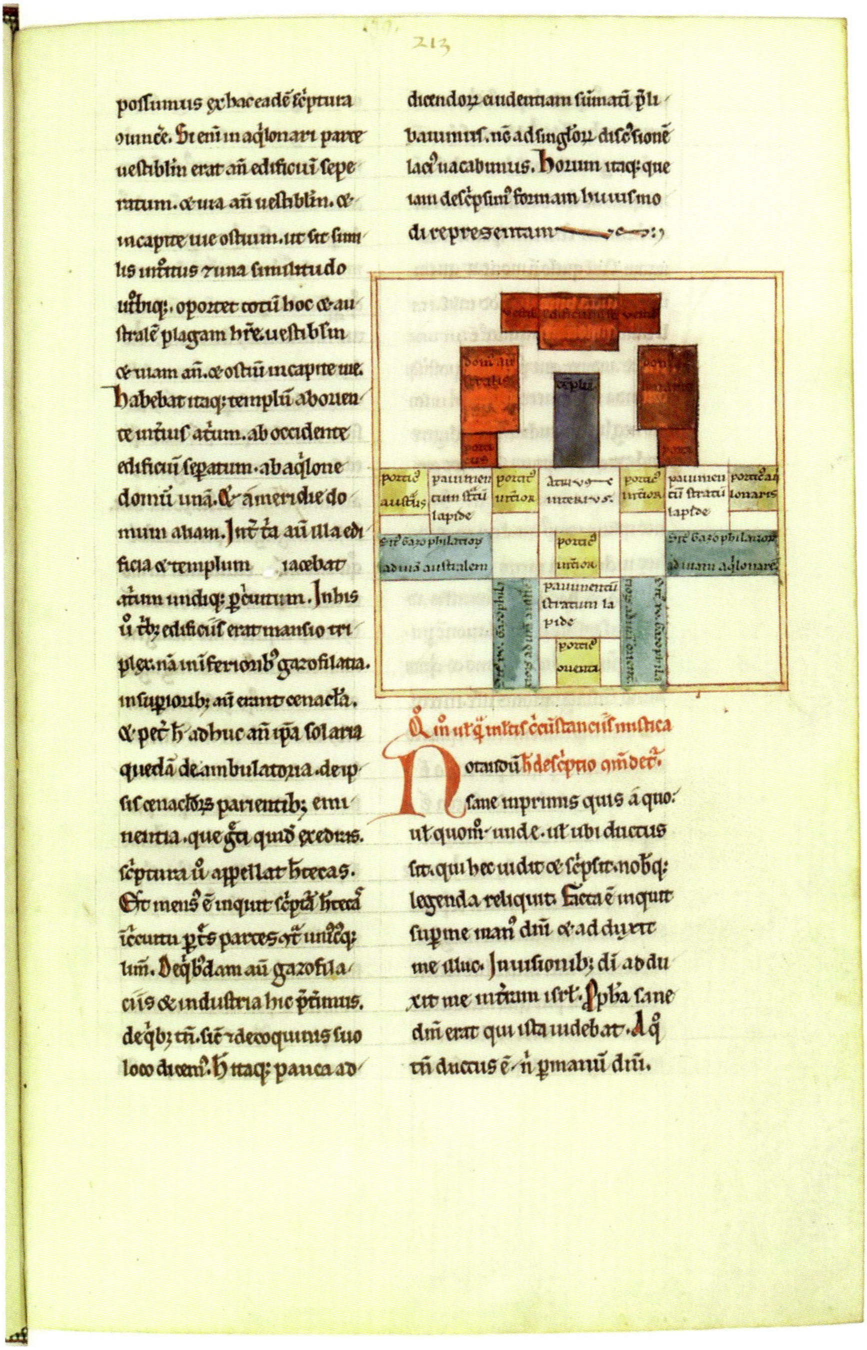

Plate 3 Richard's plan for the middle and inner atria indicating the temple's location. Paris, BnF, MS Lat. 14516, f. 213r.

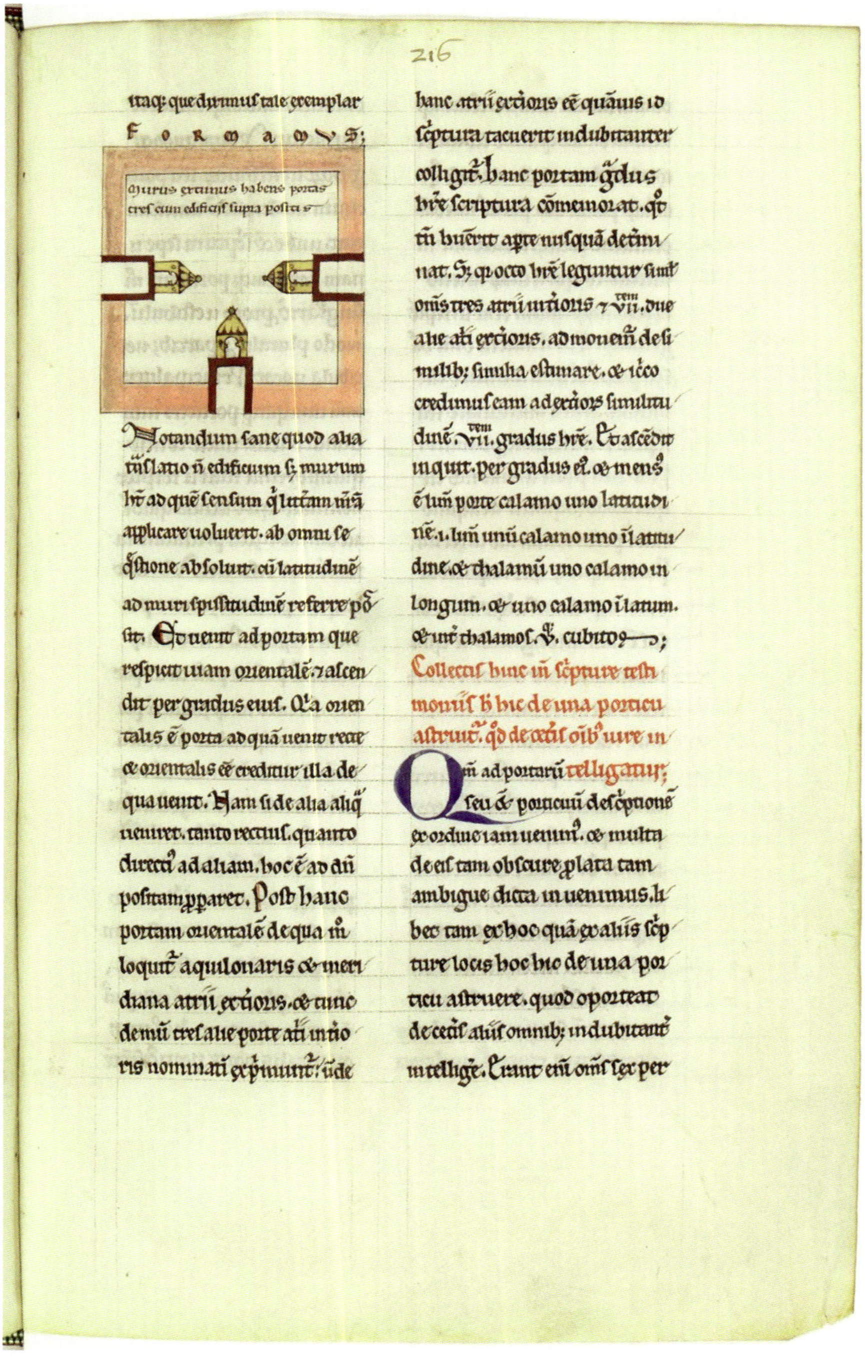

Plate 4 Richard's hybrid plan of the inner atrium with elevations of the gatehouses. Paris, BnF, MS Lat. 14516, f. 216r.

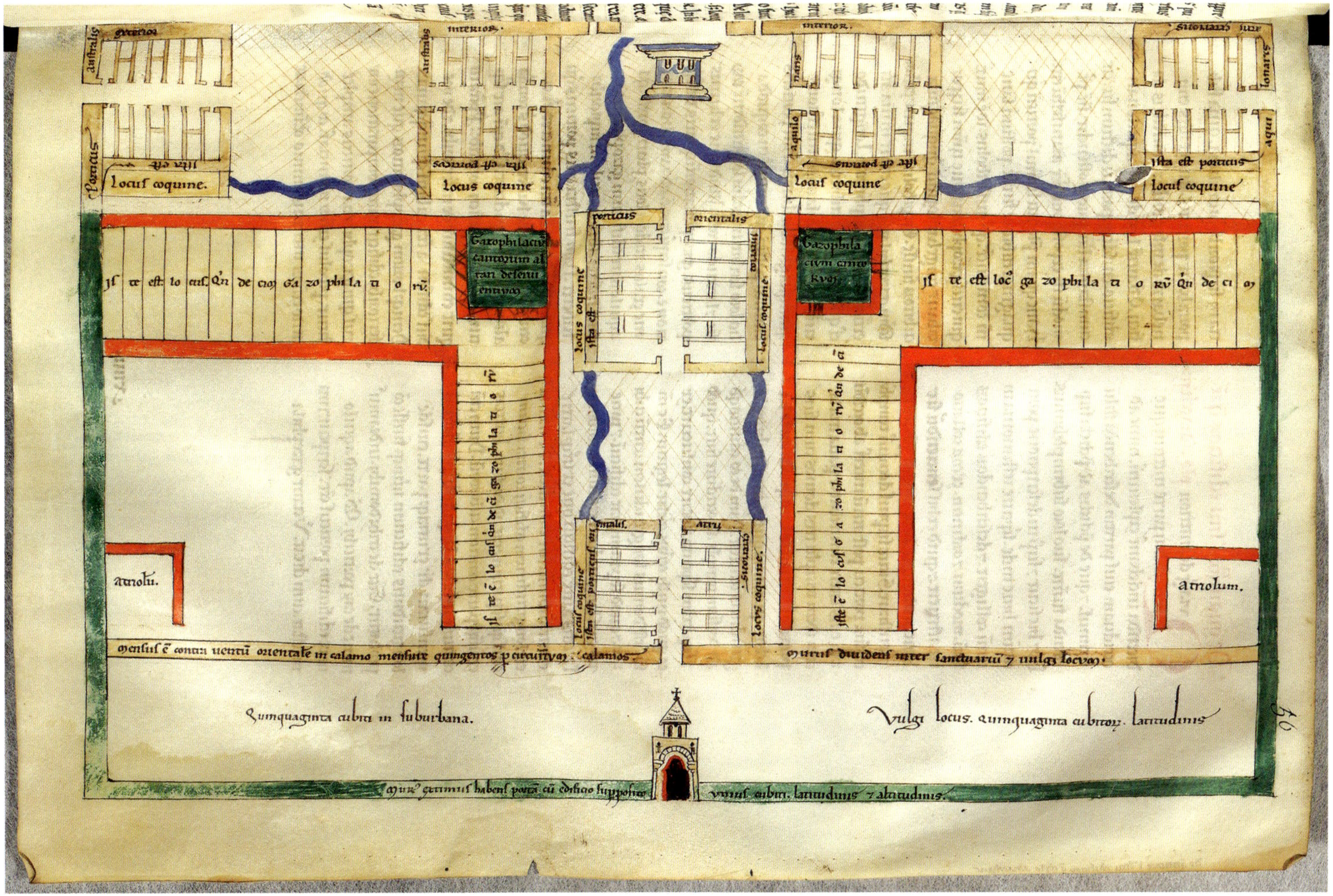

Plate 5 Richard's detailed plan showing the gatehouses and *gazophylacia*. Paris, BnF, MS Lat. 2165, f. 56r.

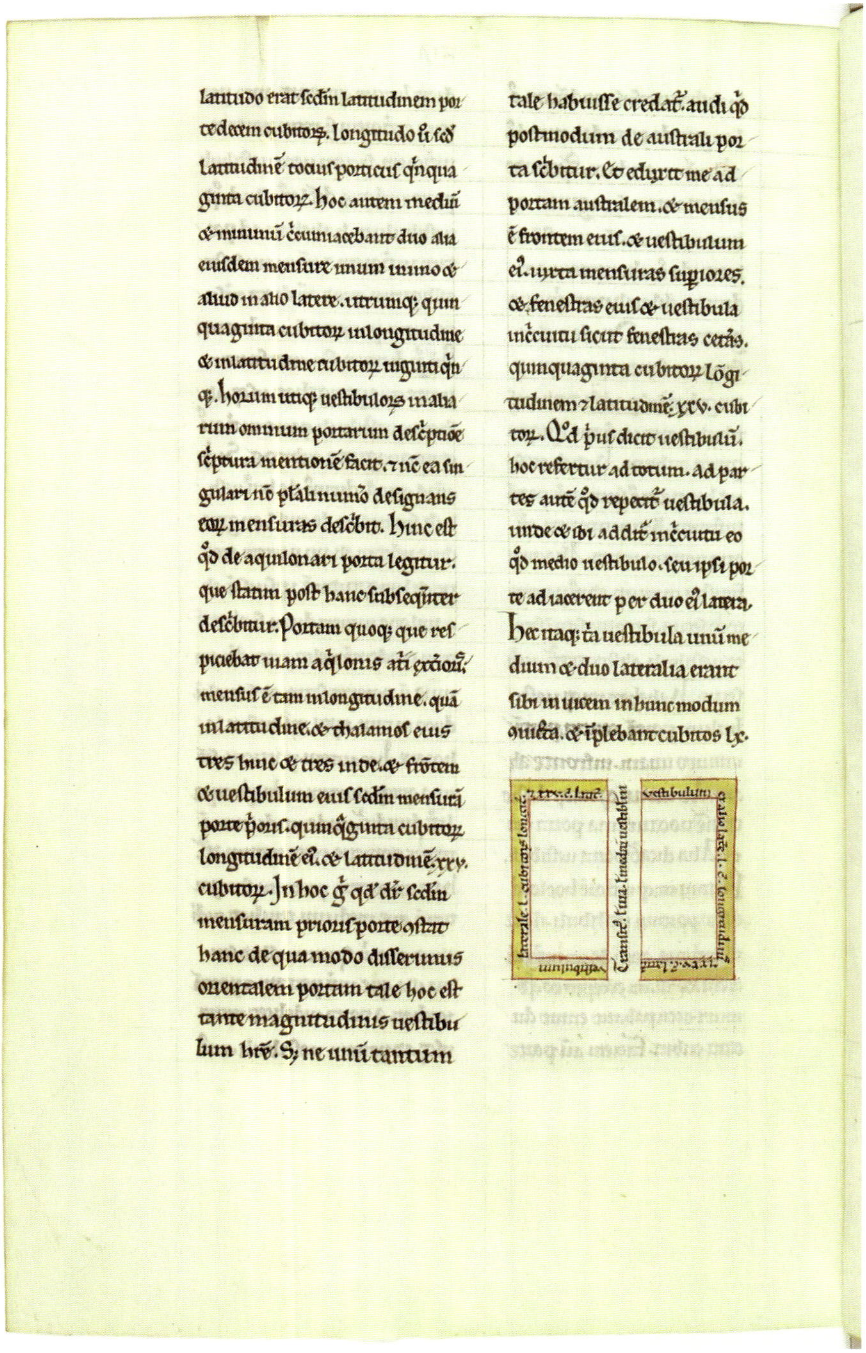

Plate 6 Richard's plan for a gatehouse. Paris, BnF, MS Lat. 14516, f. 217v.

Plate 7 Richard's plan for half a gatehouse. Paris, BnF, MS Lat. 14516, f. 219r.

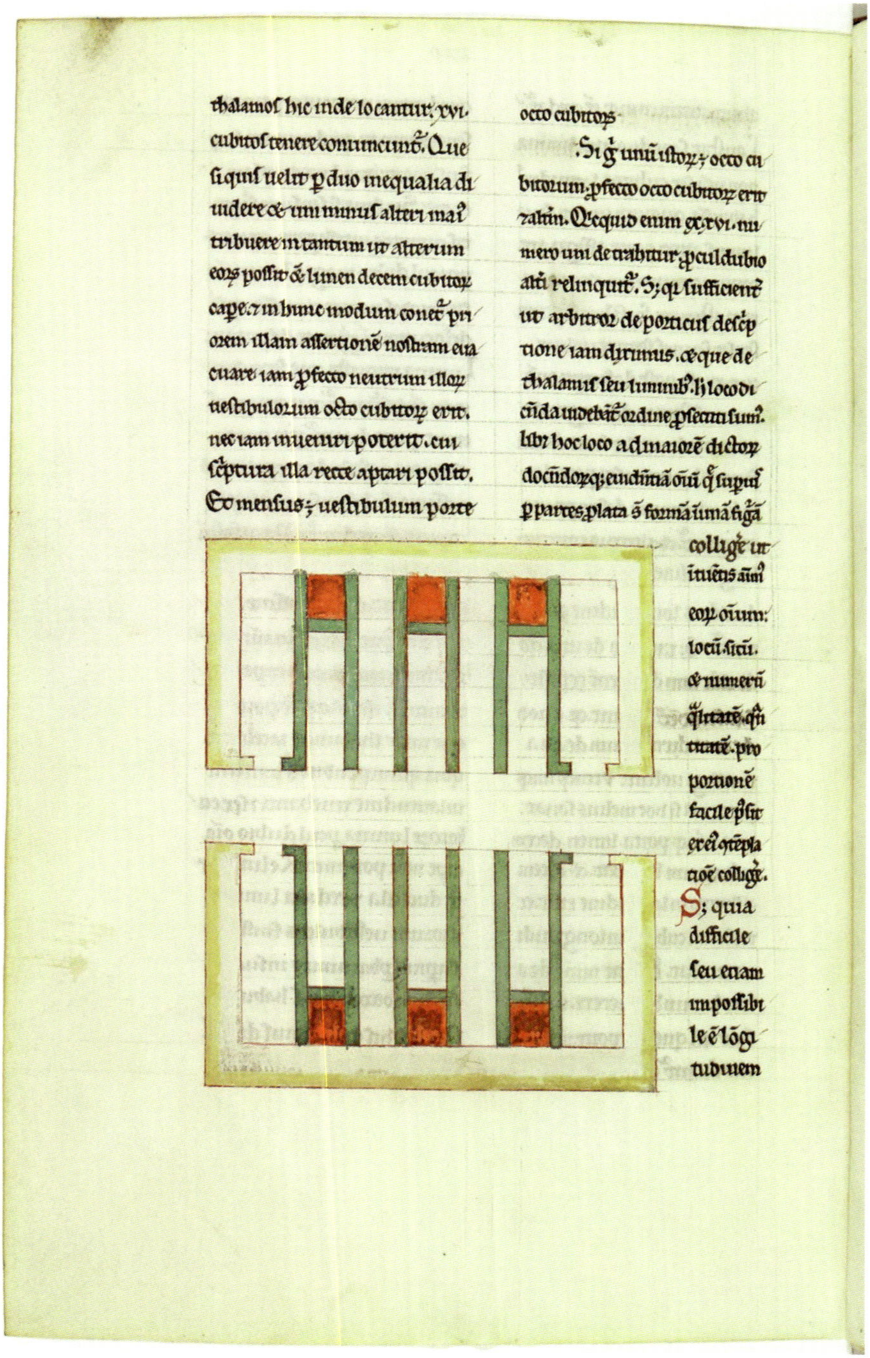

Plate 8 Richard's detailed plan for a gatehouse. Paris, BnF, MS Lat. 14516, f. 220v.

Plate 9 Richard's front elevation for a gatehouse. Paris, BnF, MS Lat. 14516, f. 240r.

Plate 10 Richard's lateral sectional elevation for a gatehouse. Paris, BnF, MS Lat. 14516, f. 240v.

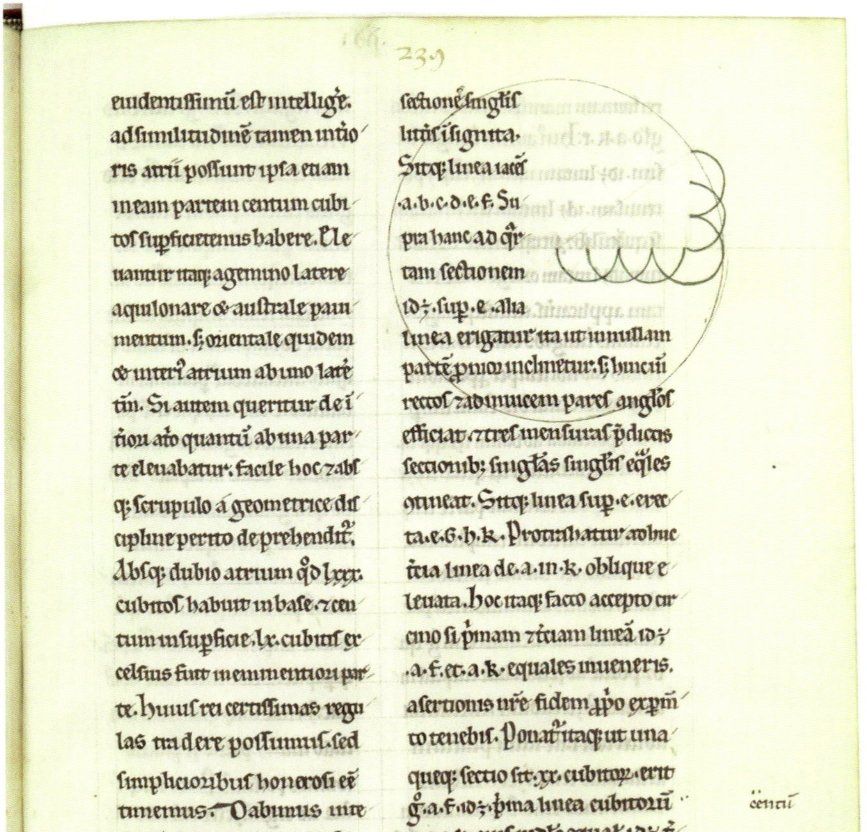

Plate 11 Geometrical diagram showing the slope of the mountain. Paris, BnF, MS Lat. 14516, f. 239r.

Plate 12 Front elevation of a gatehouse. Oxford, Bodleian Library, Ms Bodl. 494, f. 155v.

Plate 13 Lateral elevation of a gatehouse. Oxford, Bodleian Library, Ms Bodl. 494, f. 156r.

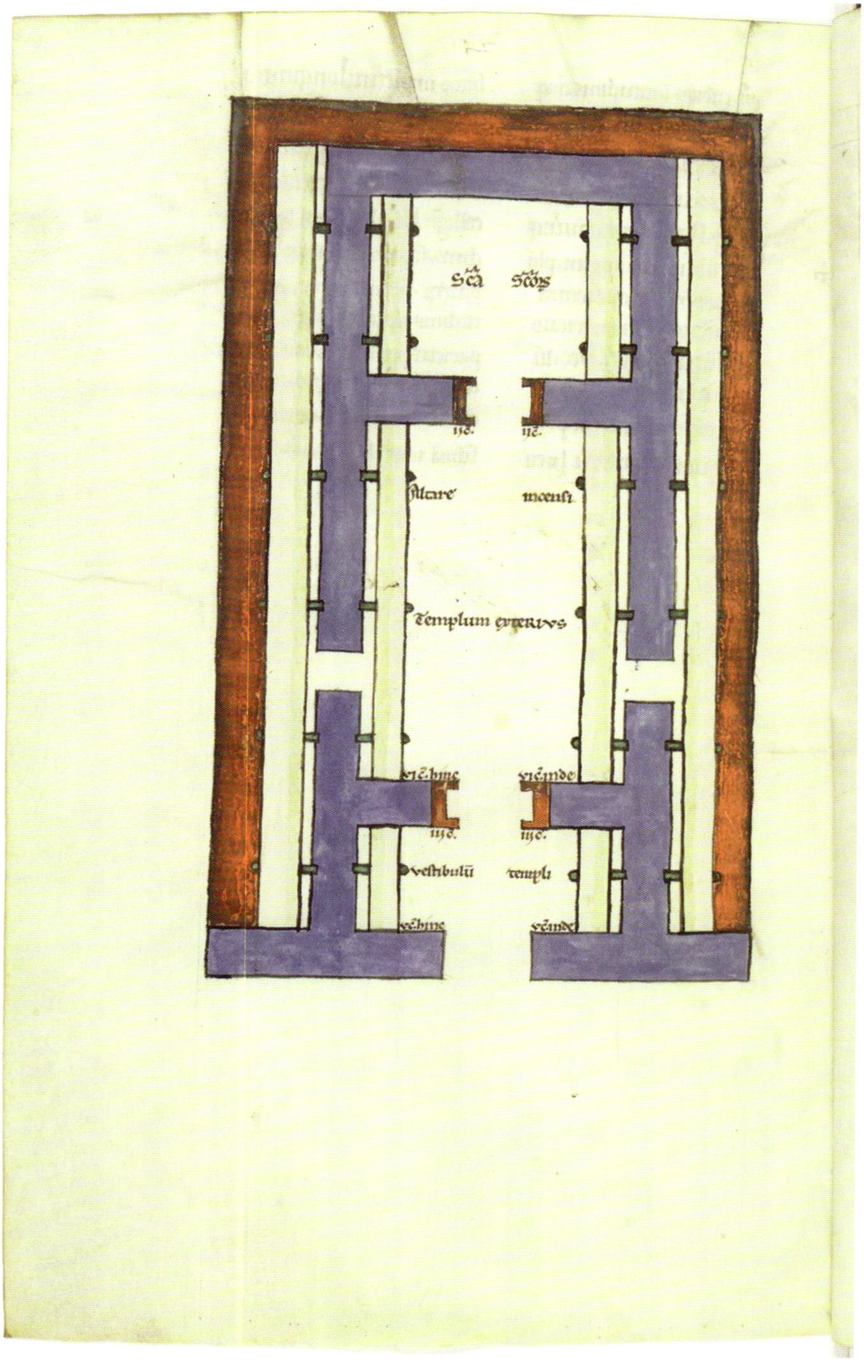

Plate 14 Richard's plan for the temple. Paris, BnF, MS Lat. 14516, f. 244v.

Plate 15 Richard's lateral elevation of the building beside the temple. Paris, BnF, MS Lat. 14516, f. 248r.

Plate 16 Richard's elevation of the altar in the inner atrium. Paris, BnF, MS Lat. 14516, f. 252r.

Fig. 4.9 Detail of the front elevation. Paris, BnF, MS Lat 14516, f. 240r. Detail.

door is placed at the bottom with a single columnar order, with a round arch and tympanum, above which is an inscription reading "the roof of the porticus" (*tectum portae*), implying that it is separate from the elaborate gate below. Richard's visual strategies for the elevations are more complex than first appears. These are not simple elevations, but embody twelfth-century ideas of what could and indeed should be shown in the picture of a building. Richard is not held back by strict rules of perspective and as a result can include important elements of the plan in the elevation, which may confuse the modern reader but no doubt helped the twelfth-century reader to orient themselves. Richard's priority is to show as much as possible, combining interior and exterior both visually, as in the vestibule, but also textually by including the internal dimensions on the façade.

The lateral elevation (fig. 4.8) is also concerned with showing the viewer as much of the interior as possible. Its visual strategies are much more legible to the modern reader than those of the frontal elevation with its unfamiliar hybridity of plan and elevation. Richard provides an exact description of the drawing's content, again set just below the crenellation at the top. It reads, "a representation of the gatehouse as if seen from the side."[30] From this view, the gatehouse's precarious location on the side of the mountain is much more obvious. We can see for the first time that the vestibule running through the middle does not lie flat on the ground as it appears to do in the plans and frontal elevation but is divided into seven steps. Each step corresponds to one of the rooms that comprise the side sections. The first floor holds only a single opening, with crenellations situated behind it, and the top retains the double opening of the frontal elevation.

The viewer can see the interior of the ground floor, indicating that this is a sectional elevation—and is probably one of the first of its kind in the history of architectural drawing.[31] Each of the seven arches shows the interior rooms that appear in the plan, so the arches are not blind arcades placed along the side of the building. Both the *tituli* and the content are key to understanding this point. In the first place, the gatehouse is set within the atrium walls, which are not shown here.[32] The artist must have removed the walls in order to make room for the viewer's perspective. The *tituli* in the arches make clear exactly what is being represented. The first reads, "vestibule 8 cubits"; the following, "place of the first *thalamus*"; then, "five cubits between the *thalami*."[33] The sequence follows that laid out in the large plan (fig. 4.3), with the individual *thalami* numbered one, two, and three. It is clear, then, that the individual spaces defined by the arches on the ground floor and running up the hill show the interior spaces and not exterior blind arcading.

The only way the viewer can see the interior in an elevation is if it is a sectional elevation. Richard's creation of the elevation seems to be not a systematic attempt to create new visual forms but a consequence of the exegetical process, since for Richard it is important to give information about the interior as well as the exterior. The text describes the building as a series of vertical measurements of the interior space, and to illustrate the arrangement of these spaces, they had to appear as part of the drawing. The *tituli* underline this fact: Richard identifies the internal spaces according to their biblical descriptions and presents them to the reader as an illustration of the entire interior. This interpretation of the elevations is consistent with the full plan of the building, where we see that there is a solid unbroken wall, with no doors or windows, placed between the lower *thalami* and the gatehouse's exterior. Thus, the only way the vestibules and chambers could be seen in the lateral elevation would be if it were a sectional drawing, where Richard has "sliced off" part of the building's side so the viewer can see inside. The capitals above the columns, set in the vestibule stairs, may seem problematic because they do not normally support barrel vaults, but the drawing's orthogonal perspective can explain this: the column could be positioned at almost any point in the vestibules or chambers, and so may have no close spatial relationship to the barrel vaults depicted. In reality, the measurements make little practical sense, because the stair risers are too high, making it very difficult for people to move through the building.[34] Another obvious problem is that there is no clear indication of how a person could get from the ground floor to the building's upper levels. Such problems are of little concern to Richard, because the commentary's purpose is to show that the complex could be recreated, not necessarily the exact steps Ezekiel walked. The problem may be a relic of the biblical text itself, which contains little information about the height of the building or how it was situated on the slope of the mountain (a key issue for Richard, as we will see in the next chapter). Richard's stated purpose is to recognize that the buildings can be understood historically, even if elements are unlike those of the buildings of his own day. It is, perhaps, the responsibility of an exegete who approaches the same material allegorically to explain the historical appearance of the unfamiliar and strange parts such as the immense depth of the risers.

The hybridity of the gatehouse's elevation is one feature that overlaps frequently with earlier architectural drawings; indeed, the earliest medieval example of an architectural diagram uses this combination of points of view to illustrate the appearance and form of a structure. This example is a mosaic in the Musée Aquitaine, found in the mid-twentieth century, which depicts the Holy Sepulchre at Jerusalem (fig. 4.10).[35]

The mosaic is from the late fourth century, only a few decades after the Sepulchre was completed. The mosaic's lower part shows three concentric circles that represent the Sepulchre's rotunda, the round building within which was Christ's tomb. Above the circles are two gabled roofs that illustrate the basilica; the semicircular shapes set within it are most likely the apsidal end of the church. The image is rough and does not show any part of the rotunda or church in detail. Here, however, we have the beginnings of a distinctly medieval language of architectural

Fig. 4.10 Fifth-century mosaic showing the Holy Sepulchre. Bordeaux, Musée Aquitaine.

representation that does not appear in antiquity. The mosaic's artist chose to represent the two buildings in both plan and elevation simultaneously, combining both, albeit rather awkwardly, by placing the elevation on top of the plan. The result is an extraordinary amount of information in a relatively small space, giving a sense of both the space as one can walk through it, and also the building's appearance as one might stand in front of it, from the point of view of the rotunda.

The combination of plan and elevation remained a consistent representational mode throughout the Middle Ages, seen in one of the period's most well-known architectural drawings, the Codex Amiatinus. This codex is a pandect—a complete Bible in a single volume—created in Bede's Northumbrian monastery of Wearmouth-Jarrow in the early eighth century.[36] It is the last of three pandects created at this time in the monastery, and certainly the largest of them.[37] The Codex Amiatinus contains several images and diagrams at the beginning of the manuscript, one of which is an architectural drawing of the tabernacle described in Exodus (fig. 4.11). The source for the Codex Amiatinus is thought to be another, larger pandect called the Codex Grandior, which was commissioned by the famous Roman writer and monk Cassiodorus (c. 485–c. 585). This Codex Grandior was brought back from Rome by the abbot of the Wearmouth-Jarrow monastery, named Ceolfrith, when he traveled there.[38] In Northumbria, Bede connected Cassiodorus's description of the pandect he had "caused to be made" with the book Ceolfrith had brought back from Rome.[39] Hence, Bede makes direct statements about Cassiodorus's pictures of the tabernacle.[40] Cassiodorus, however, describes another image, one of the temple which has never been included in Codex Amiatinus.[41]

The tabernacle image in Codex Amiatinus shows the structure from above.[42] It presents a large rectangular enclosure framing the courtyard. Another rectangular structure shows the tabernacle proper which, like Richard's temple, is made up of two spaces: the sanctum, and the smaller space at the end identified as the Holy of Holies (*sanctum sanctorum*). It is another hybrid drawing, similar to the mosaic plan and Adomnán's drawings for *De locis sanctis*.[43] The enclosure that frames the entire tabernacle shows columns in elevation, forsaking the restrictive plan style of simple circles used to represent columns as we might see them. The liturgical vessels are exclusively shown as if from the side, although

Fig. 4.11 Plan of the tabernacle. Florence, Biblioteca Medicea Laurenziana, Amiatino 1, ff. 2v–3r.

their form may result from an iconographic tradition.[44] While the impression of the entire layout is given, the artist went to great lengths to give as much information about the tabernacle as possible. For example, the interior and exterior of both the outer set of columns and the tabernacle itself are shown. The columns to the top and right are clearly seen with the curtains passing on the outside of them and must illustrate the interior side of the tabernacle's boundary.[45] The left and bottom sides, however, only show the capitals and bases of the columns, with the curtain passing in front of them; as a result, this must illustrate the exterior. The same method is used for the tabernacle itself. The top and right sides show the interior, while the left and bottom sides show the exterior. The consistency with which the artist uses this system indicates a deliberate approach to the depiction of architecture, and especially the problem of how one shows an interior without the need for *tituli*.

Hybridity was a common visual strategy in medieval architectural drawings. By combining plans and elevations in a single view, an immense amount of information could be inserted into an image. More importantly, the established nature of the technique meant that Richard could be reasonably confident that his audience could properly interpret what they saw in his drawings, even if it does look strange to modern eyes. By including the vestibule in the front elevation, Richard gives a sense of the building's internal structure, while still developing the audience's understanding of the building's appearance in detail.

The clearest analogue to both of Richard's elevations appears almost half a century later, and is Villard de Honnecourt's portfolio of architectural drawings. The portfolio contains sixty-five pages with approximately 250 drawings, many of which depict architectural subjects. The schematic and detailed nature of the drawings, specifically the molding profiles of mullions, make it appear that the drawings could have been used on medieval building sites, although few modern scholars agree with this suggestion.[46] It has been commented that Villard's drawings "reflect a milestone in the formation of the conventions for the representation of architectural works."[47] They are important because they illustrate Villard's attempt to depict entire structures using architectural conventions one might recognize today, such as elevations, plans, and sectional elevations, which may or may not echo the techniques used by contemporary masons and "architects."[48]

For example, on page sixty-one, Villard provides an internal and external set of elevation drawings that accord with each other accurately (fig. 4.12).[49] The drawing shows a concern for the entire structure, not just individual parts of the building as was characteristic of earlier Romanesque architectural representations. Villard's portfolio may have formed part of a movement toward technical drawing during the early thirteenth century; nevertheless, he was still bound by certain "conventions."[50] In his portfolio, an entire edifice, both internal and external, becomes the object of observation for the first time since Richard's theologically motivated drawings; nevertheless, Villard's portfolio stands as an example of how one artist interpreted his actual architectural environment, reflecting and interpreting the world around him, whereas Richard's world belongs to the imagination.

Of particular interest is Villard's transverse elevation of Reims cathedral (fig. 4.13). The drawing shows the buttresses flanking the cathedral's nave, as well as the niches, columns, and other architectural elements there. The indication that it is a sectional elevation, like Richard's, is the clear soffit profile on the lowest level of the nave's exterior wall. Above the short column is a rolled soffit that could only be seen if Villard imagined a slice taken through the building that shows the profile. Both Richard's and Villard's elevations lack consistency regarding what is shown and where the viewer stands in relation to the building under observation. In the case of the lateral elevation in *In visionem Ezechielis*, while the ground floor is clearly in section, the rest of the building is probably not—or at least it is not as clear. The viewer can, for example, see the crenellations at the top of the building, but it would only be possible to see these if the drawing were not in section, thus complicating the drawing even more. In Villard's transverse elevation, while the visible soffit profile makes it clear that the view is a section, there is no indication in the drawing's other parts that the same view applies. The lack of consistency several decades after Richard's drawing suggests that sectional drawings were not a widespread visual strategy in twelfth- and thirteenth-century France, indicating that Richard must have been among the first to do them.

Richard's elevations borrow the methods of representing elevations insofar as it is possible to call hybrid views, such as in the Codex Amiatinus, elevations to some degree. But *In visionem Ezechielis* represents them and uses the elevations in new ways, ways that become more common in the twelfth century; there was nothing like them before Richard created his. There is a sense that Richard is searching for a way to represent both the interior and exterior of a building; but without knowing it was possible to slice away a section of a building to show the interior, it would be a difficult problem to solve. Anyone attempting to represent a building faces this problem, whether they are an architect or not; it is an issue of representation and communication. Richard approached the problem in two ways. First, he used text in the front elevation, marking the extent to which the *thalami* extended into the building. This worked only to a certain extent, since the reader is forced to look closely and to imagine the appearance of the *thalami*; thus, it is not a visual solution but a textual one. In the lateral elevation, however, Richard had the inspired notion to cut the building in half at the ascending ground floor so the reader can see the internal composition in some detail. The drawing's legibility is helped by the *tituli* that correspond between the plans and the elevation, but most importantly this is a visual solution to a visual problem, and as a result drives forward a language of architectural representation that is used even today.

The Drawings' Purpose

In visionem Ezechielis contains the first sectional elevation as well as other ways of allowing the reader to read the interior and exterior together. Prior to the twelfth century, architectural drawings are rare, so why did Richard include the drawings in the first place? Peter the Chanter's criticism of the drawings imply that they were made at great intellectual and financial cost. In light of this critique, how can pictures actually help a medieval reader? From the early Middle Ages, the church fathers' theory of images and their epistemological value differed and even contradicted one another. The pedagogical potential of pictures is an important point to further our discussion of why Richard took the time and expense to make the drawings. From the beginning of the Middle Ages, there was some concern over the propriety of pictures' presence in the context of Christian worship because their content is inherently ambiguous. Saint Augustine, for example, prioritized "knowledge of certain essential things," lacking which a scriptural commentator could be led astray by the ambiguity of images.[51] The most famous statement in response to the validity of images for learning is from the late sixth century

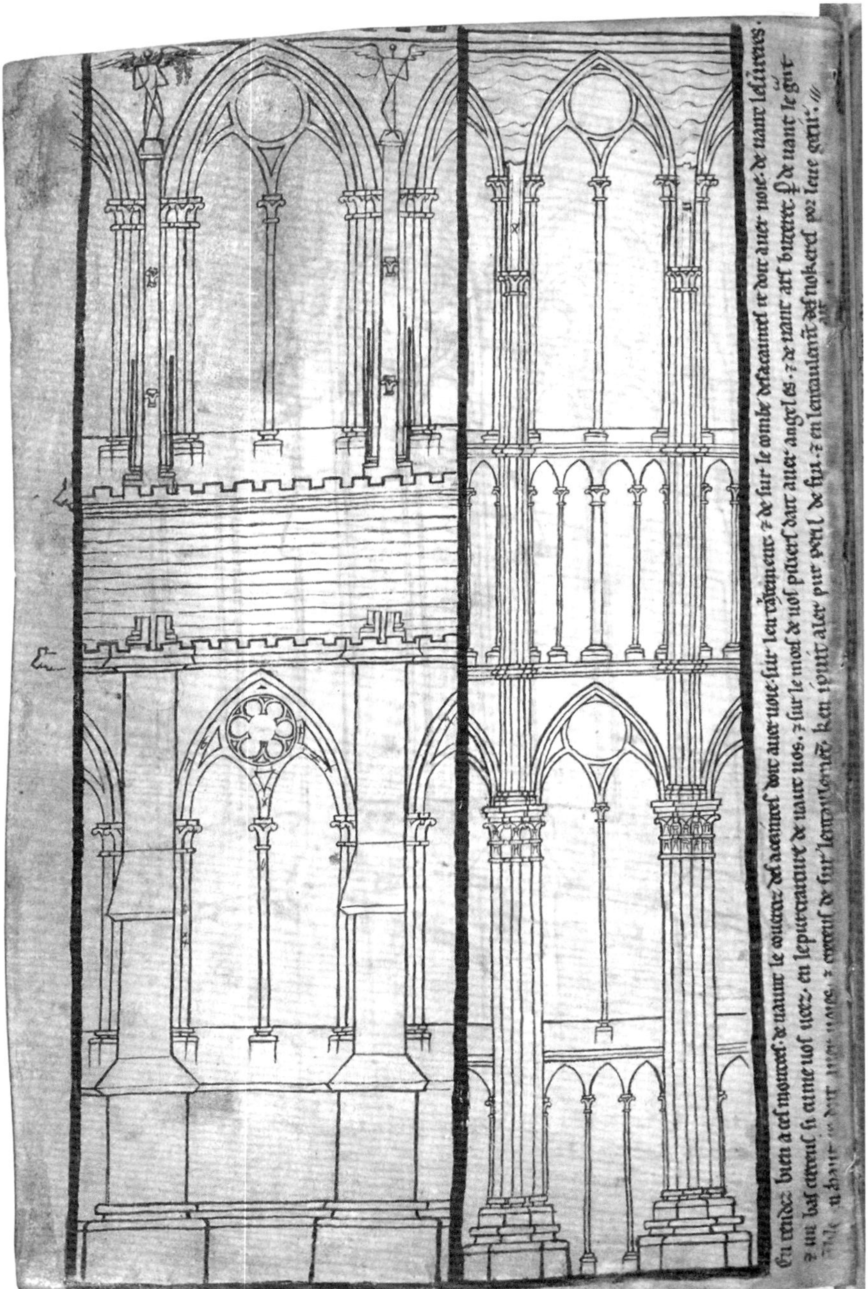

Fig. 4.12 Villard de Honnecourt, interior and exterior elevations of Reims cathedral. Paris, BnF, MS Fr 19093, f. 31v.

Fig. 4.13 Villard de Honnecourt, transverse section of Reims cathedral. Paris, BnF, MS Fr 19093, f. 32v.

when Gregory the Great was confronted with the problem of the overzealous bishop Serenus of Marseilles and his destruction of images in an iconoclastic rage. Gregory wrote two letters to the bishop defending the placement of images in churches. In the first letter, dating to 599, he writes, "For a picture is displayed in church on this account, in order that those who do not know letters may at least read by seeing on the walls what they are unable to read in books."[52] He follows this in a second letter, where he writes, "For what writing offers to those who read it, a picture offers to the ignorant who look at it, since in it the ignorant know what they ought to follow."[53] Gregory's claim has often been reduced to the idea that images are books for the illiterate; that the laity could engage with the historical content of their religion through images when texts, such as Scripture itself, were often locked behind the barrier of education and literacy. During almost the entirety of the Middle Ages, the letters were taken as a wholehearted acceptance of pictures in churches for teaching the lives of the saints, and Gregory's sentiment was often repeated when the issue was raised.[54]

Gregory and the many later writers who repeated his certainty about the didactic power of images raise an epistemological question: If pictures can be used to teach, or at least communicate the narrative of historical events, *how* does that happen? What processes occur when a viewer attempts to learn from an image? The issue gets to the heart of Richard's rationale for the images; he tells us that he included them so that everyone would know the truth of his commentary, hence the reader was expected to learn from them. And yet, even today there is much debate about the value of images as a medium for information, let alone truth. Some reject the idea that anyone can learn something new from an image, especially orthodox claims on the past, arguing that an image can only reaffirm what is already known from reading or from other forms of teaching.[55] In some sense, even Gregory would agree with the inherent limitation of images, as he wrote: "He is a very stupid man whose attention is so captured by the colours in the picture that he does not know what is depicted. For we, if we embrace the words which are said outwardly and ignore the sense [within,] are like those who do not know what is depicted, but only grasp the colour."[56] A picture's content, its inner significance, is its most important property, and a viewer should not be distracted by the "color" alone or its surface appearance, a danger when looking at anything other than text. The "sense" is locked within the image, partially hidden by the color and appearance of it, requiring skill and education to gain access to that content.

There is a problem in these doubts about the role of images in learning. While Gregory's validation of image-making was quoted throughout the Middle Ages, theories about images did change; thus, while Gregory's likening of image-gazing to reading was reused over and over, concepts of how images functioned changed, especially by the twelfth century. By that time, Augustine's uneasiness about the inherent ambiguity of pictures had started to be questioned in some quarters; more than that, during the twelfth century, "true reality belonged to the intelligible world, which was alone unchanging and which alone, therefore, was true."[57] "Intelligible" in this sense refers to the highest plane of thought, one that needed no text or image, a place of pure understanding and wisdom. For the purposes of understanding Richard's commentary, the claim that it is impossible to derive factual knowledge from pictures does not matter, since that is an issue of epistemology and not history. Instead, the question that concerns us is whether history writing at Saint Victor assumed that material objects, and by extension representations of them, could convey knowledge of some sort, of any sort.

The problem of how images could be misinterpreted played out a few decades after Richard's death. At the beginning of the thirteenth century, Odo of Châteauroux gave a sermon in which he describes looking at an image of stained glass when he was a boy but being unable to grasp what the subject was.[58] The scene would have shown three people sitting, one clearly being Christ and another two in conversation, and whom it could be difficult to identify without context. Odo, however, was lucky, since a young man who was nearby walked over to help him. This young man explained that the picture was of the Good Samaritan, Jesus' story about a traveler stripped and beaten, left for dead, and finally helped by a Samaritan who traditionally despised Jews. It is a story with a surprising ending, and Odo echoes this with the end of his own story. The young man explained the allegorical meaning behind the biblical tale, saying the window shows that laypeople were more likely to offer aid than a priest—a rather pointed comment when stated within a church. Now, Odo's sermon is most likely rhetorically inflected, but the point remains that an image—in this case, a piece of stained glass—causes confusion, and two people set out to understand what its subject is. They grasp its literal meaning, its iconographical origin in the Bible, but their reading goes beyond this and into a commentary about contemporary affairs and about their local priest. The result is certainly an unorthodox reading of the subject, but one modified and helped by their surroundings. Pictures mattered to a medieval audience. The subject matter of images was not taken for granted, and pictures were recognized to form an important part of how people communicated with one another. According to this view, vision is an epistemological action where knowledge is gained, and the "truth" of that knowledge is neither here nor there; it is inflected by the culture and people around the image. Vision and image are connected, but when trying to unpack why Richard included images, it would be wrong to mistake one for the other.

Saint Augustine was aware of images' unique power to communicate ambiguously, and criticized those who would engage with them instead of text, because they were in danger of being directed away from orthodoxy.[59] Elsewhere, however, Augustine also understood the preference of some people to engage with images in order to learn, recognizing the value of pictures to teach, albeit imperfectly.[60] Augustine writes, "But no one disputes that it is much more pleasant to learn lessons presented through imagery, and much more rewarding to discover meanings that are won only with difficulty."[61] Imagery offers an easier point of access, a way of flattening the learning curve for certain people, but that same imagery needed to be interrogated for its meaning to be understood. This is exactly why Richard states that he includes the drawing so that everyone, "no matter how simple," can understand the truth of his historical reconstruction.[62]

"Simple" in this sense parallels today's use of the term in that Richard has one eye on students or even adult readers who cannot engage with text with the same ease as with images. But, at the very least, Ezekiel's description cries out to be realized with a pen and parchment in the first place, once the commentator has the tools of architectural drawing at hand. The real question is why no one had made such drawings sooner than the twelfth century. Even Ezekiel's words echo this desire, when he calls the measuring rod carried by the man escorting him around the complex a "calamus," which is also the word used for a pen.[63] Richard's drawings speak the language of architecture as a means of making Ezekiel's vision accessible for every type of reader, opening up the complexity of biblical commentary for all to see. The language of architecture in this case is defined by geometry as it was known in the twelfth century.

5 The Slope of Ezekiel's Mountain and the Language of Architecture

In our eagerness to reach the brilliant elevations, we have skipped past a geometrical figure whose plain appearance hides its importance. It is a key element in Richard's construction of the commentary, and the intellectual heart behind it. Just before the front elevation, on folio 239r, there is a large circle set within a right-angled triangle that is barely visible against the cream-colored parchment (fig. 5.1). A series of green overlapping semicircles are on two sides of the triangle. The figure appears in all complete copies of *In visionem Ezechielis*; a thirteenth-century English manuscript gives slightly more information, with a label running along the hypotenuse stating that it represents the slope of the mountain on which Ezekiel's temple is built. In response to the figure, this chapter focuses on the importance of geometry for Richard's architectural drawings. The previous chapters made comparisons between the figures of *In visionem Ezechielis* and other medieval examples, but the truth is that Richard's drawings are founded on a clear sense of practical geometry and a recognition of what geometry offers architecture, and for this reason *In visionem Ezechielis* is unlike anything before or immediately after the 1170s.

Earlier chapters focused solely on drawings, but there is also a textual language of architecture—the terms and phrases used to make sense of those drawings—and just like his images, Richard's

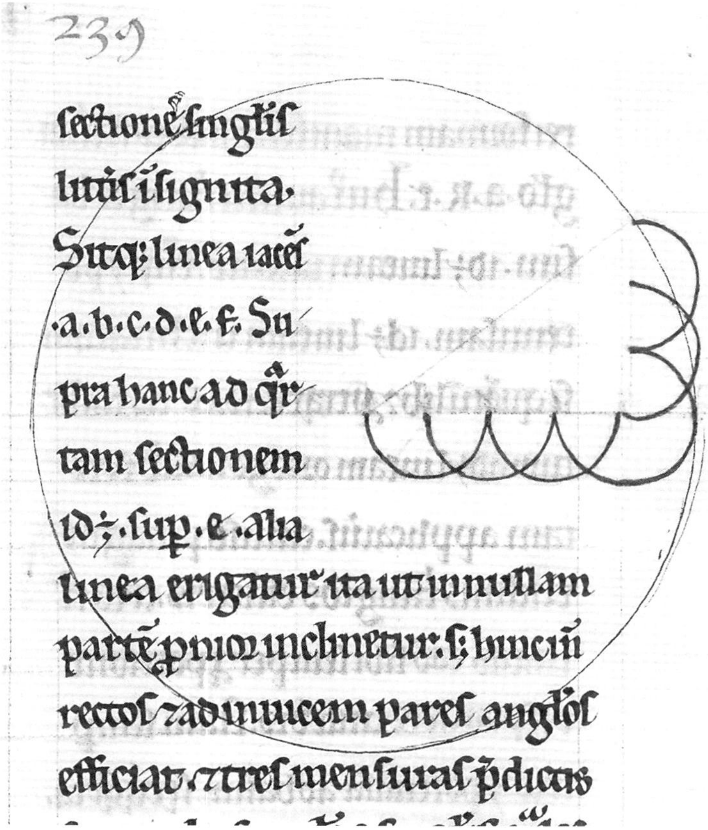

Fig. 5.1 Geometrical diagram showing the slope of the mountain. Paris, BnF, MS Lat. 14516, f. 239r.

language has a distinct sense of modernity. A simple question needs to be addressed first: What were plans and elevations called during the Latin Middle Ages? Even Richard is not always consistent on this subject, calling them at different times *forma* (shape), *exemplar* (example), and *magna figura* (large figure). He refers to the geometrical figure on folio 239r as a "documentum," singling it out as different from everything else in the commentary. The diagram points to the Latin language of architecture in the twelfth century.

Creating an architectural language that could fully describe a building was a concern in the Middle Ages, as it is today. Referring to the tower of Babel, Dante illustrated the problem rather dramatically: "Almost the whole of the human race had collaborated in this work of evil. Some gave orders, some drew up designs;

some built walls, some measured them with plumb-lines, some smeared mortar on them with trowels; some were intent on breaking stones ... and the more skill required for the type of work, the more rudimentary and barbaric the language they now spoke."[1] God punished all of humanity for building the tower, breaking us into linguistic groups that were unable to communicate with one another, but God reserved special punishment for those directly implicated in the challenge to his power, and the architects were the guiltiest of all. Even by Dante's time, the language of architects seemed "barbaric" and "rudimentary," and it was inadequate for the purpose for which it was used. In the case of *In visionem Ezechielis*, the drawings were intended to make things plain, but the commentary also relied on a Latin lexicon that was arguably as deficient as the visual strategies available to Richard at the time. As a result, creating *In visionem Ezechielis* required innovation in both image and text. This chapter examines the work's Latin text and argues that Richard used the platform of geometry to explain his vision to contemporary readers who were already accustomed to geometric practice, a subject developing rapidly by the beginning of the twelfth century. The language of geometry resonates throughout *In visionem Ezechielis*, with Richard using it to build his unique vision from the ground up and to make sense of a three-dimensional drawing on a two-dimensional surface. It would be wrong, however, to think of text and image as two separate entities within the commentary; instead, they were intertwined, with the language of geometry used to make sense of the images and to draw attention to both their potential and their inherent limitations.

Latin is not a medieval language but an inheritance from antiquity, and its formative period was set in a world very different from twelfth-century Paris. Thus, its architectural lexicon was not inherently suited to describing the architectural world of such a different time and place. The word *porticus* is a case in point. The word is "a multi-purposed rendering of several words differing more or less in meaning,"[2] with various meanings that run from "gatehouse"—as in *In visionem Ezechielis*—to a colonnade of some sort. There are differences even in the modern meaning of "portico," especially between the United States and elsewhere, which is a warning not to be definitive in the translation of architectural terms from Latin to English. Even Richard recognizes the problem of his Latin source and the problem of equivocation, as we discussed in the first chapter, where the first step in writing the commentary is to be clear about what each individual word means. To fulfill his own aims, Richard must strive for accuracy but is hobbled by the poverty of the language at his hands, addressing the problem through well-established exegetical methodologies. The issue underlines the close connection between word and image in *In visionem Ezechielis* and the wealth of potential opportunities when examining the text as closely as the images. Ultimately the question is how to determine a building's appearance if you do not have the words to describe it in the first place.

Despite these linguistic limitations, Latin was still the only means at Richard's disposal to create a scriptural commentary, but, as this chapter will make clear, his innovations in this arena are as impressive as those in his drawings. His Latin is infused with the intellectual disciplines he brought to bear on the problem of the commentary, and gives us the opportunity to draw connections between his language and those disciplines. In the context of the twelfth century, Richard's drawings are unique, an interesting but frustrating situation, since comparisons can be made only loosely with other images. Language is different. Recognizing that word and image are connected, we will examine the close relationship between them by, for example, determining what words Richard uses to refer to the drawings and to trace the words' origins to their disciplinary contexts, which, in this instance, is geometry. As a result, the drawings are a manifestation of twelfth-century practical geometry because the theoretical foundations of the commentary are rooted in the practice of this subject, as seen in the liberal use of geometrical terms throughout the commentary, not least in the first use of the word "plan" to describe an architectural drawing.

By placing the drawings within the discipline of geometry, we can partly define them as geometrical figures similar to those in modern textbooks; indeed, it is possible to think of them as diagrams that help "prove" the details in Richard's work, echoing the appearance of geometrical manuscripts produced at the time with various shapes and forms in the margins.[3] The drawings can function as figures placed beside geometrical theories that simultaneously demonstrate visually the content of the accompanying text and act as rhetorical pictures reinforcing any of the claims made. Works of practical geometry are relatively rare in the twelfth century, but even those produced in Saint Victor during that century contain diagrams in the margins and set into the text block, like those in *In visionem Ezechielis*.[4] Richard's work is not a guide to practical geometry but rather applies practical geometry toward a particular purpose and to what was, up to that point, an intractable problem: the historical reality of the prophet's vision. The striking modernity of the drawings can be partly accounted for because they are closely related to geometry, a subject that is, even today, closely linked to architectural practice. However, identifying the figures as a visual manifestation of geometrical proofs can only be an analogy that usefully contextualizes their presence for a modern audience; they are not literal proofs since twelfth-century practice, especially within an abbey such as Saint Victor, relied on the reader's imagination and ability to visualize figures, objects, and buildings accurately in their "mind's eye" and not to need the physical act of sight. In this sense, the drawings are only the beginning of a mental process, an invitation to readers to fully construct Ezekiel's buildings in their imagination.

Geometry and Architecture

Two significant developments in the history of geometry are relevant to this discussion. The first is the subject's great evolution during the twelfth century and the growing links between it and architecture at the same time. Richard was not the first to realize that geometry could be a useful tool when examining Ezekiel's vision. Nearly 150 years previous, the mathematician Gerbert of Aurillac (Pope Sylvester II, d. 1003) wrote, "In that image of the measuring rod for Ezekiel's temple, the heaven and earth are inclined and erected according to the dimensions of geometry."[5] Gerbert's work was immensely important and, as will become clear later, Richard was certainly influenced by it when making the drawings for *In visionem Ezechielis*. Architecture, geometry, and Ezekiel's vision were thus already considered to be connected phenomena. After all, Ezekiel guide in his vision uses a tool for geometers—a measuring rod—to determine the size of the buildings (Ez 40:3). From the early Middle Ages, the measurement of land and objects was recognized as the origin for geometry in the first place, since the word's etymology joined these phenomena.[6]

While Gerbert's work on geometry was important, there were relatively few other works on the subject available to Richard as he was writing his commentary, although important changes were happening. In the middle of the twelfth century, Adelard of Bath translated Euclid's geometrical treatise, known especially for its proof of the Pythagorean theorem, and knowledge of it spread across Europe.[7] Prior to that, the little knowledge of Euclid that seeped into western Europe appeared in a work of geometry thought to be authored by the philosopher Boethius.[8] During his prolific writing career, Boethius (d. 524) authored several works on the liberal arts, including geometry, but the two works about geometry often attributed to him were actually written centuries after his death.[9] These were important sources for the study of geometry until the twelfth century, however, and one of them preserves some of Euclid.[10] The author of the earlier of the two, known as *Geometry I*, begins by outlining the usefulness of the subject: "There are three uses for geometry, for practical skill, for health, and for the soul. Regarding skill, it is for workers and architects."[11] The author does not, however, elaborate on geometry's importance to the architect; indeed, it is not mentioned again.[12] While there is little of practical value for the architect, geometry was, at least abstractly, known to be of some use to architects and for building.

During the twelfth century, Hugh of Saint Victor separated the discipline of geometry into two parts: practical and theoretical, with the former defined as the type for which a geometer uses a compass and straight edge to create shapes and forms.[13] Geometry was, therefore, already recognized as a skill that may have been useful outside of the cloister and that needed certain tools with which to work. It is during this time that we begin to see a more certain connection between architecture and geometry. An example is in the account of Abbot Suger (d. 1151) of the renovation of the abbey church of Saint-Denis. The work is well known as a patron's account of the renovation of the church as well as the construction of one of the first structures built in the Gothic style. Frustratingly, Suger did not mention whatever part architects or architectural drawings may have played in the process. In recognizing that the awkward placement of the crypt under the ground floor created problems with the alignment between the two levels, he did, however, observe that "the old nave should be equalized, by means of geometrical and arithmetical instruments."[14] While laying the plan, that is, the accuracy of the structure was prioritized, and the builders needed geometrical instruments to gain that accuracy.[15] The brief remark suggests that practical geometry was used in the mid-twelfth century in architectural contexts. The similarity between Hugh's description of practical geometry and Suger's passing mention that the geometrical placement of the church's east end used instruments has drawn some scholars to suggest that Hugh was a key influence on Suger's design for the new Gothic renovation.[16] Any connection is speculative, but perhaps more mundanely, Suger's comment also indicates that from the viewpoint of a nonexpert, geometry was something skilled persons used to gain accurate measurements and could play a vital part in a tricky piece of architectural placement.

In the thirteenth century, architecture's link with geometry became more explicit, a state of affairs coinciding with the growing recognition of architects as a professional class and the appearance of architectural drawings.[17] The monument to Hugues Libergier (d. 1263), the architect of Saint-Nicaise in Reims, displays geometrical instruments, in this case a pair of compasses, as a way of representing Hugues's vocation; they were also, as we have seen, the tools required for practical geometry, and even God is represented holding a compass in the act of making the universe (see fig. 1.1). This use of geometrical instruments to demonstrate an architect's status and role only became consistent during the thirteenth century.[18] Whatever Villard de Honnecourt's actual profession was, his portfolio demonstrates an interest in geometry when he constructs shapes that may have been useful for an architect.[19] Also, it appears that architects from the late twelfth century and consistently afterward would draw out required shapes using precise tools and instruments.[20] Later, Euclid, as the creator of many geometrical rules, became a figure for masons in late medieval iconography.[21] The strong connections between architecture and geometry are affirmed from the genesis of architecture as an esteemed vocation. It should therefore be no surprise to see some of the most developed architectural images of the time, in Richard's work, relying and building on practices of geometry. In some sense, *In visionem Ezechielis* was, from a contemporary stance, a work of practical geometry, one that necessitated the use of compass and ruler to create its drawings.

Geometry thus provided an intellectual framework for architects and, in the case of *In visionem Ezechielis*, biblical commentators, but it is not obvious how geometry could inform the language of architecture itself. To gain a sense of this language, we must take a step back to Vitruvius's *De architectura*, the only architectural treatise that Richard could have known. Vitruvius did not include drawings, but may have originally intended to do so.[22] In his discussion of drawing, Vitruvius describes the three types:

> Arrangement includes the putting of things in their proper places and the elegance of effect which is due to adjustments appropriate to the character of the work. Its forms of expression (in Greek ἰδέαι) are these: groundplan (*ichnographia*), elevation (*orthographia*), and perspective (*scaenographia*). A groundplan is made by the proper successive use of compasses and rule, through which we get outlines for the plane surfaces of buildings. An elevation is a picture (*figura*) of the front of a building, set upright and properly drawn in the proportions of the contemplated work. Perspective is the method of sketching a front with the sides withdrawing into the background, the lines all meeting in the centre of a circle.[23]

Without showing any drawings, Vitruvius gives a good sense of their appearance, as *ichnographia*, *orthographia*, and *scaenographia* are three different drawing types representing a building from different points of view. The descriptions of *ichnographia* and *orthographia* clearly map onto Richard's drawings very well, though he never uses these terms in his commentary.

There is some evidence to suggest that Richard knew an abridged version of *De architectura* and hence was aware of Vitruvius's terminology from a copy of the text in Saint Victor's well-stocked library.[24] There is no definitive book catalogue from twelfth-century Saint Victor, but a list of books appears in a manuscript completed in a hand from late in the century. The writing is worn, but one of the works listed is *De architectura*.[25] The abbey certainly had a copy by the end of the Middle Ages, but this manuscript is lost. There is evidence to suggest that Saint Victor's twelfth-century copy of *De architectura* was not Vitruvius's complete text but a shorter edition. In his description of the large plan for the gatehouse in Ezekiel's vision, Richard describes the drawing as like "the foundation [that] had just been laid down."[26] While Vitruvius does not use this phrase when describing *ichnographia*, Marcus Cetius Faventinus, in one of the best-known abridgments of *De architectura*,[27] writes: "These, then, amount to three sorts of figure called the plan, the elevation, and the perspective. [The plan is the description of the area, ground, or the foundations.] The elevation is the setting out of the proposed side walls and height. The perspective is the display of the façade and the whole building with the help of painting."[28] Richard's echo of Faventinus's definition of the plan as illustrating the foundations suggests that he was aware of a preexisting and antique tradition of architectural representation.

The key term in Vitruvius's, Faventinus's, and Richard's work is the identification of the drawing as *figura*, a term used throughout the Middle Ages in many different contexts. The passage from Faventinus quoted above calls all three drawing types *figurae* (figures), language that Richard echoes. Just like the modern term "figure," *figura* can have many meanings, and in the Middle Ages it was frequently used in biblical commentaries as a way to mark the links between the Old and New Testaments.[29] In an architectural context, Vitruvius described the ground plan as a *figura*, but the quotation above indicated that elevations were also called *figurae*, while Faventinus, among others, seems to have thought that all three types could be called figures. It seems unlikely that *figura* would refer only to an elevation; hence, for Vitruvius any technical architectural drawing—plan, elevation, and drawing in perspective—may be called *figura*. This would mean that not all *figurae* are ground plans, but all ground plans are *figurae*.

There are few examples from antiquity that can provide clues to the appearance of Vitruvius's *figurae*. One exception is the *Forma urbis Romae*, erected between 205 and 208 CE under Emperor Septimius Severus. This city plan of Rome was monumental, 13 by 18.1 meters, and inscribed on a marble surface standing on one internal wall of the Temple of Peace.[30] It was destroyed by fire and little of it survives today (about ten percent), but its scale and ambition must have been remarkable. It appears to have fit, albeit loosely, into Vitruvius's definition of a plan: it illustrated the footprint of a series of buildings and their spatial relationship with one another.[31] While it appears to have been made with careful attention to detail, such as the location of individual columns, there are inconsistencies in scale and orientation.[32] The intention of this careful and costly map remains unclear, but there is a suggestion that it was a statement of the emperor's achievements, one that "graphically attested to his physical improvement" of the city.[33] At this relatively early stage of development, the plan—a format of drawing still taught to Roman architects in the third century—was a means to solve spatial problems as Vitruvius indicated, but could also be used for quite different purposes, as statements of power and purpose.[34] Ultimately, the plan was not confined to the production of architects, but could signify something other than the intended footprint of a building on the landscape. If this is the case, then Vitruvius's *figura* could clearly be appropriated outside of the architect's practical context, as something along the lines of "image" or, depending on the context, "diagram."

We can only speculate whether Vitruvius would have truly interpreted the marble plan of Rome as *ichnographia* let alone a *figura*; however, the language is echoed during the early Middle Ages and into the twelfth century, indicating its continued association with schematic architectural representations in that time. For example, in his *De locis sanctis*, the seventh-century abbot Adomnán uses this language along with other words and phrases. He begins *De locis sanctis* by saying he met a bishop living in Gaul named Arculf who told him about the places he had seen in his travels around the Holy Land. Arculf, Adomnán tells us, also drew the plans of four buildings on a wax tablet which were transmitted in the later manuscript copies of the work. A question hangs over whether Arculf actually existed or was merely a convenient foil for Adomnán, who could claim his description of the Holy Land derived from eyewitness testimony.[35] Adomnán's drawings have been likened to earlier drawings of maps, which were "essentially illustrations to clarify verbal text and they have no independent claim to describe reality other than what the text says. Adomnán also uses illustrations in this way: the plans/drawings are to make clear what is obscure in his writing."[36] According to this view, the drawings are paratextual insertions designed to support the textual encounter between Adomnán's fictional traveler Arculf, the buildings, and the reader's engagement with both.[37] They are still fundamental to the work's design and potential, once Adomnán refers to them in the text, which he does several times. The images reinforce Adomnán's authorial voice, demonstrating the supposed truth of his personal experience of the buildings. They act as geometrical proofs, just like earlier figures within works of natural philosophy, drawings which "were made with a compass and a straight-edge."[38] The use of these geometrical tools echoes

Vitruvius's description of *ichnographia*, which he said should be drawn with "compasses and rule," as well as Suger's description of his masons' working methods, and even Hugh of Saint Victor's definition of practical geometry.[39] In this sense, the process of making these types of architectural drawings reaffirms a picture's particular power in conveying the "truth" of experience to the reader; they have a "reality effect."[40]

In this and other early medieval works, "figures" have a particular role in that they explain the text, and are inserted to give readers who struggle with purely textual explanation something else to which they can pay attention. But the language to describe them is never clear-cut, with other words such as *formula*, *pictura*, and *figuratio* sometimes used. Such variety in architectural vocabulary implies that the object to which it referred was less fixed than in Vitruvius's language for drawings or even Richard's regular use of *figura* or *forma*.

When referring to his drawings, Adomnán uses the term *exemplar*, a word that Richard uses twice, once in relation to the fourth plan, which shows the atrium in plan but the gatehouses in elevation, and again when referring to the large plan of the atrium that is missing from most copies of the text.[41] There is little sense of how to distinguish between his use of the term and, for example, *figura*. The Saint Gall plan, however, uses a form of the term *exemplar* to refer to its drawing and offers a little more context.

The Saint Gall plan offers one of the most useful examples of Latin terminology applied explicitly to an architectural drawing.[42] In the transmission note in the upper part of the drawing, the artist referred to the drawing as an *exemplata*.[43] The most popular translation renders this as "copy," arguing that there was an original model from which the drawing was made and the term simply indicated that fact.[44] It was later shown, however, that the Saint Gall plan is unlikely to be a copy, casting doubt on this translation of *exemplata*. The most in-depth discussion of the note argues that the clearest rendering is the English synonym "example."[45] "Example," in this instance, is not a specifically architectural term and does not specify that the plan's author necessarily believes it to refer to a plan only. So, despite extensive work, the relationship between text and image in the Saint Gall plan remains unclear. Even an explicit reference to a plan in an accompanying note serves only to cloud the issue of how authors described and conceived of architectural drawings. Even at this early stage, however, we can begin to draw parallels to Richard's work.

The argument that "example" is a better translation of *exemplar*, and its cognate *exemplata*, finds support in the medieval practice of geometry. In this context, *exemplar* refers to a figure that helps to prove or demonstrate a point visually. For example, Gerbert of Aurillac uses the term in exactly this way in his introduction to geometry: "So to make it abundantly clear, for the sake of an *exemplum*, a line is drawn along the length, and it is divided into four palms in this manner."[46] Gerbert does not refer to all of his drawings in this way, but he offers a clear analogue to Richard's language by referring to accompanying figures whose purpose is to clarify visually difficult parts of a text. In this sense, then, *exemplum* and *exemplata* are an indication for the reader to examine a paratextual object that resides on or near the text itself. The fact that this approach is associated with the practice of geometry begins to hint at the genre of text through which we can come to a fuller understanding of *In visionem Ezechielis*. Even the most basic of terms that Richard uses to refer to the drawings reveals a link to common geometrical language.

Villard de Honnecourt's portfolio provides a useful snapshot of vernacular architectural terminology at the beginning of the thirteenth century.[47] A question remains as to whether new words were coined to reflect new architectural forms and building practices, and within these innovations whether a new lexis emerged out of a growing emphasis on architectural representation in the thirteenth century. Richard understands his drawings quite differently than Villard, possibly reflecting a significant perceptual gap between the two, whether due to their different aims or reflecting the difference between Villard's Picardish dialect and Richard's highly developed Latin. The different languages represent a social and intellectual gulf between artisans and patrons, as patrons wrote about architecture but in a way entirely divorced from issues of structural engineering and the concerns of medieval masons.[48] Despite this more abstract engagement with architecture, Richard's readers were also patrons who must have conversed with builders and made decisions about their buildings. This suggests there must have been alternative registers of language: vernacular for discussions about design and layout, and Latin for the significance and symbolism of an architectural form.

Figura and Geometrical Diagrams

If architecture is a language, then words and their meanings matter. A diversity of words was used throughout the Middle Ages to refer to an architectural drawing of any type, but *figura* remains the most consistent, and its links with the practice of geometry go some way to show the strong influence of that subject on *In visionem Ezechielis*. Without doubt, the most significant parallel use of *figura* appears in Calcidius's translation of and commentary on Plato's *Timaeus*, which in Richard's time was a common source for information about the natural world and creation. Completed in the fourth or fifth century, it constitutes the only written work by Plato known to early twelfth-century readers, albeit by indirect means.[49] *Figura*, in the sense that Calcidius uses it, is an indicator for the reader to look for an accompanying diagram that helps to explain a particular part of the text in a visual way. This usage implies that, in some cases, certain types of information can be best indicated visually and that a diagram is the most convenient way of making a point. Similarly Boethius in his *De arithmetica* writes that he included diagrams to help some readers understand his point.[50] Boethius's consistent use of images in *De arithmetica* and *De musica* demonstrates a pedagogical strategy at play even during the earliest part of the Middle Ages, a strategy that recognized the unique power of images to communicate specific types of information.[51]

Following the usage of the word *figura* is key to understanding the language of *In visionem Ezechielis*. Adomnán's *De locis sanctis* shows us that *figura* was used to refer to architectural plans even at their earliest appearance in the Middle Ages. However, Richard's work was rooted in contemporary geometrical practices, already implied by the use of *exemplum* but reinforced by the more extensive use of *figura*. One of the earliest examples of *figura*'s association with a geometrical diagram occurs in Calcidius's commentary on *Timaeus*. Near the beginning, Calcidius offers an outline of the contents, writing, "Now, since this book concerns the constitution of the universe and provides a causal explanation of all that the world embraces, it was inevitable that there should be many questions of various types, concerning plane figures [*de planis figuris*], solid bodies, the incorporation of the soul that vivifies the sensible world, concerning its movement and perpetual motion, concerning the courses of the fixed and errant stars."[52] The section corresponding to this statement of purpose is called

De genitura mundi. It begins, "perfect bodies are solids consisting of three things, length, width, and depth—the first expounds the *epipeda*, i.e., plane figures [*planas figuras*], which have only length and width but no depth."[53] The following section in the commentary considers the relationship between number theory and geometry. Calcidius demonstrates that certain groups of numbers, such as six, twelve, and twenty-four, may be placed into patterns to form shapes, the *figurae* to which he earlier referred. The diagrams that his editor Waszink provides with the texts were not universally transmitted in the manuscripts; hence, it may not always have been clear what exactly the *figurae* constituted.

It is clear that Calcidius used *figura* in a stricter manner than Vitruvius, Adomnán, and anyone else whose language we have examined so far. Calcidius has certain types of shapes and figures in mind, calling them *plana figurae* or "plane figures." These are two-dimensional shapes such as circles and squares, geometrical forms containing certain properties that can be examined in detail. As a result, we are very much in the domain of geometry, and the phrase *plana figura* is key to understanding how Richard perceives his own figures. While Calcidius's commentary would certainly have been known at Saint Victor, the strongest influence on Richard's use of geometry most likely comes from much later, in Gerbert of Aurillac's *Isagoge geometria* (Introduction to geometry).

Gerbert's knowledge of the quadrivium was legendary even in his own time, and it is mostly his mathematical works that have survived. Prior to becoming bishop, Gerbert was a schoolmaster at Reims, and he is best known for his introduction of the abacus into western Europe. His association with this tool, which enabled relatively quick calculations, was so synonymous that those who used the abacus were called Gerbertists. During his travels, Gerbert most likely learned from Islamic scholars on the "other side of the Pyrenees," demonstrating an eagerness to advance his own and his students' knowledge of mathematics.[54] Despite his importance in the history of mathematics, Gerbert had a somewhat notorious reputation by the twelfth century, including his ability to "cast the head of a statue that could speak" and answer questions.[55]

In his introduction to geometry, Gerbert directly references Calcidius's discussion of figures, thus demonstrating the line that reaches back to antiquity from Richard through authors such as Calcidius and Gerbert regarding the significance of figures to the geometer.[56] In fact, Gerbert also provides a definition for a figure that coincides well with Richard's usage. In his *Isagoge geometria*, Gerbert writes, "a figure, which in Greek is called a *scema*, is space [*spatium*] enclosed by lines."[57] Gerbert's definition is taken almost word for word from Saint Augustine's "On the Greatness of the Soul," a dialogue between Augustine and his friend Euodius that includes a relatively extensive discussion of geometry and the definition of terms such as "length," "point," and "sign."[58] While it may seem odd that a discussion of the properties of the human soul should include a section on theories of geometry, the work was important enough for part of it to be included in the pseudo-Boethian *Geometry I*.[59] Having asked Euodius to imagine a line, Augustine points out that "no figure results" when he does so; this leads Euodius to question what Augustine means by the term "figure."[60] Augustine responds with the definition, "For the present, I call that figure in which some space is enclosed by means of one or more line, for example, draw a circle, or connect four lines at their extremes, so that no end of any one line is unconnected with the end of another line."[61] Taken literally, Augustine's words describe the formal appearance of the figure and its properties very well; it is a shape of some sort in which there is a certain amount of space. In the following chapter, Augustine provides examples of figures by describing an equilateral triangle, a square, a parallelogram, and a circle, each of which constitutes a figure, but a line cannot be one since it encompasses no space. A figure, then, is a shape of some sort, a drawing that, according to Augustine, must have at least three lines (to form a triangle) or a continuous round line (to form a circle), so that it shows a shape with space bounded by lines. The definition is not exclusive to theological works, since it was followed so closely by Gerbert in his mathematical work. By the central Middle Ages, and specifically within the field of geometry, *figura* had a formal definition: it is space with lines around it, or space bounded by some form.

Augustine's and Gerbert's definitions could as easily define architectural drawing as a two-dimensional figure, especially if we take *spatio* as a representation of physical space.[62] Indeed, in some sense these definitions describe architecture better than they do the figures in Augustine's and Gerbert's texts.[63] Much of Gerbert's imagery is, necessarily, abstract, comprised of parallel lines and other geometrical shapes, examples of which are included at the end of the modern edition of Gerbert's works.[64] Similar shapes line the margins of many copies of geometric works from the Middle Ages, and they were probably understood as *plana figurae*. According to Gerbert's definition, the figures were interpreted as whole entities, and not as separate schematic lines. The medieval *figura* is an object which contains geometrical space; it is not simply an assortment of straight lines arranged to form a diagram of some sort; instead, it has a form defined by the entirety of the space it takes up.

Gerbert provides a fuller explanation of *plana figura* as a specific type of figure:

> They are called plane figures, those lacking in depth, that is height, and only length and width are considered. These are, if rationally considered, either with straight lines, which are called *euthyae* by the Greeks, and those with angles, which are called *euthygrammae*, or curved ones with round lines, which are called *cyclicas* or *elycoydas* or *campellas* by the Greeks; round and oblong ones are included, which are named *campylogrammae*, or those composed of both, that is straight and curved lines, part angled, part curved, the type called a *micton* by the Greeks.[65]

This passage and its discussion of "plane figures" echo Calcidius's commentary. Gerbert outlines particular types of *figurae*—that is, "plane figures"—offering some examples of their type and their Greek roots. They are plane because they are two-dimensional shapes that bound an inner space of some sort and possess only length and width. Gerbert envisions these plane figures as part of a more complex environment, out of which the reader may construct three-dimensional forms.[66] For example, Gerbert describes the process of dividing a square into separate sections to create sixteen new squares, highlighting the difference in method between the division's application to plane and to solid figures. At the end of the text he writes, "it will be more easily understood, when it is drawn in plan [*in plano*]."[67] Taken in context, Gerbert's use of *in plano* refers to the plane drawings that he goes on to describe in detail. He is, however, clearly aware of the relationship between representations of two- and three-dimensional objects, the latter of which are able to provide more information about a structure or object than the former. Gerbert's statement has two implications: first, that a plane figure may be one part of a solid figure; second, that plane figures are necessarily limited in what they can depict because they lack the dimension of height. We will see that Richard understands *figura*, and *plana figura*, in exactly the same way, but he is able to adapt Gerbert's simple diagrams to an architectural context.

This rich vocabulary for discussing any associated diagrams within a text demonstrates these authors' awareness of the issues and limitations of diagrams and images. It provided Richard with a technical vocabulary to discuss aspects of his work that were peculiar to him. More importantly, it established a means through which he could articulate his vision within a mathematical framework. Gerbert's *in plano* representations are only approximations of three-dimensional forms, but, according to Gerbert, they offer a sound foundation on which to build a firmer understanding of solid shapes and their properties. This relationship between three- and two-dimensional shapes is exactly the intellectual content that Richard takes from Gerbert's introduction to geometry.

The perceived relation between two- and three-dimensional shapes is more than the former lacking the height of the latter, but also concerns the way in which medieval artists could represent those shapes on the surface of a page. The making of forms using perspectival lines is apparent in Vitruvius's *De architectura*, as alluded to in his definition of *scaenographia*, but the consistent use of this technique fell out of practice during the early and central Middle Ages, as if forgotten. It was eventually rediscovered in the fifteenth century by Filippo Brunelleschi, who created a form of mathematical perspective that had a large impact on painting at the time.[68] To say that perspectival lines were used inconsistently in drawing during the Middle Ages is different from suggesting that artists of the time had no concept of portraying solids or even that they did not want to. As Calcidius and Gerbert make clear, solids were an important component of creation, and so understanding their appearance was an important part of training in geometry. The problem is that the technology to represent three-dimensional objects "clearly" [*aperte*] did not exist.[69] As a result, it was best for the medieval reader to simply picture these objects in their imagination, which they could do with relative ease.

Gerbert explicitly calls for his reader to picture a solid object "in the imagination" and not on the parchment, noting that planes "must be understood by the intellect, because of their incorporeity."[70] Since solid objects could not be shown clearly, according to Gerbert there was no point trying to represent them in the first place, and the imagination was the best tool for the job. Despite such caution, some authors inserted their representation of solids where they thought it to be appropriate. One of the most instructive examples to study is Isidore's representation of the "cube of the elements," which appears in his *De natura rerum*. The cube is intended to visually represent the relationship between the characteristics of the four elements, allowing his reader to understand it at a glance. Some examples show a three-dimensional cube as we would understand it today. John E. Murdoch, however, traces the later iterations of the cube and highlights the difficulties artists had in understanding what exactly they were supposed to draw.[71] Early medieval artists could not grasp how to represent a cube, drawing two rectangles instead and shading certain areas to give a sense of depth; the result is garbled in comparison with Isidore's intended cube drawing. This example clearly shows the reason for Gerbert's hesitancy in asking his readers and copyists to draw a solid object.

Richard's *plana figurae* are the plans that appear in *In visionem Ezechielis*, and they are the first architectural drawings referred to as "plans."[72] He uses this term to describe their properties and limitations, echoing Gerbert in doing so. Richard is making only an approximation of what the building looked like; it is not exact. It is, after all, impossible to represent a building perfectly. This is an inherent problem in any representation and cannot be solved with ingenuity or technology, whether medieval or modern. Lewis Carroll summarizes the issue with characteristic brilliance in his children's story *Sylvie and Bruno*: when a cartographer is asked about the different and best possible scale for a map, he concludes that the answer is 1:1—essentially, that it is best to use the land itself as a map.[73] Richard is faced with a similar problem: how can one best represent a three-dimensional object or topography without simply recreating it like-for-like? More precisely, the issue for Richard is that Ezekiel's gatehouse is built on slope, as shown in the elevations. The plans' orthographic point of view makes the area seem flat and hides the slope, because when compared to the flat surface, the oblique angle on which the gatehouse is situated changes the dimensions slightly. Richard highlights this discrepancy when he notices that "the slope of the mountain will have reduced the size in this central hundred [cubits] from the west according to the reckoning of the plane figures [*plani*]."[74] The *plana figura*'s limitation is the same that Calcidius and Gerbert discussed when they defined the phrase as excluding all measurements of height. Richard's plans are plans because they show only two dimensions, but they offer excellent approximations of a historically and structurally sound reality.

Richard addresses this point directly when discussing the large gatehouse plan (fig. 4.3). He writes: "But because it is difficult or even impossible to represent the length, width, and height of buildings in plan [*in plano*, i.e., in two dimensions] within the same figure [*figura*], for all the things we've talked about, I judge it sufficient to have described the site and place, and to have drawn all of them using proportional lines, as if I have laid down the foundations."[75] Here Richard correctly points out the limitations of the plan: namely, it is only able to illustrate one flat section of the entire building; the upper levels cannot be represented in conjunction with a representation of the floor plan, at least not as clearly.[76] No fewer than five drawings illustrate the gatehouse, and Richard was concerned about representing it as clearly as possible, so it is no surprise that this statement, one directly concerned with the plan, is about an image of the gatehouse, the most fully realized building in the entire commentary. The limitation of the plan, showing only two dimensions, applies to the other plans in the commentary as well.

Richard certainly understands the plans and elevations to be *figurae*, in much the same sense as Vitruvius classified *orthographia* and as Faventinus called all three types of drawings. The figures, taken together, attempt to represent all three dimensions of a building, but including height in a plan is, for Richard, "impossible." The impossibility of doing this reflects the very nature of a *planum figura*, in that it only shows length and width. Height, in this instance, would mean showing the slope and dimensions of the mountain on which the temple stands, as Richard does later in the work. More detail is provided about the drawing that accompanies this section, however: namely, that it demonstrates an image of the building as if Richard had "laid down the foundations."

Having established that Richard's plans are two-dimensional geometrical figures that do not contain any information about a building's height, we can now determine how he set about discussing the three-dimensional appearance of the gatehouse, or of any building. This, after all, is the point of including the drawings: they must reflect a believable historical reality and hence should be identifiable as three-dimensional structures, not merely abstracted two-dimensional figures in a manuscript. A key part of how Richard differentiates between two- and three-dimensional representations is his use of the terms *planum* and *superficies*. In this context, Richard uses *superficies* to indicate a measurement that takes the mountain's slope into account. For example, he writes, "Let us first consider how many cubits from east to west the inner atrium has inside, according to the consideration of the plan [*planum*], of which the actual surface [*superficietenus*] was 100 cubits on every side without doubt."[77] Earlier, in chapter three, when considering a discrete 500 cubits and the structures placed within it, he writes: "This, however, was said according to the consideration of the two-dimensional or flat surface, for the slope of the mountain has added nothing to this measurement, about which more will be considered in its correct place."[78] There are clearly two types of measurements that Richard uses in his commentary; one is two-dimensional and the other is more accurate because it accurately reflects the mountain on which the prophet walked.

Outside of *In visionem Ezechielis*, the term *superficies* is used almost exclusively in a geometrical context. For example, we can compare Richard's phrasing to pseudo-Boethius's in *Geometria I*, "A plane surface [*superficies*] is one which is equally contained in its straight lines."[79] Adelard of Bath's Latin translation of Euclid's treatise on geometry appeared before the latest recension of *In visionem Ezechielis*, around the middle of the twelfth century.[80] In this work, Adelard writes, "A surface figure [*superficies plana*] is an extension from one line to another, enclosing them at their ends."[81] In *In visionem Ezechielis*, *superficies* refers to the surface on which the prophet would have walked. It comprises the space between the straight lines in the geometrical figures, corresponding to the three-dimensional structures which Richard attempts to recreate, but this does not fully align with contemporary use, such as found in Boethius and in Adelard's translation of Euclid. Richard is, in a sense, appropriating developments in geometry to solve the problem of discussing a three-dimensional vision, and extends the significance of certain terms to suit himself. Richard's association of *plana* and *superficies* with geometry becomes explicit when he begins to explain the effect of the slope of the mountain on the measurements.

Richard clearly has a predictable correlation between *planum* and *superficies* measurements, one that can be recreated by the reader to make sense of the vast array of measurements, without Richard having to explicitly spell it out each time. His more detailed discussion of the subject appears in the section between the plans for the gatehouse and the elevations—that is, between the *plana* figures of the gatehouse and the elevations that take the height into account, which is an ideal moment to explain his reasoning. To fully understand the relationship between these two types of measurements, we must turn to the only nonarchitectural image in the text (fig. 5.2).

This diagram has received much less attention than the other drawings and has, to an extent, been mischaracterized. Some describe the figure merely as the most obviously geometrical in Richard's work, without considering its function.[82] Others refer to it but do not explain how it fits into his wider methodology, recognizing only that it is a consistent presence in copies of the work.[83] The diagram shows a right-angled triangle set within a circle. The bottom and side of the triangle are broken into equal segments with sequential letters attached to each one. In some examples (fig. 5.3), the hypotenuse is called the "side of the mountain."

Richard provides a step-by-step process for creating the diagram, one any reader can follow along with. First, a horizontal line is drawn and divided into five equal sections, with the letters A, B, C, D, E, and F along equally spaced points on the line. A vertical line is then placed above point E. This second line is divided into three sections (G, H, and K), of equal length to the sections contained in the first line (A–F). Richard points out that if a circle is drawn with a radius of A–F, it demonstrates that the distance between A and F is equal to the distance between A and K. A line is then drawn from A to K, which completes the construction of a right-angled triangle. Richard suggests that each section, such as A to B or B to C, should be assigned the length of 20 cubits, and that, as long as the triangle is constructed in the

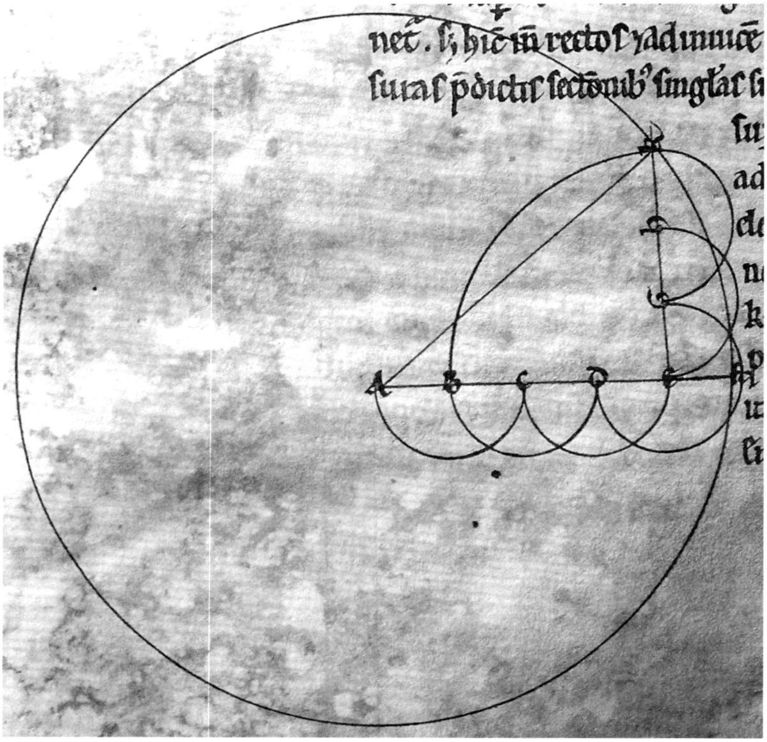

Fig. 5.2 Geometrical diagram showing the slope of the mountain. Oxford, Bodleian Library, MS Bodl. 494, f. 154v.

manner he describes, the actual size of the figure does not matter because it will have the same proportion as the one in the text. As a result, the line A–F is 100 cubits in length, and the line E–K will be 60 cubits (obviously, in this construction, with Richard having demonstrated the equal length of A–F and A–K, the latter will be 100 cubits as well).[84]

The drawing's purpose is to demonstrate the relationship between the plans and the three-dimensional structure that the prophet saw and walked on. The bottom line (the adjacent side) is that which runs from A to F, and the opposite side is the vertical line containing the segments E–K. If we follow Richard's suggestion that each segment corresponds to twenty cubits, then the distance from A to E—where the adjacent and opposite sides meet—is eighty cubits. According to Richard, this adjacent line is the *planum* dimension, the two-dimensional length that assumes the gatehouse was located on a flat surface. In a right-angled

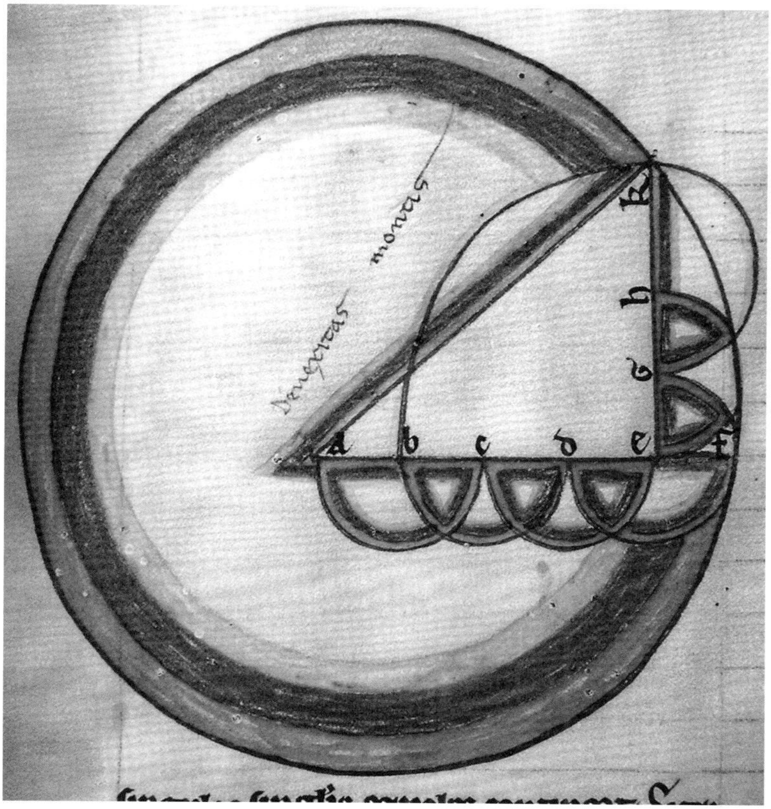

Fig. 5.3 Geometrical diagram showing the slope of the mountain. Oxford, Bodleian Library, MS e Mus. 62, f. 96r.

triangle such as this, Richard proves that the hypotenuse is 100 cubits because it is the same length as the bottom line that runs from A to F. The hypotenuse represents the *superficies* measurement, the one that incorporates the slope of the mountain into its calculations. Knowing what each side of the triangle represents, we can then translate from one type of measurement to another. If we were to look at the diagram from above, as if floating above the triangle and looking down, we would see something like Richard's plans. From that perspective, the *planum* measurement, which represents the entire width of the gatehouse, would be eighty cubits; that is, the line running from A to E. It is only when we shift perspective to how the diagram is actually presented, as if viewed from the side, that we can see the eighty cubits is an illusion resulting from the orthographic perspective of the plans, and that the same length covered by the hypotenuse is in fact 100 cubits. This geometric diagram is more like the elevations than the plans because it incorporates the three dimensions and makes the slope of the mountain and its influences on the gatehouse's overall width plain to see.

The consistent ratio that Richard provides accords with another of his claims—that he created the drawings using "proportional lines." Claims that architectural drawings should be in proportion appear in Vitruvius's definition of *orthographia*, where he states that this type of drawing illustrates the front of the building and must be "in proportion" (*rationalibus*).[85] We can understand the term *rationalibus* to mean drawings in which an artist used a consistent measurement to scale a drawing from its life-size appearance to a reasonably accurate representation on a two-dimensional surface. However, this practice was not common until after the twelfth century and in the later Middle Ages.[86] Richard's claim corresponds to a much narrower understanding of proportion, which he took to mean an ability to consistently and accurately translate measurements from one type to another; this is the way Hugh of Saint Victor understood the term as well.

Recall that Hugh defines practical geometry as the use of "instruments, and [getting] results by working proportionally, from one figure to another."[87] Richard's sequence of drawings requires the reader to work in exactly this way, between the plans, elevations, and the triangular diagram, so as to fully understand the whole structure. The similarities between Richard's and Hugh's work continue in their view of triangles. If we compare Richard's description of the triangle, summarized above, with Hugh's *Practica geometria*, we find a similar description of the lines of a triangle. Hugh writes: "Consider a right[-angled] triangle. Its base is the lower line, set along the ground. Its perpendicular is a line at the base end, raised straight up, so that it inclines to neither side, but makes a right angle, where it meets the base. The hypotenuse is a line from the top of the perpendicular to the far and opposite end of the ground line (i.e., the base). It descends obliquely, and so makes an acute angle at both ends."[88] Discussing the proportional properties of the right-angled triangle, Hugh writes, "This triangle can never have all its sides equal. Sometimes there are no equal sides; sometimes two, i.e., base and perpendicular. The hypotenuse never equals the other two."[89] The proportionality between a triangle's sides, as Hugh describes it, allows

Richard to identify an equivalence between the hypotenuse and the base line. Manuscripts of Hugh's work tend to include drawings that illustrate the point in more detail. In one, for example, Hugh provides an illustration of the triangle under discussion, but there is no suggestion of how it was made or to what use it could be put.[90] Richard's illustration and the process through which he constructs it thus demonstrate that *In visionem Ezechielis* was produced as part of wider practices in practical geometry at Saint Victor.

Richard's application of practical geometry to an architectural problem, by combining it with Gerbert's theories of *plana figura*, demonstrates a more sophisticated awareness of the triangle's properties than Hugh's. By discussing the proportional properties of the triangle, Richard touches on Pythagoras's theorem that "in right-angled triangles the square on the side subtending the right angle is equal to the sum of squares on the sides containing the right angle."[91] From Richard's figures, it is a relatively easy process to determine the truth of this statement.[92] Richard, however, never explicitly states or refers to any aspect of the theorem, and could have determined the truth of his proportions without necessarily being aware of the axiom. Strictly speaking, he only illustrates that the hypotenuse is in a proportional relationship with the base line to some degree, but he does not define the exact properties of that relationship (in other words, that the square of the hypotenuse is the sum of the squares of the other two sides). Yet his geometrical figure offers a visual key to Richard's measurements. Those measurements which he cites as *secundum planum* should be interpreted as correlating with the base of the triangle.[93] Knowing this, it is possible to determine the *superficies* measurement by applying the same processes Richard describes in the creation of the triangle.

Planum, in the sense that Richard uses it, then corresponds to two connected properties of the drawings: first, the two-dimensional nature of the representations; second, the type of measurement that results from using this type of shape and not a three-dimensional figure that must incorporate the dimension of height. If this is in fact the first time that "plan" is used to refer to an architectural drawing in medieval literature, the term would have come about because of these two characteristics. Richard's vocabulary is a key part of how he integrates architecture and geometry, and how he expects the reader to know that geometry is the key foundation for understanding the drawings. Yet the detail in which he works is in stark contrast with the lack of equivalent detail in the elevations.

Looking at every reference Richard makes to his drawings, we find that he never draws attention to the elevations in the text, never including any phrases to capture and direct the reader's attention to the nearby drawing. All of the words discussed above (*figura*, *forma*, etc.) appear alongside the plans only. This raises the question of whether Richard had a word for the elevations in the first place. The only bits of text that directly reference the elevations are the titles that are set within the drawings themselves, something that Richard does not include in the plans. For example, in the sectional elevation of the gatehouse, just below the crenellations, is a title reading: "a representation [*representatio*] of the gatehouse as if seen from the side." The front elevation of the same building has the title: "a representation of the gatehouse as if seen from the front," while the lateral elevation of the building near the temple has the title: "The building sloping toward the north." The use of *representatio* here is not a technical term for an elevation, in the way that *planum* is for the other drawings.[94] Richard simply offers this term as a noun to describe what the picture is attempting to show: the appearance of the building in a particular way without strictly defining the view from which one sees that building.

In a strict sense, the elevations are two-dimensional figures because they are drawn on parchment; but because they represent the height of the gatehouse, taking them together with the plans the reader is able to know the building's three dimensions. The lack of visual examples similar to Richard's work reflects the uncertain vocabulary that surrounds it. Later, Villard uses the vernacular term *montee* for an elevation in his thirteenth-century portfolio.[95] If we accept the conclusion that "Villard possessed a sophisticated architectural vocabulary, probably learned from his talks with masons in the various workshops he visited," we cannot say that Richard has borrowed any term or concept from masons.[96] Where we might expect him to use *orthographia*, derived from Vitruvius's word, it does not appear, and similarly, there is no suggestion that Richard has attempted to render the vernacular *montee* into Latin.

Understanding the words that directly impact the reading of the drawings, and especially the elevations, is a key method of interpreting these drawings properly. Directly after chapter fifteen and the description of the theory that defines Richard's interpretation of the mountain's slope, he presents the two gatehouse elevations.[97] It is only by presenting his theory about the biblical measurements and the slope of the mountain that he can introduce the elevations, and he does so at the earliest opportunity.[98] In the lateral elevation of the northern gatehouse, Richard presents the three-story structure comprising the ground floor (with the *thalami*) and the two upper rooms (*coenacula*). The outer side—that facing away from the inner atrium—is much taller than the inner side because of the mountain's slope, correlating with Richard's description in the text that describes the outer part (*exterior parte*) as rising to ninety cubits, and the inner part as forty-five.[99] The importance of Richard's incorporation of the slope is clear in terms of the length of the building. Comparing the lateral elevation with the previous figure of the right-angled triangle, we can clearly see that the length of the gatehouse is affected. Using Richard's dimensions, we see that the measurement along the base line (*in plano*) would be fifty cubits; however, the measurement along the sloped base of the gatehouse (*superficies*) would be sixty cubits, which is the measurement given in Scripture. The longer measurement allows for Richard to incorporate the full size of the structure in a highly sophisticated process of proportional measurement.

To demonstrate the height of the building, Richard divides the building into three primary parts, an arrangement that helps define the two elevation drawings and their *tituli*. The total height of the building is ninety cubits. The top part is made up of two upper rooms, each measuring twenty cubits in height, and an additional five cubits for the crenellations. The bottom forty-five cubits extend from the ground to the top of the chambers.[100] Richard's descriptive technique is to separate the building into discrete parts, measure each of them individually, and then add the results at the end. We have already seen a similar approach in the gatehouse's plans, where the two walls on either side of the vestibule were given as twenty-five cubits long, which lengths were added to the central passage's width of ten cubits, leaving the reader to come to a total of sixty cubits. This additive method works well in text form, but the conceptual approach to the drawing is surprising. Richard envisions an internal structure with stairs ascending through the central hall. The stairs are shown in bright red lying on top of a series of curving lines which represent the mountain (see fig. 4.8).[101] The columns spring out of the ground without any bases, but are aligned perfectly with each step.[102] Set on top of the stairs are the chambers (*thalami*), which are shown as small barrel-vaulted spaces; in each chamber is an accompanying *titulus* that describes the depicted space.[103] The first *coenaculum* on the outer side is accompanied with the note, "From here rises the first-floor room, the outer side."[104] The top floor on the inner side of the building has multiple *tituli* attached. The one that appears underneath the vaulted space states, "The floor of the first floor and directly above the chambers." Above this, set within the space, is the *titulus* "the measurement of the gatehouse from the chamber roof to the top is twenty-five cubits."[105] Also set within the vault of the top floor is, "the roof of the entire gatehouse."[106] Finally, placed just under the crenellation at the top of the drawing, a *titulus* notes that this is a representation of the gatehouse "as if seen from the side."[107] The close connection between the text and image, in this instance, allows Richard to illustrate the stages of the building and then reflect this in the visual material.

If we accept that this drawing is the first that is explicitly shown in section, then Richard's rationale for that choice begins to make sense. He explains the height of the building by means of the different heights of the individual elements and stories inside. For the text to relate to the image, it was necessary for the reader to see the interior; otherwise, the drawing does not achieve the objectives laid out by Richard (that is, to explain the text and to bring the prophet's vision vividly to life).

Even though text and image are closely aligned in the elevations, which likely plays some role in his inclusion of a sectional elevation, there does not seem to be a Latin term for an elevation that derives from a geometrical context, in the same way that *planum* does. Villard's use of *montee* suggests that thirteenth-century masons had a vernacular term for this type of drawing, but the lack of Latin terminology certainly hints at the poverty of Latin when it comes to describing architectural matters in twelfth-century France. Since Richard did not use any Vitruvian terms, his word choice seems to be deliberate rather than due to ignorance of the matter; perhaps he felt that the strange-sounding Greek roots of *orthographia* were an innovation too far for his readers.

The geometrical diagram demonstrates Richard's careful and proto-scientific approach to the representation of architecture.

We cannot make comparisons to earlier drawings because nothing like it, from an architectural context, exists in medieval Europe. If the language of architecture is in the drawings, the grammar dictating that language is geometry. The little diagram of the right triangle in *In visionem Ezechielis* is the first time this relationship is made visually explicit. It pales in comparison to the complex plans and elevations that surround it, but embedded within it is Richard's true innovation and the beginning of architectural drawing as we know it today.

6 The Temple Precinct

Following the gatehouse's lateral elevation, there are remarkably few pages left in the manuscript; the commentary, left unfinished by Richard in the twelfth century, still has a few more surprises, however. Moving four pages forward, the viewer is greeted with another plan. This one includes *tituli*, but how the parts of the building relate to each other can be confusing, as it seems to have been to some medieval readers as well. It is at this point, having walked up Ezekiel's slopes, through the atria and the gatehouses, past the *gazophylacia*, and into the inner atrium, that we come at last to the vision's focal point, the temple. The building was the central point of religious worship for the Israelites, and its representation is one of the most remarkable drawings in *In visionem Ezechielis* (fig. 6.1). Looking at the third plan (fig. 3.3), one can orient oneself, as the temple was west of the central atrium, with its entrance facing the viewer in each of the plans up to this point. There is, as in the rest of Ezekiel's architectural descriptions, some ambiguity as to its appearance. The prophet divides the building into three parts: the porch or vestibule, the temple, and the Holy of Holies.[1] The porch is the narrow section at the front, the temple is the largest part in the center, and the Holy of Holies lies just beyond that and would have contained the Ark of the Covenant, which contained the commandments Moses accepted from God. Though Ezekiel gives a clear overall sense of

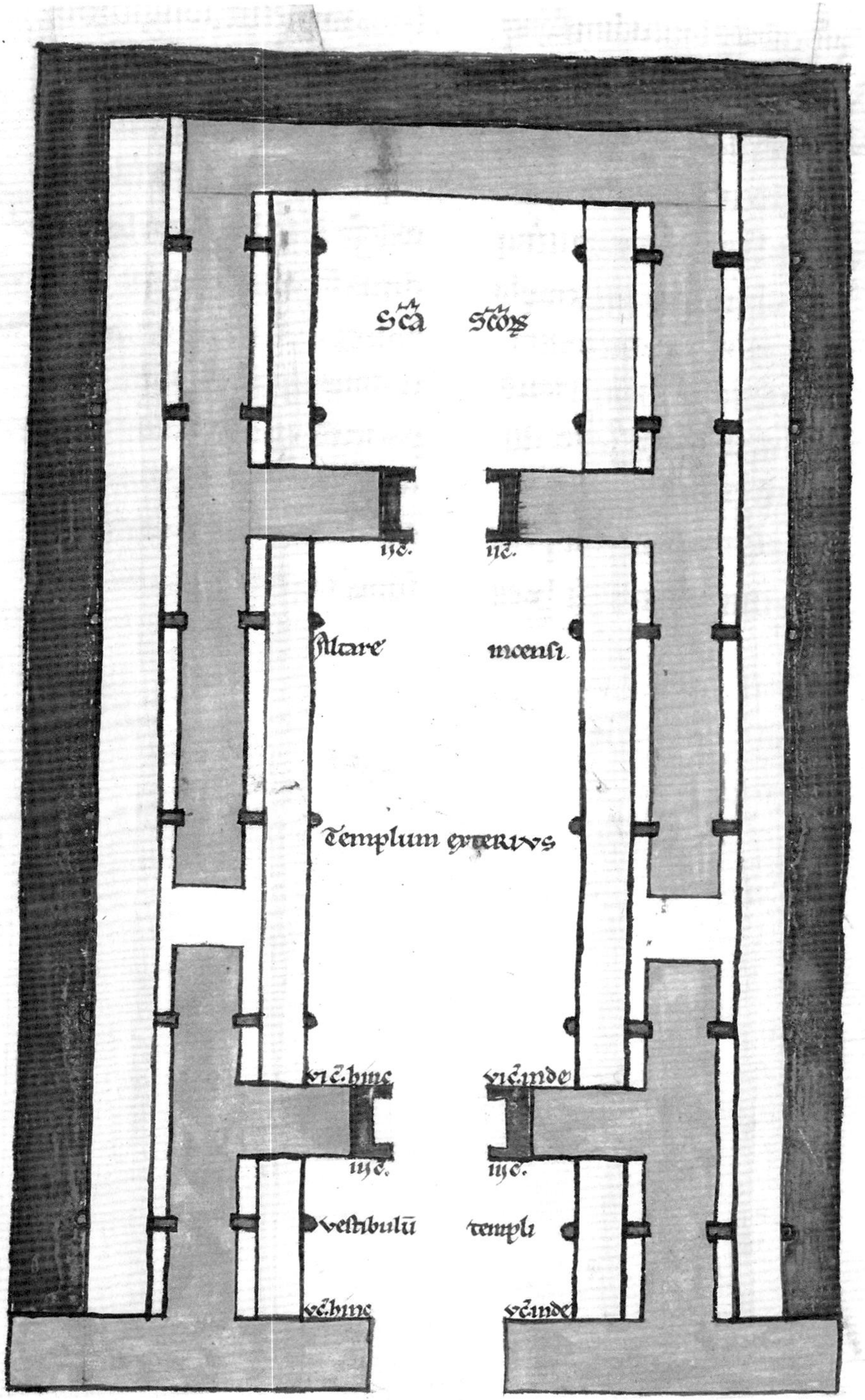

Fig. 6.1 Richard's plan for the temple. Paris, BnF, MS Lat. 14516, f. 244v.

the building, much remains unclear. We are told, for example, that when Ezekiel was brought into the temple, the man "measured the fronts six cubits broad on this side and six cubits on that side" and that "the breadth of the gate was ten cubits: and the sides of the gate five cubits on this side, and five cubits on that side."[2] It is not obvious what "fronts" are in this description or how they relate to the doors set in the middle of the wall.

This chapter focuses on the so-called temple precinct, an area for which Richard provides three drawings: the temple plan, an elevation of one building near it, and finally an elevation of the altar located in front of the temple in the central atrium. The temple's status as the vital monument to God's presence on earth cannot be overstated; for the Israelites, it was literally the home of the divine presence and, for Christians, the prototype for all churches. While Noah's ark was the first man-made structure, the Israelite temple was the first permanent building designed for worship, its construction and destruction consistently referred to throughout Christian history. It acted as a waypoint for Christians who focused on the relatively detailed description of it in two separate books of the Bible (2 Kings and 1 Chronicles), with numerous attempts made to recreate it in the medieval and early modern periods. When Richard looked at this plan, he knew its historical importance, but there is no doubt that his own church was at the front of his mind as well. In this sense, history and the strange ways it plays with the interpretation of the present provide an important mode of engaging with not just the three temple precinct drawings, but the entirety of *In visionem Ezechielis*.

Despite the temple's importance, Richard only made a single drawing of the building. There is no elevation, and so we are left with little idea of how a twelfth-century visualization of the building would have appeared. While we could only speculate that other drawings in the earliest version of the commentary were left unfinished, the temple drawing certainly is. As a result, we will need to draw on a number of other examples to flesh out Richard's intentions for the plan and his readers' interpretations of it. Located just before the second entrance, the one leading to the *sanctum sanctorum*, the altar of the holocausts is indicated in the Paris manuscript by a *titulus*, but there is no drawing of the structure. Most other manuscripts do have it, although it is inconsistently represented. The altar in Bodl. 494 is small relative to the temple space and appears to be an afterthought, although it is the same brown color as other parts of the temple itself, indicating it was drawn at the same time. The altar in e Mus. 62 is the most substantial of all, shown as three consecutive squares in different colors. This variation in the altar's design suggests that its absence in the Paris manuscript was common in the copies used by the later versions, leading the artists to improvise when they chose to add it.

A second significant change between the versions indicates that some artists were confused about what the drawing represented in the first place, and suggests that we really are in the early stages of architectural drawing's development. The early Paris manuscript includes the *titulus* "temple exterior" (*templum exterius*) in the central space, and this is followed by the Cambridge manuscript (fig. 6.2). The two Bodleian manuscripts, however, change this note so that it simply reads, "the temple."

It is difficult to determine how the entire drawing or its central space could be construed as the temple's exterior. Yet the Paris copy was produced when Richard was still alive in Saint Victor, and he must have known this copy was being made. The "temple exterior" label may indicate that the artist responsible for the *titulus* believed that the drawing was an elevation, similar to the frontal elevation for the gatehouse. Indeed, this is certainly possible in the case of the Cambridge manuscript, which follows the Paris manuscript closely. The central core of the wall is indicated in blue, and while all artists attempted to differentiate the spaces by applying different colors, the Cambridge artist included a masonry pattern in a darker blue tone within this temple space, very similar in design to this manuscript's version of the gatehouse elevation. The artist may have believed that the drawing showed the building from the front. The temple, after all, contained three levels, but the relative sizes and the entrances between the different sections demonstrate clearly that the drawing can only be a plan. The two Bodleian artists and copyists seem to have recognized the drawing as a plan and removed any indication in the *titulus* that it shows the building's exterior only.

Of note is Richard's inclusion of the wooden beams that extend from the temple's interior through the walls and jut out into the "place of prayer" outside. A plan is, essentially, a sectional drawing where the roof is removed so that the viewer can see the interior, but of some concern in the case of the temple plan is where that horizontal slice occurs. If Richard had provided an

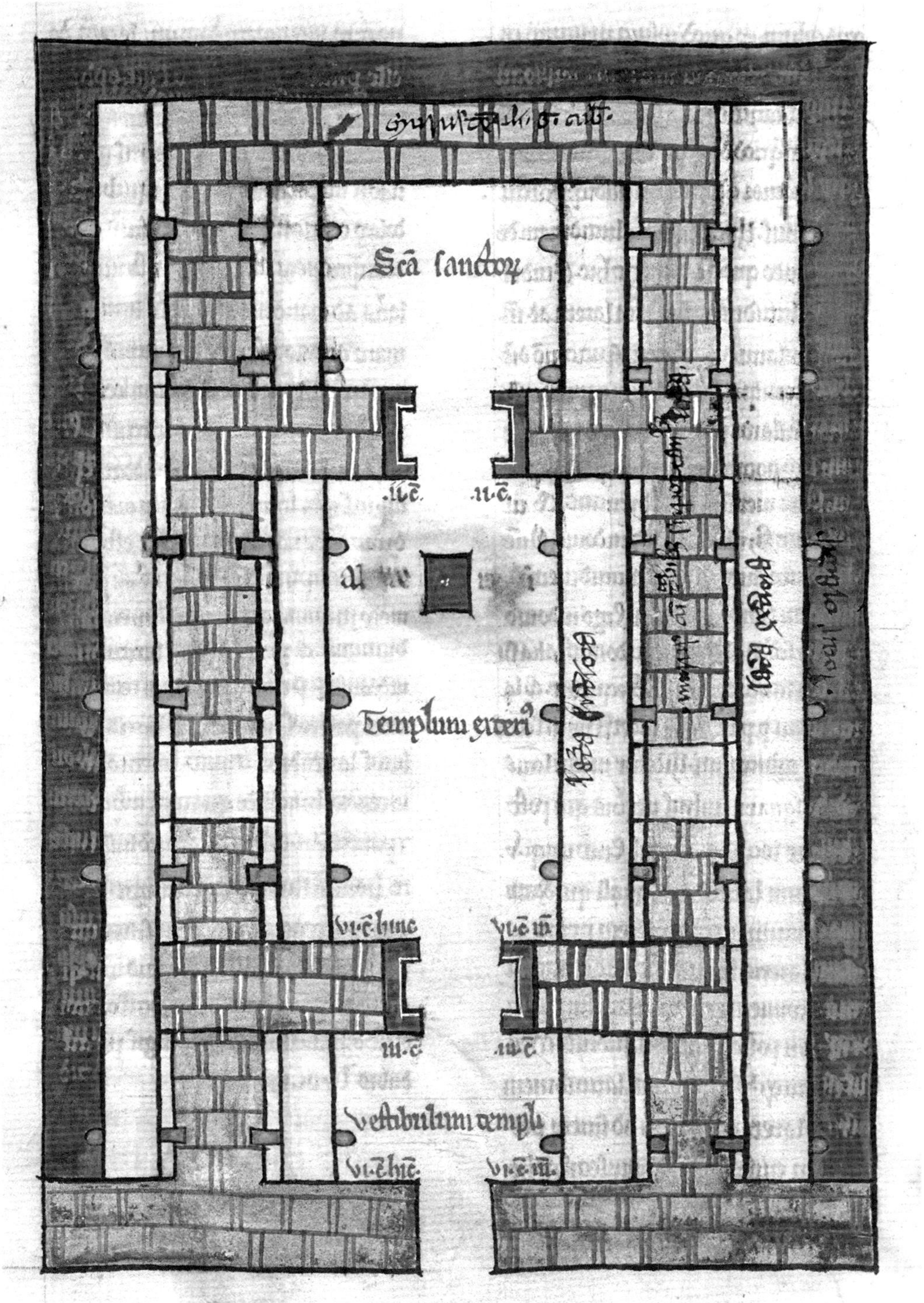

Fig. 6.2 Richard's plan for the temple. Cambridge, Corpus Christi College, MS 315, f. 104v.

elevation of the temple, it would have been possible to see the walkway that runs around the building's exterior. These are supported by the wooden beams that pierce through the temple's walls, and are discussed in Richard's text: "timbers extended from the walls, and supported planks, but the surrounding floors, which were placed on them, did not extend wholly to the wall."[3] The plan cuts at the level of these timbers, allowing the viewer to see more information about the structural characteristics of the building. The timbers are not given *tituli* in the drawing, however, making it unclear to the viewer what they might do. In this sense, Richard undermines his insistence that the purpose of the plan is to show his interpretation to those unwilling or unable to follow the text. Instead, the text is needed to explain this particular aspect of the drawing; otherwise, the timbers seem a strange addition to such a detailed drawing.

Richard's chapter on the temple in *In visionem Ezechielis* is primarily concerned with the measurements of the doorways, jambs, and the total width of the building. Chapter sixteen's first line is taken from Scripture: "He brought me into the temple's vestibule and measured the temple's vestibule as five cubits here and five cubits there."[4] Over and over again Richard is at pains to explain what exactly the prophet means when he writes "hinc et inde" (here and there) and to what structures he refers. Richard acknowledges that the width of the threshold must include the doors (*valvae*) and the jambs that join them to the walls (*ejecturae*). A similar concern is found in the plan, where the width of the jambs is given in the Victorine manuscript. The jambs at the entrance to the temple, after one has passed through the vestibule, are three cubits on each side, while those at the entrance to the *sanctum sanctorum* have a slightly smaller width of two cubits. Only the Cambridge manuscript contains the same measurements and objects, but with the addition of the total width of the temple entrance on both sides (*hinc et inde*) as six cubits, further reinforcing this manuscript's strong relationship with the French manuscript. With a doorway six cubits wide, this gives an internal width of eighteen cubits, and thus a total width that includes the wall width would be twenty cubits, which is exactly that given by Ezekiel. The two Bodleian manuscripts do not include this information and have removed the jambs as well. This is particularly noticeable in e Mus. 62. Here the Cistercian artist quite drastically changed the appearance of the temple. Here the widths of the three entrances make little internal logic. He has given the widths for the vestibule entrance, taking them from Scripture: "v cubitis hinc et v cubitis inde." The entrance to the temple, however, is shown as significantly wider than the vestibule entrance, despite Richard's arguing that the walls should extend further into the space—six cubits, as given in the Cambridge manuscript. There are no jambs in Bodl. 494 either, and no *tituli* indicating the relative width of the walls on either side of the apertures.

Overall, the temple plan is one of the few examples in *In visionem Ezechielis* where the drawings diverge. We are left with the impression that the Cambridge artist most likely had a version close to that of Lat. 14516 and copied it closely, except for the addition of the altar of the holocausts. This artist has, however, attempted to interpret the information, believing that the drawing also illustrated the temple's exterior since the masonry pattern is remarkably similar to that in the two gatehouse elevations. It may also be possible that the artist simply wanted to illustrate the core section of the wall. The interior and exterior walls, each indicated clearly in all drawings, would have been made of wood, as only the core *murus* used stone. The Cambridge artist has made the structural materials explicit in their particular depiction. The thirteenth-century e Mus. 62, despite having two exemplars, which in other drawings seems to suggest a closeness to the Victorine original, diverges drastically and is a lot less precise than the other three drawings.

Adjacent Building Elevation

Richard devotes approximately half of chapter seventeen to the description of the buildings to the north and south of the temple. In fact, he only needs to describe one of the two since they are mirror versions of each other. The buildings appear to the left and right of the temple in the third plan of the complex near the beginning of the work (fig. 3.3), and so Richard does not need to provide much detail explaining its location in relation to the other structures. He provides no plan of the building, only a lateral elevation, which is indicated by the *titulus* set under the crenellations, "the building sloping to the north" (fig. 6.3). The lack of other accompanying drawings for both the temple and the south building suggests that Richard was starting to run out of steam in providing the visual parts of his commentary.

The drawing is similar to the lateral elevation of the gatehouse and comprises three levels. Also like the gatehouse, but

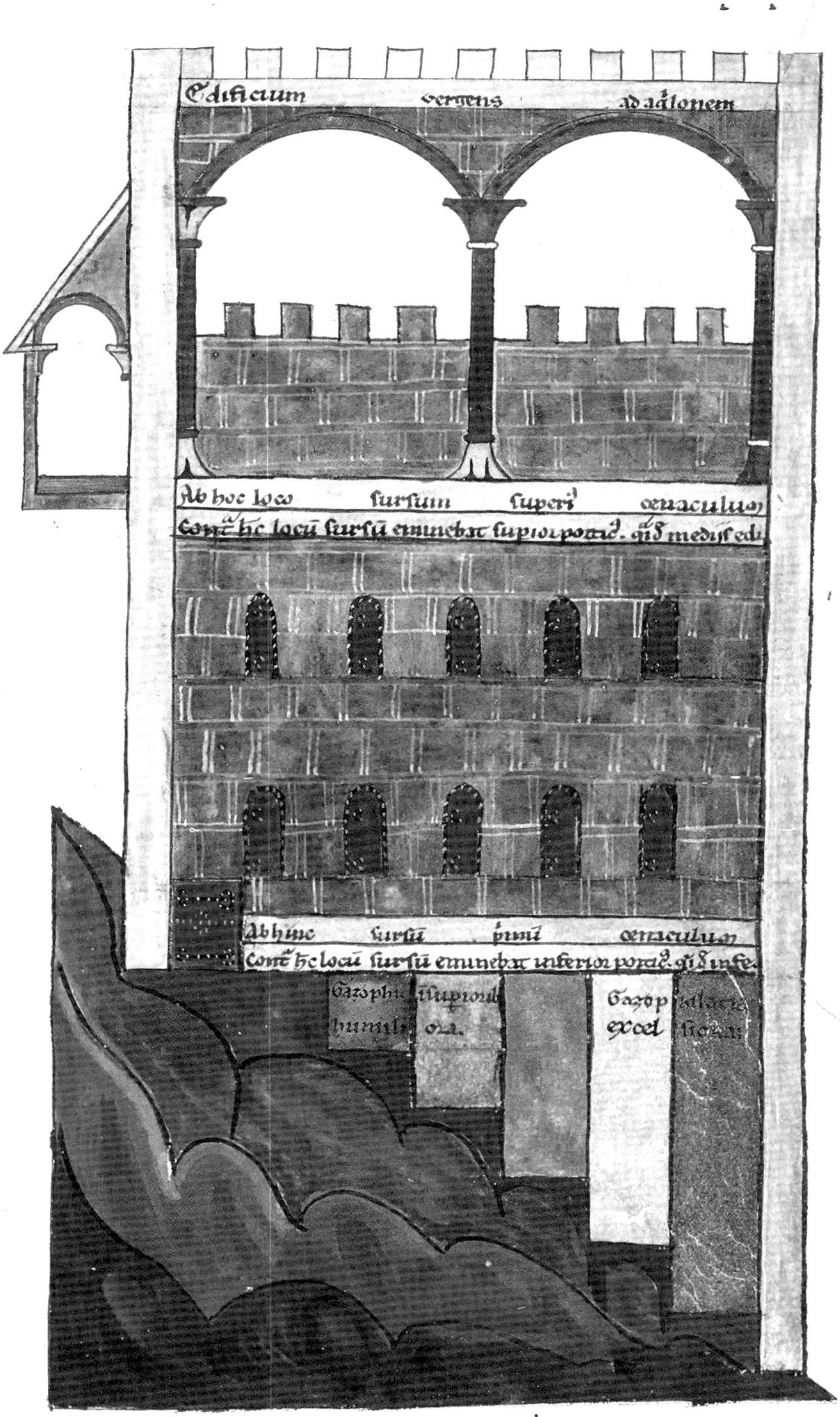

Fig. 6.3 Richard's lateral elevation of the building beside the temple. Paris, BnF, MS Lat. 14516, f. 248r.

unlike the temple, this building is situated on the slope of the mountain, which needs to be accommodated. The gatehouse elevation was an important touchstone in creating this elevation. Here, the elevation looks to be a very similar size, but this building's dimensions were very different: Ezekiel gives them as fifty cubits wide and one hundred cubits in length.[5] The building is thus much longer than the gatehouse, something that might have been obvious if a plan of the building were included (other than the brief outline of it in the plan of the inner atrium [see fig. 3.3]). There are two upper rooms and a lower level with steps running through the building and descending along the mountain's slope. Two large arches open at the top, and the ground-floor level is shown with windows and a masonry pattern, which indicates that we see the exterior wall and not the interior composition. There is a balcony on the upper left side that runs around the shorter façade and faces the temple. It is difficult to map the rough plan that appears in the first part of the commentary (fig. 3.3) onto the elevation, suggesting that as we come to the end of the commentary, Richard no longer includes redundancy in his images, and is no longer interested in repeating elements over a number of drawings to ensure the reader does not get lost between the descriptions.

The different versions of this building in the four manuscripts discussed so far look remarkably similar to one another, especially considering the building's complexity and its many individual parts. The most significant difference between the manuscripts is the presence of a door on the ground floor in the Paris manuscript, toward the lower left side, something that does not appear in any other version. The door's location corresponds with the text, which focuses on the composition of the building's lower part, especially the placement of the smaller *gazophylacia* (*gazophylacia humiliora*) and the larger *gazophylacia* (*gazophylacia excelsiora*).[6] The door is necessary to gain access to the building's lower levels; otherwise, there is no obvious way to enter the building. The door is at ground level, facing the pavement leading to the temple, meaning it was essential for the building.[7]

The drawing is like the lateral elevation of the gatehouse in that both are complex sections, showing the façade and the interior simultaneously. Also, as with the gatehouse drawing, Richard's text reflects what he chooses to show in the elevation: where parts of the buildings receive attention in the commentary, that same attention is reflected in the drawing's content. Richard takes some care explaining the internal composition of the ground floor and the location of the *gazophylaciae* in the upper and lower levels. Their presence in the text requires their appearance in the drawing, and so a section is required at the very bottom or basement level. In fact, Richard not only takes away the exterior wall here, but also the mountain's slope that runs alongside the building. Underlining this relationship between the text and image, the first floor and the windows that are set within the walls are important to understanding the building's situation on the mountain's slope. Richard writes that the earth went up to the windows, and "we should understand this to be the first-floor windows."[8] In order for the reader to relate this sentence to the drawing, it was necessary to include the windows, which, in this instance, mark the location of the first floor. A section of this part of the building would, in fact, have hindered the interpretation of the drawing. What we see, then, is a strong correlation between text and image, with the latter directly informed by the former, allowing Richard to bring his words to life.

The Altar

The final main drawing for *In visionem Ezechielis* depicts the altar set within the inner atrium (fig. 6.4). It is referred to in Ezekiel 40:47 and 41:22, where it is described as three cubits high and two

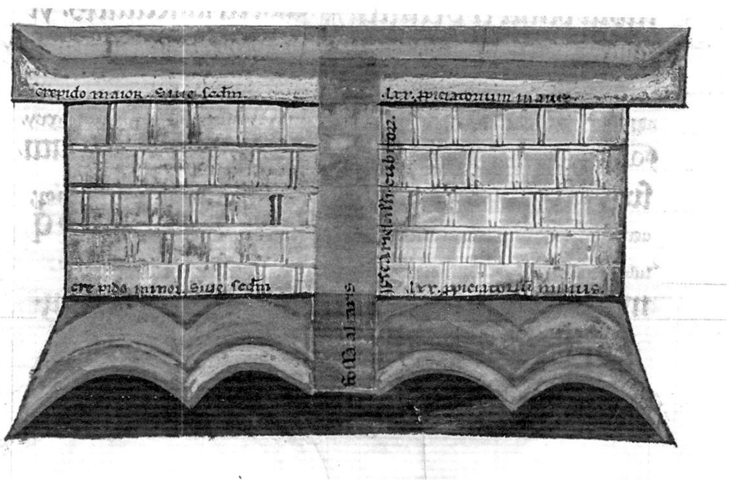

Fig. 6.4 Richard's elevation of the altar in the inner atrium. Paris, BnF, MS Lat. 14516, f. 252r.

cubits in length, and with "walls" made of wood. Certainly it is not a building, such as Richard has focused on up to now, but he nevertheless describes it architecturally. By giving the altar's measurements in cubits and referring to its construction material, Richard brings it into line with the other drawings. The drawing for the altar is an elevation, illustrating a single side of the structure. It has three parts: an inclined section of earth at the bottom that tapers as it rises, the altar's body above this, and finally, the top surface, which is approximately half the height of the body, projecting slightly over the altar's body. The Paris manuscript shows a narrow rectangular section running from the middle of the top section to the bottom. This is the final drawing in the text, appearing just before the interlinear gloss, which makes up the last chapter. When we compare the altar drawing across the four manuscripts that include it, we can see that the artists struggled with their understanding of the drawing's content and how to illustrate it accurately.

Possibly the clearest version of the drawing appears in the Cambridge manuscript (fig. 6.5). The opening running through the middle of the altar (*fossa altaris*) is depicted much more clearly here than in the other drawings, extending from the bottom of the upper section of the altar's surface down to the altar's base, near the earth, allowing the blood and water to drain. The top part of the altar has two horizontal sections, the top one colored in brown and the bottom section in yellow, where the *titulus* indicates that they are the *crepido maior* and the *propiciatrium maior.* The two Oxford manuscripts do not include any *tituli*, and the drawings are vastly different from the Paris and Cambridge versions. Bodl. 494 (fig. 6.6) retains the two tones for the altar's top sections, a flat brown for the body—where the other two simulate stonework and pointing—and a blue for the lower part of the altar's top surface. The drawing in e Mus. 62 (fig. 6.7) makes little sense, indicating a complete breakdown in the transmission of the drawing in what must have been both of that manuscript's exemplars. Similar to Bodl. 494, e Mus. 62 does not include the bottom section showing the earth to which the central openings run; indeed, the opening is completely absent and does not run through the middle of the altar but is only implied by its top and bottom ends. The top of the altar is divided into three sections but retains the upward curve on each end (*cornua*), which appears in all examples. The Paris manuscript includes three

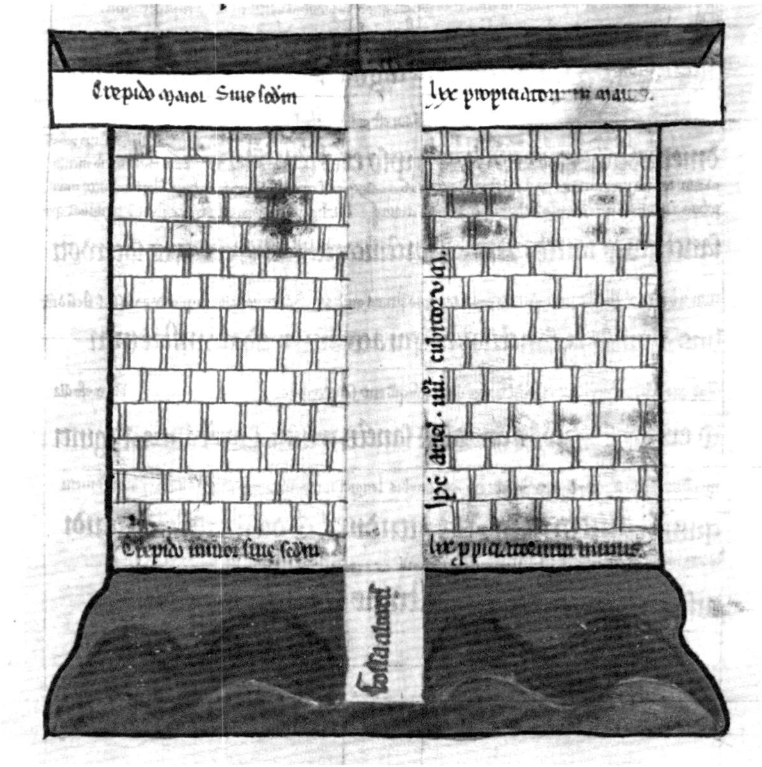

Fig. 6.5 Richard's elevation of the altar in the inner atrium. Cambridge, Corpus Christi College, MS 315, f. 111r.

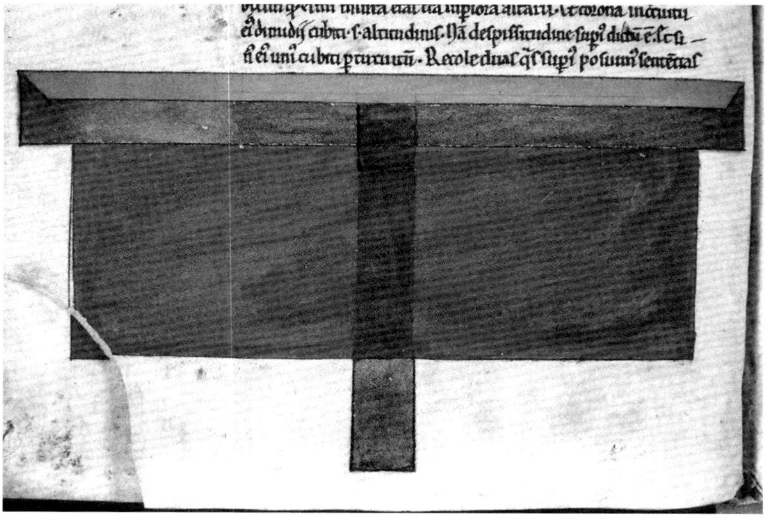

Fig. 6.6 Richard's elevation of the altar in the inner atrium. Oxford, Bodleian Library, MS Bodl. 494, f. 165v.

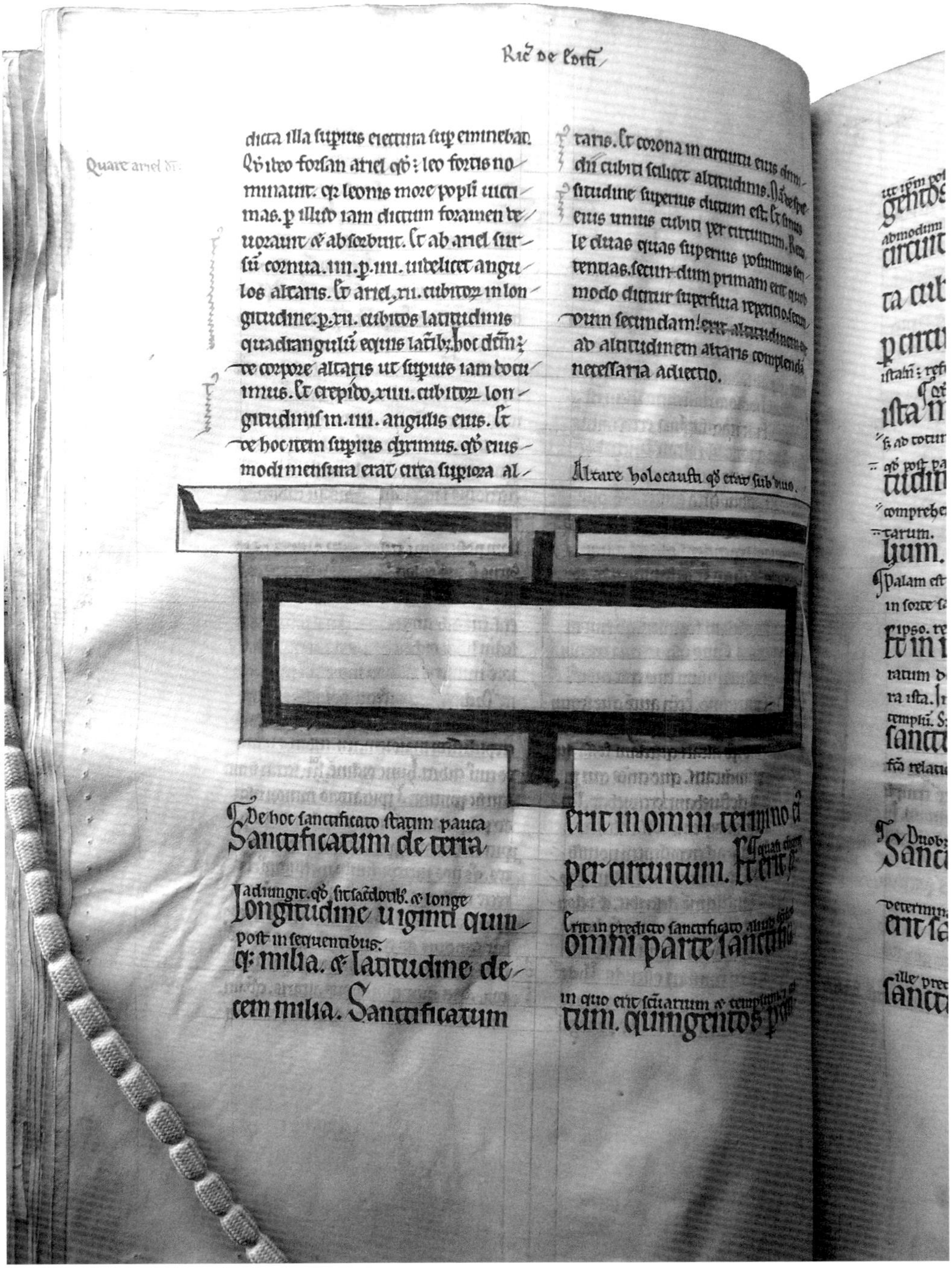

Fig. 6.7 Richard's elevation of the altar in the inner atrium. Oxford, Bodleian Library, MS e Mus. 62, f. 105v.

sections at the top of the altar, but they are not divided clearly, appearing only as three tones of red, making the structure quite difficult to read.

The purpose of the opening from the altar's top to the ground was to facilitate disposal of ashes from the burnt offerings placed on the surface. At first glance, the altar appears to be a section where Richard has removed a part of the structure, as in the gatehouse elevation, allowing the viewer to see inside to the chute. Comparing the image to the text, however, we see this is not the case. There was an apparent need to include the chute in the drawings because Richard devotes almost half of the chapter to explaining its placement and purpose. The drawing shows the altar from the back, and the different colors were used in the Paris manuscript—and the dark outlines in the other manuscripts—to separate the different parts from one another. Richard writes, "Its length is seen to begin from the back part under the altar's base and to extend along the altar's back, so that the blood is able to escape, which is poured to the base, and the altar's back was opened to the remaining ashes flowing into it."[9] The chute thus seems to have run down the back of the altar, perhaps open to the air. This interpretation would suggest that the drawing illustrates the back of the altar, from the point of view of the priest, but it also demonstrates some interesting ideas of how to represent a relatively complicated structure in a manner that was, as the later manuscripts suggest, incomprehensible to some later artists.

Since the Cambridge version of the altar (fig. 6.5) is the clearest, it is best to take that example as the main source for analysis. The lip (*labia*) that runs around the edge of the top is shown by separating the colors (brown and yellow). Importantly, the artist has darkened the tapered corners, reinforcing the bowl shape of the altar, which was useful for containing the blood and ashes of the sacrifices. There is no lip at the back of the altar because this enables the remains to be washed down the chute running down the back of the entire structure to its base and, ultimately, to the soil beneath it. Any difficulty in reading the drawing results from its orthographic point of view, which makes the relationship between the chute and the top of the altar unclear. This seems to be the problem with the drawing in e Mus. 62, where the artist struggled profoundly to understand how the different parts fit together, possibly due to a lack of understanding about what exactly is being depicted. Such difficulty underlines the problems that elevations posed for twelfth-century artists and readers, as they had few tools to interpret the orthographic presentation of a structure, so much so that some fifty years later Villard de Honnecourt still struggled with the approach, as we have seen.

Richard does not refer to the drawing of the altar in the text. Since there is no introduction to it, the question arises of whether it was intended to be included in the first place. The drawing appears in every manuscript, suggesting that it was issued from Saint Victor along with the rest of the text. It is, however, not as well integrated into the overall argument of the commentary, and it is unclear why, of all the structures described by the prophet, Richard chose to include an image of the altar. The problematic nature of the drawing is, most likely, linked to its placement next to the unfinished final chapter of *In visionem Ezechielis*. Richard may have broadly worked out the need for a drawing, yet his commentary on the upper part of the altar is at times confusing. The drawing is certainly a help for the reader who can understand it; however, its details were not completely worked out, leading to a breakdown in its transmission from copy to copy.

History and Exegesis at Saint Victor

The temple and the altar are two structures that medieval Christians like Richard knew well. The temple was nothing less than the prototype for every Christian church: both were divided into two main spaces, with the nave and chancel of the church being the sanctum and sanctum sanctorum, respectively. The experience of history through the material reality of everyday life in medieval Europe was intrinsic to the practice of religion, and when Richard attempted to recreate the temple, he says as much about his own historical methodology as he does about the temple itself.

No doubt the unfinished nature of *In visionem Ezechielis* is reflected in Peter the Chanter's criticism of the commentary's expense and the intellectual effort of making the drawings. Why then does Richard expend so much time and effort recreating their literal and physical appearance, as if they were real structures to be brought back to life and to the attention of a twelfth-century audience? Perhaps more significantly, why does Richard's vision of the past appear so similar to his own twelfth-century world, filled with crenellations, Romanesque arches, and floriated capitals? The drawing of the altar could almost be an image of a Christian altar from Richard's time. At this point, it is worth remembering that Ezekiel's buildings, courtyards, and pavements never existed; they were, after all, images in a vision, a glimpse of a future that the Old and New Testaments demonstrate never came true. But Ezekiel's vision was set within a historical framework that was extensively theorized in twelfth-century Saint Victor. The status of *In visionem Ezechielis* as a work of history, albeit an idiosyncratic one, is made clear in the prologue, where Richard defends his application of certain historical methodologies to Ezekiel's vision. The roots of *In visionem Ezechielis* within a specifically Victorine disciplinary context go some way to address an important question: why did *In visionem Ezechielis* appear at Saint Victor when it did and in the form it takes?

History lay at the heart of all exegetical practice at Saint Victor in the twelfth century. Even in another work by Richard known as *Benjamin minor*, which was devoted to the mystical sense of Scripture, he wrote, "History holds the first place in sacred Scripture."[10] "First place," in this instance, is not simply an indication of history's importance, but partly defines the exegetical system used by Richard and other Victorine authors. In the prologue to *In visionem Ezechielis*, Richard reiterates this stance: "Then, as it is seen in these things, the structure of the spiritual sense is more firmly established when it is properly and firmly founded in the historical sense."[11] This firm belief in history's importance comes from Hugh of Saint Victor's threefold approach to exegesis. According to Hugh, all exegesis should begin with literal and historical interpretations of the biblical text. Even Richard's language of "foundation" and "structures" echoes Hugh's description of history.[12] At the beginning of book six of his curriculum for students known as the *Didascalicon*, Hugh provided an architectural allegory for the relationship between these three ways of understanding Scripture: "In this question it is not without value to call to mind what we see happen in the construction of buildings, where first the foundation is laid, then the structure raised upon it, and finally, when the work is all finished, the house is decorated by the laying on of color."[13] History belongs both at the beginning of the interpretation of Scripture and in the systematic exegetical process, where it supports all subsequent readings. The architectural metaphor of history as an "intellectual" foundation is a pun on Richard's intention for his commentary, filled as it is with explanations of architecture and plans that show the buildings' foundations.

Architectural metaphors such as these can be an important way to communicate complex ideas, serving Hugh and Richard distinctively.[14] At its simplest level, the metaphor makes the idea of progress more "concrete," underlining the "reality effect" toward which Richard aims.[15] For example, Hugh seeks to explain the relationship between the different exegetical approaches (historical, allegorical, and tropological), marking them as distinct but structurally related to one another. Visualizing concepts in this way—creating an explicit link between idea and object through analogy with a recognizable form such as a building—was common during the twelfth century, appearing in works such as those written by the prolific and popular author Honorius Augustodunensis with his "love of views and vantage points."[16] Richard echoes Hugh's architectural metaphors throughout the introduction to *In visionem Ezechielis*, hinting at the true object of his attention. For example, near the beginning of the work, Richard writes, "Often they are tempted to fall, while they would be better to build."[17] The consistent use of architectural terms, such as "building," "founded," and the verb "to build," hints at the commentary's content and its intention to set out an architectural vision according to the literal and historical sense of Scripture. At the same time, it echoes Hugh's language of historical exegesis. The result is a playful interaction between Richard's intention—historical exegesis—and his use of architectural drawings to make his argument.

Such architectural metaphors reaffirm Richard's commitment to Hugh's curriculum, as well as the literal approach to Scripture at its "foundation." Richard devotes a significant portion of the prologue of *In visionem Ezechielis* to defending the importance of literal and historical exegesis, discussing how earlier authors failed to approach the book of Ezekiel in this way, thus undermining their own work.[18] On this subject, Richard expresses his thoughts forcefully: "But, having ignorance of these matters, they are numb in their laziness, they deride, mock, and blow away the work of others in the search for and discovery of truth; he who resides in heaven ridicules them and the Lord mocks them."[19]

Gregory the Great is introduced in this vein; Richard explains, "Behold that miraculous vision of the celestial animals, which the prophet Ezekiel saw, and which Saint Gregory examined according to the mystical sense. But he did not say in what way the literal interpretation is able to stand."[20] Richard tacitly refers to Gregory's *Homilies on Ezekiel*, where Gregory argued that the buildings did not lend themselves to a literal or historical interpretation. Gregory writes, "What is clearly indicated in these words, unless that you will see nothing is written according to the literal understanding? For he speaks spiritually and contemplates according to the spiritual sense."[21] Gregory's aversion to the literal sense was well known in the central Middle Ages, and especially in relation to Ezekiel's architectural chapters, so much so that Hugh of Saint Victor was suspicious about Gregory's influence and his "sublime disregard for the letter of Scripture."[22] By invoking Gregory in this way, Richard makes a point about Victorine historical methodologies and their application to one of the most problematic visions in Scripture: not only could Ezekiel's words be understood for their plain meaning, but that meaning could be visualized to make the exegesis more believable.

Up to the twelfth century, there were relatively few commentaries on the book of Ezekiel, with Gregory's being the most substantial.[23] Gregory argued that not only was there no literal way of understanding Ezekiel's vision, but that the contradictory dimensions the prophet gives were actually a sign that one should not take the description literally in the first place. For Hugh's threefold exegetical approach to succeed, however, there must be a literal and historical interpretation. As Hugh writes, "Nor do I think that you will be able to become perfectly sensitive to allegory unless you have first been grounded in history."[24] Hugh did not believe that the entirety of Scripture could be interpreted historically, yet it was still important for the exegete to fully rule out such an approach first.[25] During the Middle Ages, the sense of history being founded in truth was associated with an underlying belief that seeing the world was the best way to gain knowledge. According to the medieval etymology of the term "history," it was rooted in personal experience. Isidore of Seville writes that "History is so called from the Greek term ἥστορειν, that is, from 'seeing' or from 'knowing.'" Isidore continues, "Among the ancients no one would write a history unless he had been present and had seen what was to be written down, for we grasp with our eyes things that occur better than what we gather with our hearing."[26] Despite Isidore's optimism regarding the veracity of historical accounts, he believed there was an innate epistemological relationship between history, observation, and knowledge.[27] Indeed, no history can be written or known without the act of seeing, a fact that applies to text—we read through our eyes, after all—but also to drawings. Ezekiel, as a prophet of God, must of course have written what truly happened and must, therefore, have "seen" the things he described; thus Gregory's suggestion that there was no plain meaning to his words made little sense to Richard.

Hugh's theory of historical exegesis is obviously a key influence on Richard, but it does not fully demonstrate Richard's own agency in the matter; he was not, after all, a slavish devotee to Hugh's practices, but an innovator himself. For both authors, however, the first stage in the analysis of a text was to uncover the *sensus litteralis*, which was the plain or literal meaning and for which the trivium was employed.[28] The exegete explained facets of Scripture in several ways, but Richard's primary way in *In visionem Ezechielis* was to "explicate individual words in a verse with the goal of helping the reader understand how they function within that particular book."[29] In essence, it was necessary for readers to understand the words on the page before they could even begin to understand the appearance of things, let alone more advanced allegorical meanings of Scripture. A comprehensive approach to the past, one that attempted to encapsulate all of its material reality, is emphasized in all of Richard's historical writings. One such work is Richard's *Liber exceptionum* in which materiality and its importance to history are consistently reiterated. In the *Liber*, Richard placed strong emphasis on the liberal arts as a necessary foundation for understanding and interpreting historical events, with a particular focus, in one instance, on the quadrivium, just as Hugh did.

The *sensus litteralis* is the "literal interpretation [of Scripture] as a ground for spiritual interpretation, using the trivium ... and the spiritual meaning of a passage."[30] To address Gregory's denial of any literal reading for Ezekiel's vision, Richard clarifies the meaning of particular words in the biblical text; after all, "The interpreter cannot discover the spiritual meaning of a passage without a technique allowing for a literal investigation of the objects [*res*] found within it and their characteristics."[31] To do this, Richard first distinguishes between equivocal words that might refer to several objects. For example, when discussing the entrance to Ezekiel's temple, Richard attempts to differentiate between many possible meanings of the word *porta*: "For another [object] by the name for a portal we may sometimes assign an opening which opens and closes. One is the *hiatum* or an entrance which is crossed. Another is the *ambitum*, which the *hiatus* is surrounded by. It is the part of the wall which goes around the opening; it is distinguished and decorated by objects or by its form so as to highlight or emphasize it from the remaining wall."[32] The problem Richard hints at here is what he calls *aequivocatione*, namely, that Ezekiel's use of the term *porta* may be unclear for a twelfth-century audience. The first step is noticing the equivalence of the term, which must first be discussed in relation to its grammatical/syntactical placement within the text, and only then can the *res* (the real object) to which it refers be identified. While the discernment of *aequivocatione* is determined by the trivium, the next step of determining the historical object—that is, the form and nature of the *res*—relies on the quadrivium. And it is the quadrivium (that is, the mathematical subjects of arithmetic, geometry, music, and astronomy) on which Richard relies to make sense of Ezekiel's words.

Res ("objects" or "things") are not just objects that exist in the world but the visible manifestation of God's creation, and hence are clues to his power and purpose. Richard's *Liber exceptionum*, which considers the physical nature of the universe and its history, is partly concerned with understanding the significance of these *res* and explains what exactly they are. The *Liber* begins with an assumption that Hugh laid out in his *Didascalicon*: no learning goes to waste when interpreting Scripture.[33] As if to reinforce the importance of education, book one of the *Liber* concerns the "origins and division of the [liberal] arts."[34] By placing the division of knowledge first in his work, Richard prioritizes the methods of history before moving on to a description of past events. Perhaps significantly, he includes specific chapters on the quadrivial and mechanical subjects, such as geometry, astronomy, and farming, all of which are vital for the study of *res*.[35] The second book considers the materials of the world, and acknowledges that these materials are "subservient to the divine."[36] In chapter five of the second book, Richard follows Hugh's discussion of *res*, explaining that they are composed of "form" and "nature."[37] He follows by giving examples: first, that the nature of snow is cold and can mean the "annihilation of desire." The form of snow, "because it is white, designates cleanliness of good works." So, for Richard, there is an inherent correlation between form and nature, between what we see and the meaning that lies behind the materials of this world. The *Liber*'s structure gives some clues as to his thoughts on epistemology and history. At the basis of all inquiry is the physical makeup of the universe, the raw matter of which it is made. Only then do the events, people, and objects come into focus through the study of the liberal arts. For example, Richard continues to give the seven circumstantial meanings of snow, demonstrating the flexibility of the semantic system.[38] There is little sense that he is reading a language signified through creation, but instead that the significance of snow, in this instance, is intrinsic and not in any way arbitrary. The subsequent books of the *Liber exceptionum* are concerned with historical events, with each book and chapter focusing on a particular period. For example, book four, chapter six, is titled, "History from Adam to Moses."[39] The objectivity of Scripture—that is, the significance of the objects within it and Richard's reading of them—is key to understanding why he would create the drawings in the first place. They are literal visions of divine creation, otherwise unseen and therefore unknown by the medieval mind. Richard recreates *res* in front of the reader: his own divine act of creation, in a sense.

The identification of *res* is part of *In visionem Ezechielis*' purpose, as it helps the reader to visualize what the prophet saw in both text and image. These *res*, similar to Richard's discussion of snow in the *Liber*, are made of visible "form" and invisible "nature," and the relationship between the two parts is intrinsic; they are two sides of the same coin, with the visible form acting as a gateway for understanding the invisible reality and nature of the buildings in Ezekiel's vision. Having established the meaning of Scripture's words, such as the word *porta*, the next step is to subject them to a mathematical analysis. As this book has shown, in *In visionem Ezechielis*, geometry is the key to understanding that mathematical basis. At this point, however, what concerns us is one of the most astonishing aspects of Richard's commentary: how much the buildings resemble his twelfth-century world. Parallels between the reader's world and Ezekiel's were important for the literal exegesis to be successful; by making the prophet's world appear like his own, Richard can draw readers' attention outward toward their environment and how its many details overlap with the biblical world.

One way Richard does this is by moving "the biblical text toward the contemporary reader," and drawing readers toward the physical world around them for comparison.[40] For example, when he discusses the tower attached to the temple's front, he writes: "in this manner we daily see, in high towers or even lofty buildings, the ways in which the stairs ascend and are bending around."[41] Elsewhere, writing about the buildings beside the temple, Richard explains that walking to them from the temple side leads one to a door with a series of windows beside it, and from there one can descend downward following the mountain's slope. He writes that "by 'window,' we ought to interpret this as the first floor, thus the entrance was descended to by certain steps, as we see in the manner of cellars."[42] Richard takes advantage of the reader's world to bring the *res* of Scripture within a solid and familiar framework of understanding. The effect is like Hugh's comparison between Noah's ark and the boats on the Seine, where both the objects of the past and the physical world they inhabit become instantly recognizable in the perception of the present. As a result, the reader can understand what the prophet saw, which simultaneously makes Richard's account easier to accept.

Unlike in Hugh's exegesis of the ark, however, the most obvious presence of the medieval world in *In visionem Ezechielis* is in the drawings. Richard's stylistic choices are very much drawn from the world around him, even if not directly from specific buildings. For example, the section of the gatehouse uses typical Romanesque elements to define the style of Ezekiel's buildings, giving them a sense of familiarity to twelfth-century readers. Many of the capitals depicted in each version of the drawings are simple cushion capitals, with no elaboration. MS Bodl. 494's version uses floriated capitals, but this is a rare exception and still parallels the Romanesque style. In Richard's approach to literal exegesis, the present was brought to bear on the past in visual and material ways, and thus introduced the reader to the fleshly reality of the historical events, people, and buildings in Scripture.

The success of *In visionem Ezechielis* in borrowing contemporary architectural styles has led to a false equivalence between the drawings and twelfth-century architecture, leading even to suggestions that Richard was referencing specific buildings as far away as Jerusalem, even though there is no evidence that he traveled there. Such a striking resemblance between Richard's world and his biblical subject results in a "reality effect," where the forms of twelfth-century Europe are transposed to Ezekiel's vision and grab readers' attention by giving them the opportunity to experience exactly what the prophet saw without being alienated by strange and unrecognizable architectural forms.[43] The effect is reinforced by the inclusion of certain elements that may seem unusual but were commonly believed. For example, Richard suggests that the gatehouses' roofs were flat because that was common in Palestinian buildings. The round arches that appear in all manuscripts of *In visionem Ezechielis* are not automatically synonymous with the Romanesque style, but they do show that Richard is not seeking to innovate through the content of the drawings; instead, he prioritizes their familiarity to the reader. Such familiarity is a key component in bringing Richard's reconstruction closer to his readers, in the text through references to the cellars and towers, and through the images by means of recognizable stylistic forms.

The presentation of Romanesque architecture within a pseudo-historical context transforms the commentary's exegetical strangeness into something more quotidian. Noah's ark, in Hugh's imagination, floats because it resembles the boats of twelfth-century Paris; the remarkable structure becomes more manageable as an image as long as comparisons are made between it and the world the reader already knows. If Richard was interested in presenting the historical reality of ancient Middle Eastern architecture, however, his result is anachronistic.[44] The obvious anachronism should not be read as a mistake by Richard and is clearly influenced by Hugh's commentary on the ark; instead, the medieval forms speak to Richard's engagement with the present as much as with the past. Anachronism in medieval objects and images reflects premodern modes of reading the present, where the anachronistic objects act as substitutions for historical objects, embodying their earliest exemplar, and yet still read as intrinsically authentic.[45] In this instance, the colors, crenellations, and round arches are both twelfth-century examples of architecture and the actual buildings in Ezekiel's vision, circling each other in a dialectic relationship and collapsing in on each other to form a singular object. In Victorine terms, they are *res* where their "form" is modern but their inner "nature" is ancient. Our modern view of anachronism would make little sense to a twelfth-century reader such as Richard, where the outward form of a thing (*res*) was only one component used in interpreting its significance.

Addressing the question of history's role in *In visionem Ezechielis* leads to a conclusion that focuses on the possibilities within twelfth-century history writing. The commentary's purpose was not to create an archaeologically accurate picture of Ezekiel's world, but to transport Richard's readers to Ezekiel's world, where the prophet's "vision" and its universal elements helped twelfth-century readers to see that immutable reality in their own world. The architectural drawings, as a result, become vehicles for the imagination. Above, we saw that the geometrical nature of these drawings ensured that readers knew their imagination needed to be engaged to fully understand what they were seeing, and that they needed to imaginatively take a step further to understand that the forms or *res* of Ezekiel's prophecy could be interpreted in light of their much more recognizable environment.

7 The Map of the Promised Land and Jewish Exegesis

We have arrived at the end of *In visionem Ezechielis*. There is, however, one more drawing that appears in about half of the extant manuscripts, and it can tell us something profound about the richness of Richard's sources. This is because Richard's utter belief in the veracity of a historical framework, underpinned by architectural drawings, partly derives from medieval Jewish commentaries and drawings. In fact, Victorine authors recognized that if they wanted to access the best possible information about the world before Christ's incarnation, Jewish scholars were the most knowledgeable sources. Richard's borrowing from contemporary Jewish sources provides one of the commentary's most remarkable images. Eleven copies of *In visionem Ezechielis* include a map illustrating the land given to the twelve tribes of Israelites, as well as the sizes of the sanctuary and the city, all of which the prophet describes in the final chapter of his vision (Ez 48).[1] The map is highly schematic and lacks the detail given in the architectural drawings. Its presence or absence constitutes the most significant difference among the manuscripts. There are two versions of the drawing, although they are very similar.

In Bodl. 494 (fig. 7.1), for example, the map appears on a single page with the title at the top, which reads, "A description of the Promised Land's division." The map has three major vertical divisions: on the left are the names of six Israelite tribes and on

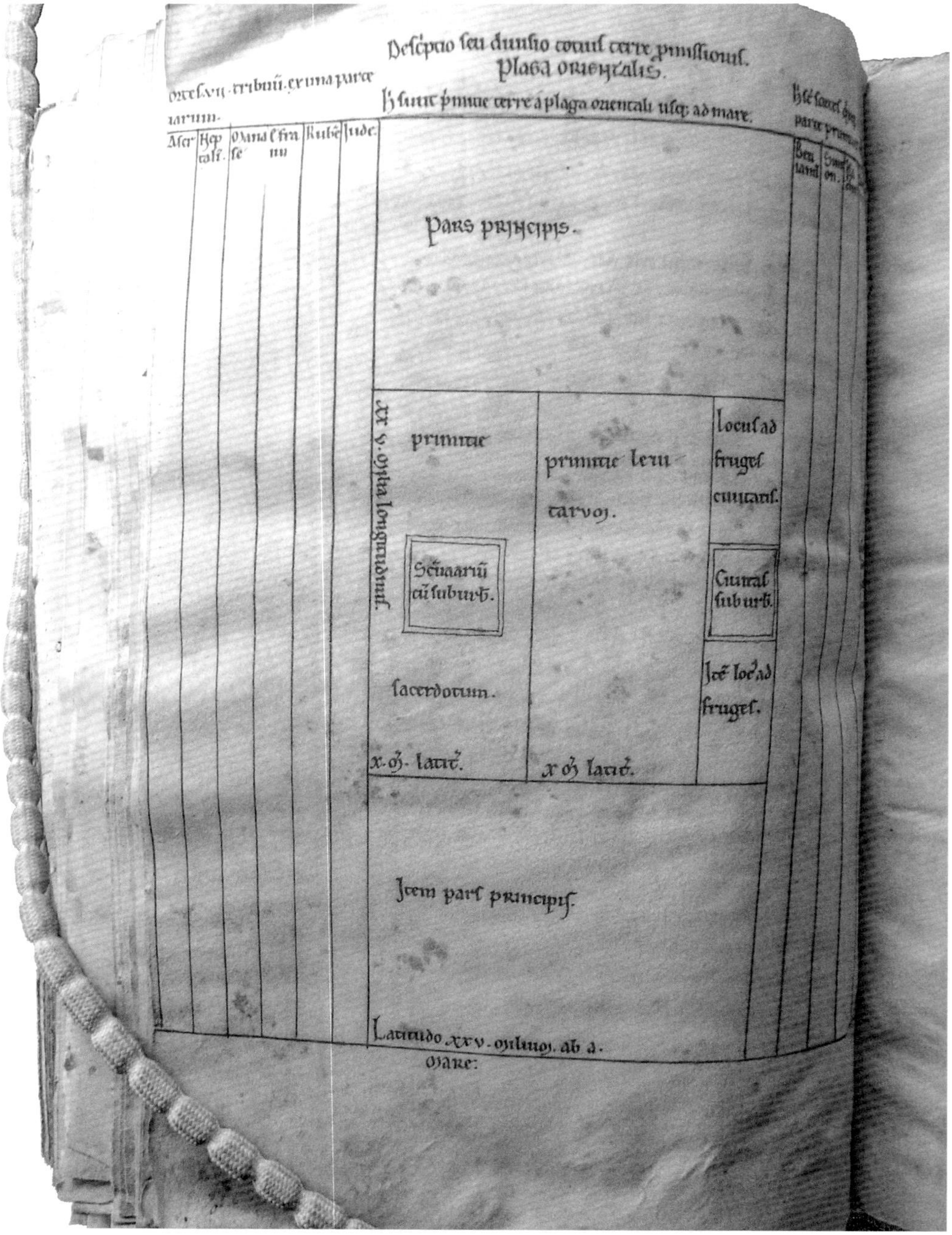

Fig. 7.1 Plan of the Promised Land with locations marked for the Israelite tribes. Oxford, Bodleian Library, MS Bodl. 494, f. 166v.

the right the names of five tribes, with the extreme right indicating a southern expanse. The central section is subdivided vertically: at the top (east) and the bottom (west) there is land for the prince, while within the middle portion the sanctuary appears in the left (north) subsection and the city in the right, as described by the prophet. Finally, the central subsection is given to the Levite tribe since they comprised the priestly order. The artist gives some measurements in *tituli*; for example, the width of the section containing the sanctuary and that of the Levites' portion is 10,000 cubits each; also, the length running from east to west in the middle section is given as 25,000 cubits.[2] The second type of map is spread over two facing pages, as in the Cambridge manuscript (fig. 7.2). Despite being larger, this second type contains slightly less information; for example, where Bodl. 494 tells us there are six tribes to the north, no such *titulus* appears in the Cambridge manuscript.

In all versions, the map appears after the commentary's final chapter, and so the text makes no mention of any map. Significantly, the earliest copy of the commentary, which Richard almost certainly supervised, does not contain the map. Its absence suggests either that Richard did not intend to include it or, as has already been established, that some of his drawings were left unfinished, and so the artist never had the opportunity to include the map as well, although it is difficult to be sure. Since the map appears in Bodl. 494, made in twelfth-century England, it was closely associated with Richard's commentary soon after his death, if not before, and then continued to appear in later versions. The map's content aligns with Ezekiel's description of the land in his final chapter, but in fact the source drawing was not done by Richard or anyone else at Saint Victor; it originally derives from a Jewish commentary on Ezekiel's vision. The map was made at the end of the eleventh century by a Jewish scholar to illustrate the general appearance of the Promised Land and its borders. Its presence in *In visionem Ezechielis* raises significant questions about the nature of architectural drawing in the twelfth century and the types of influences on Richard. Before examining the details of the map and its origins, we need to assess the importance of Jewish scholarship on members of Saint Victor during the twelfth century. The overlap between Christian and Jewish approaches occurs in both text and image; we will consider the text first before moving on to the map.

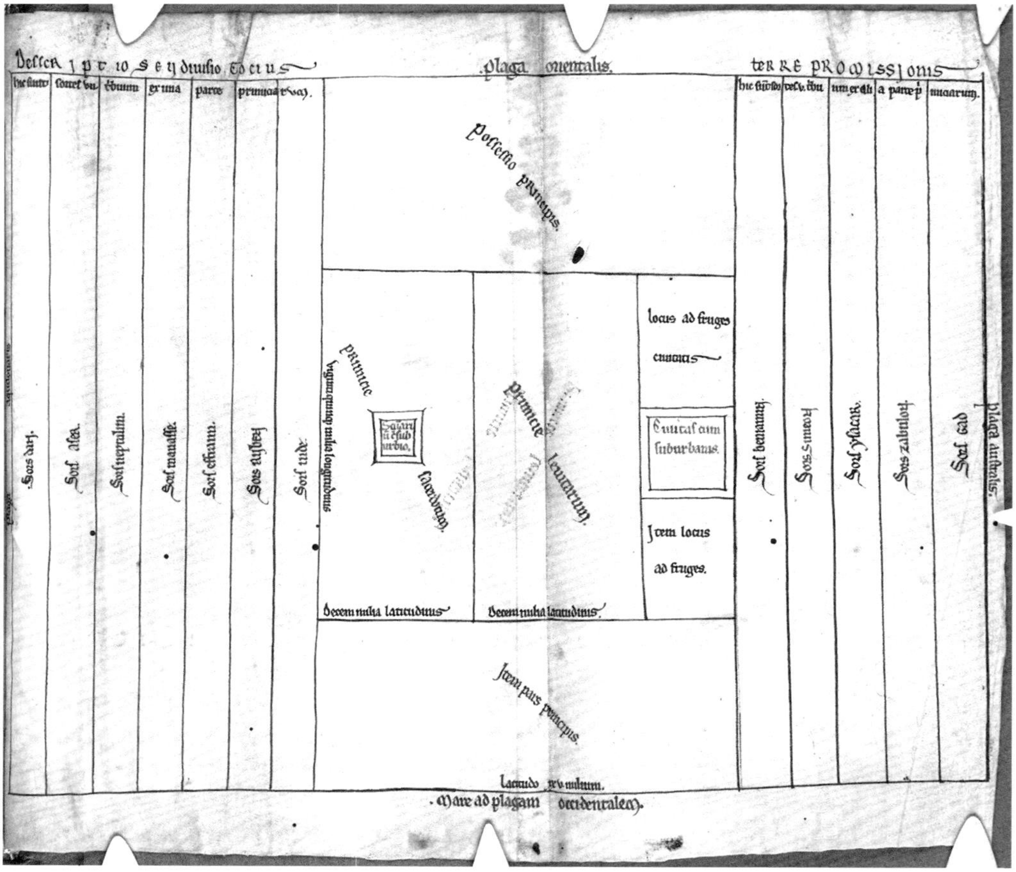

Fig. 7.2 Plan of the Promised Land with locations marked for the Israelite tribes. Cambridge, Corpus Christi College, MS 315, f. 113r.

In the early Middle Ages, Christian authors such as Saint Augustine argued that Jewish communities in Christian lands were a testament to Christian truth and would be converted at the end of time. As a result, up to the end of the first millennium, Jewish communities remained relatively unmolested by Christian authorities. By the end of the eleventh century, however, and as a consequence of the call for the First Crusade, Jews were violently attacked in places such as along the Rhine and in Rouen, where one Christian author suggested that the local people were thus attacking God's enemies without having to travel to the Middle East.[3] In 1182, Philip II expelled Jews from the Île-de-France, forcing approximately 5,000 people to leave. While the king's motives were likely financial, his actions demonstrate the uneasy nature of Jewish communities in twelfth-century France.[4] Despite these problems, Robert Chazan points out that "the broad (though unprovable) consensus is that the Jews of northwestern Christendom simply flourished during the 12th century."[5] And so there is a tension between the decline of Jewish communities' fortunes in northern Europe and their intellectual and artistic flourishing, with some Christian authors, such as the Victorines, eager to speak to them and learn from their enduring knowledge of the Old Testament in particular.

Saint Jerome wrote that if his Hebrew was incorrect, one should "go and ask the Hebrews; consult the rabbis in various cities," and this is exactly the advice Hugh of Saint Victor followed. This sort of intellectual relationship has been described as one where, "when the medieval scholar talked to a Rabbi he felt that he was telephoning to the Old Testament," because Jewish knowledge of the strictly historical aspect of the Bible—though not the allegorical or tropological—was stronger than that of Christians.[6] The presence of Jewish material in a Christian context, especially a text associated with Saint Victor, reflects the strong element of Hebraism within twelfth-century theological methods in Paris. Andrew of Saint Victor, a contemporary of Richard, stated that Hugh of Saint Victor learned the literal sense of Scripture from the Jewish community, and so even the basis of examining the historical context of Scripture, so vital to Saint Victor's intellectual identity, at least partly derives from conversations with contemporary Jewish communities.[7] Certainly for the purposes of historical narrative, Jewish knowledge of their own history would have proved useful to Hugh. In fact, there are at least sixty-seven "Hebrew notes" (notes taken from Jewish authors) in Hugh's work, implying Hugh's willingness to acknowledge contemporary Jewish learning.[8]

One of the primary influences on Saint Victor's use and development of literal exegesis was the French Rabbi Solomon ben Isaac, or Rashi (d. 1105). At the age of thirty, Rashi established his academy, the Yeshivat Ge'on Ya'aqov, to the southeast of Paris in Troyes.[9] Rashi's primary concern was to expound the literal meaning of Scripture. For example, in his commentary on the first verse of Lamentations, he says, "there are many haggadic midrashim, but my purpose is to explain the scriptural passage according to its *peshat*."[10] Signer draws a parallel between the term *peshat* and the Christian use of the term *sensus litteralis*, in that both refer to uncovering the plain or original meaning of the biblical author—exactly the approach Richard takes to Ezekiel.[11] The literal interpretation of a text, as in the Christian context, was not unknown to Jewish scholars, but it received new emphasis in the eleventh and twelfth centuries.[12] While Rashi's death in 1105 precluded direct connections between him and mid-twelfth-century exegesis at Saint Victor, his academy and students emanating from Troyes continued to have an effect on Christian readings of Scripture. For example, in the later part of the century, Andrew of Saint Victor (d. 1175) continually references Rashi's work, and that of his scholarly grandson Rashbam, in his commentary on Isaiah.[13] This continued influence may have been due to extant copies of Rashi's work or the work of numerous students of the master. As the twelfth century progressed, Jewish exegesis emphasized the literal reading much more strongly, as seen especially in the work of Joseph Kara (d. 1125).[14]

Although the parallels with Victorine exegetical methods are clear, the incorporation of Jewish content into Latin commentaries could be problematic, especially during such a fraught phase in the relationship between the two communities. Andrew of Saint Victor was particularly focused on historical exegesis and tended to follow Jewish readings closely—so closely, in fact, that Richard publicly disagreed with his reading of the past, as seen in the latter's *De Emmanuele*.[15] In his commentary on Isaiah, Andrew examined the prophet's words, "Behold a virgin shall conceive, and bear a son" (Is 7:14), focusing on the historical situation of Isaiah's words without referring to the obvious Christian dimension of the virgin birth and the Incarnation.[16] Richard believed that Andrew had gone too far in his emphasis on a Jewish interpretation of Scripture, and criticized his historical commentary for not referencing any typological interpretation of the prophet's writing. One scholar comments that Richard's "essential criticism of the Jewish interpretation is that it can never confirm or add to the Christian faith, which should be the purpose of all exegetical activity."[17] Despite his emphasis on the higher modes of exegesis, as we have seen, Richard recognized the importance of a complete historical understanding of Scripture, one which begins with the historical context but has its purpose directed toward allegorical and tropological ends, which were, according to Richard, inherently Christian in their truth.

In other striking parallels with Richard's and even Hugh's work, Rashi attempted to bring the past into the present by referencing the reader's world; in this way, the familiar is used as a platform to discuss the unfamiliar. For example, one of the most important elements in literal exegesis was a requirement to be clear about equivalent terms, as Richard and Rashi were; however, the two authors went about the work differently. In his biblical exegesis, Rashi tended to use *lea'zim*, vernacular words used to explain a piece of text appropriately.[18] For example, when discussing Ezekiel 41:17, he referred to a *planchez* as a balcony, such as ran around an inner courtyard, shifting away from the Hebrew in the rest of the text to Old French, and drawing the reader's attention to an architectural structure that would have been recognizable.[19] This is the same structure that appears in Richard's elevation for the building beside the temple, as a balcony running along the inner side of the building (fig. 6.3). Like Richard's, Rashi's purpose in making comparisons with the twelfth-century world was to identify a particularly problematic word whose literal meaning might be confusing for the reader. Many architectural terms were explained through the use of *lea'zim* in Rashi's exegesis of Ezekiel 40–48, highlighting the problems such terminology caused exegetes.[20] The first step for both Richard and Rashi was the discernment of problematic terms, which would help form the foundation for the second part of a literal exegesis.

The next stage for Rashi, as for Richard, was to make the images described in Scripture understandable to the reader. He carried this out in two ways: the first likened the twelfth-century reader's environment to that described in Scripture; the next used images in a literal sense to clarify what was meant in Scripture. In the first instance, worldly images were drawn upon to influence particular passages. For example, Rashi writes:

> When it comes to Ex 19:4, when God says "I bore you on eagles' wings and brought you unto myself," God is using the image of the Eagle [or Rashi is interpreting it in this manner] that God is protecting the people, as Eagles are only frightened by man and their arrows, saying to itself "better that the arrow should pierce me than my young."[21]

Having identified the images of Scripture, Rashi attempts to interpret them based upon experience. Here, a particular characteristic already associated with the eagle, its protective nature, is used to explain a piece of Scripture. This form of literal exegesis becomes useful when Rashi attempts to explain various miraculous events described in Scripture. For example, when discussing Exodus 19:18 and the term "furnace," he compares it with Deuteronomy 4:11, "'and the mountain burned with fire unto the very midst of the heavens.' This is said in order to make intelligible to the human ear as much as it can understand: Scripture offers human beings a pattern which is well known to them."[22] This "pattern" is around the human already, a pattern which is reflected in Scripture. For Rashi, it is important that his exegesis makes use of the human environment to explain Scripture. As in Richard's exegesis, this drawing of the historical environment toward the reader is a vital element in literal exegesis.

Rashi wrote his commentary on Ezekiel at the end of the eleventh century, and as an illustration of chapter 48 he included the map that was used as a model in some versions of *In visionem Ezechielis*. Several versions of Rashi's map exist, including the one in BnF Hebr. 161 (fig. 7.3), and its parallels with the map in *In visionem Ezechielis* are striking. The most significant difference between the two is the presence of seven portions of land to the left side (north) instead of the six that appear in Richard's version. Other versions of the Hebrew map are almost identical, such as Vatican City, Vatican Library, MS Ebr. 94 (f. 174r) and many others, which suggests that Rashi's map was relatively widespread in Jewish communities at the time. Both Richard's and Rashi's maps place east at the top of the page, which is significant because none of the other plans in *In visionem Ezechielis* are oriented in that direction, and so the map marks a departure from the rest of the drawings. It is clear that the drawing that appears in some copies of Richard's commentary, deemed to be useful for the final part of *In visionem Ezechielis*, is drawn from the parallel architectural drawing tradition in twelfth-century rabbinic circles.

One of the many similarities across the Latin and Hebraic examples is the representation of the city to the south of the middle portion. In the examples of Rashi's maps, such as Vatican, cod. Ebr. 94, and Paris, MS Hebr. 154, the city is represented as extending the entire way from north to south across the width of the section, giving it a width of 5,000 cubits, with no passage between the city and the boundary of its section.[23] Such an interpretation seems at odds with Ezekiel's description, which says the

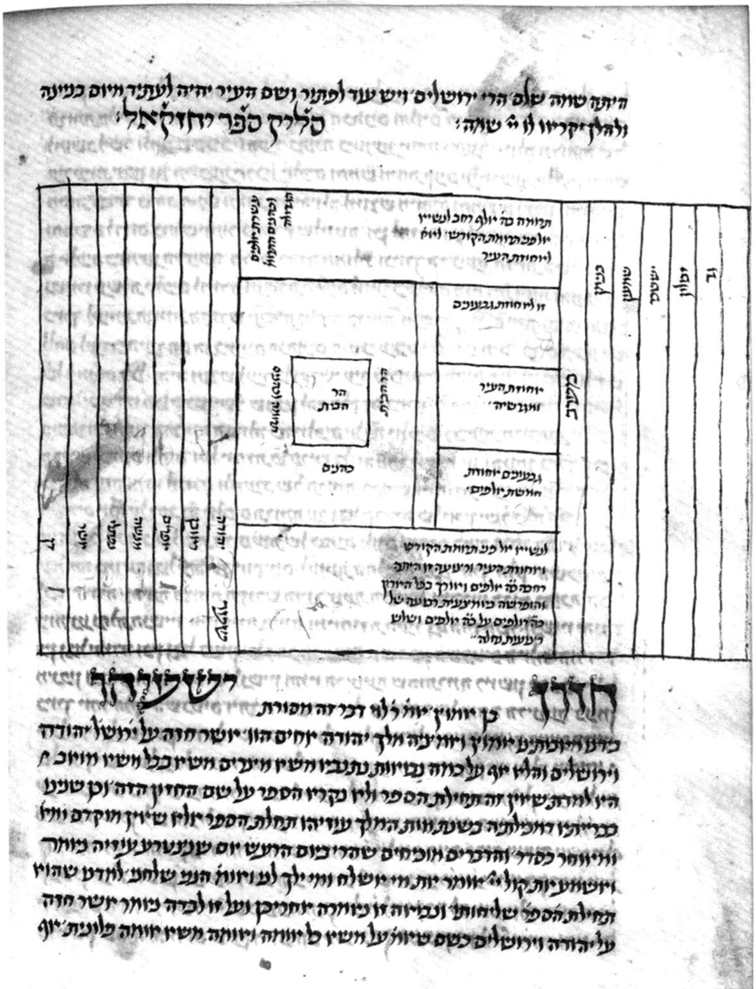

Fig. 7.3 Rashi's plan of the Promised Land with locations marked for the Israelite tribes. Paris, BnF, MS Hebr. 161, f. 206v.

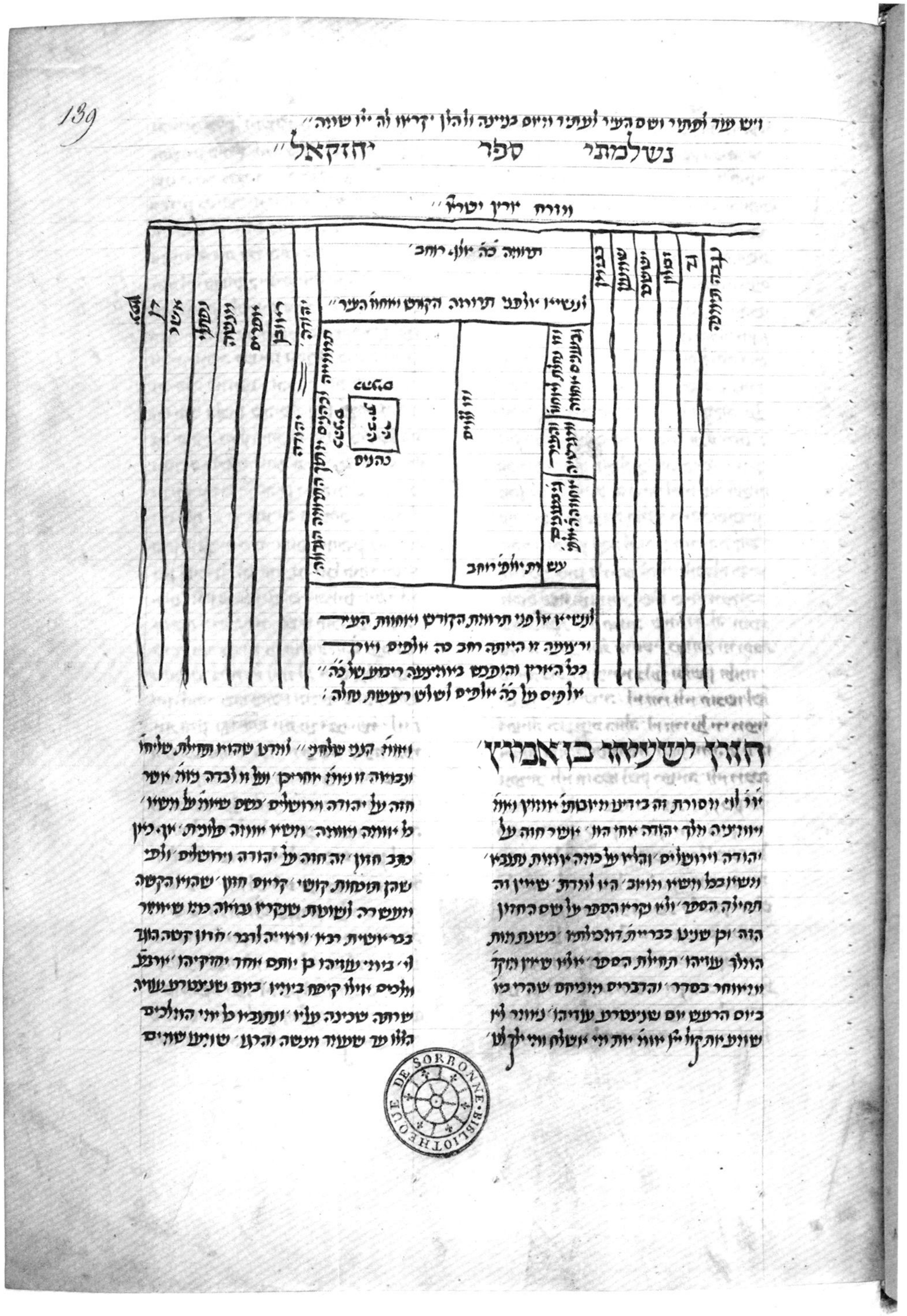

Fig. 7.4 Rashi's plan of the Promised Land with locations marked for the Israelite tribes. Paris, BnF, MS Hebr. 154, f. 139r.

city was only 4,500 cubits on each side. The same way of representing the city appears in a number of manuscripts of Richard's commentary, although not all of them. For example, the city is represented as spanning the entire width in BnF, MS Lat. 2165, CCCC MS 315, and Vatican City, Vat. Lat. 13014. It probably would have expanded to the same width in Vat. Lat. MS 1053, but the artist has not extended the line marking the southern boundary from west to east, making it impossible to tell. The biblical text would seem to indicate that there should be a space between the outer suburbs of the city and the boundary line, but it is not represented in some Latin maps or in any of the Hebrew examples.[24] It appears that the second type of Latin map, such as that which appears in CCCC MS 315, is closer to Rashi's original in this regard than the other type. Either way, both Christian and Jewish artists struggled to keep the measurements consistent.

The presence of a drawing from a Jewish rabbinic scholar in a Christian commentary parallels Victorine appropriation of Jewish historical models, such as an emphasis on the literal meaning of Scripture. It suggests that Richard, Hugh, and other Victorines were not only discussing Old Testament history among themselves but incorporating images into that discussion. Indeed, the use of images must have made such discussions easier since neither Hugh nor Richard understood Hebrew; they were essentially illiterate within the realm of Jewish exegesis, but at least had a starting point for a conversation through the drawings. To borrow Richard's own language, they were too "simple" to understand the Hebrew text, and so needed the drawings to help.

Rashi's drawings are not unique within Jewish theology either, although they are the only ones to directly affect Richard's work. Later examples of Jewish architectural drawings appear in Maimonides's commentary on Solomon's temple (fig. 7.5). Maimonides was a Jewish author who wrote in Arabic, and he included both plans and elevations in his commentary on the *Tractate Middoth* in a bid to clarify the structures and vessels in the second temple. The slim dark lines on the page give the sense of a simple diagram, very much like Rashi's map. Their purpose is also shared with Rashi's map in that both are included to make sense of a historical question, one that can be easily explained by drawing a picture instead of laboriously explaining an architectural space with words. While there were very few architectural drawings in Christian works, important and precocious examples existed

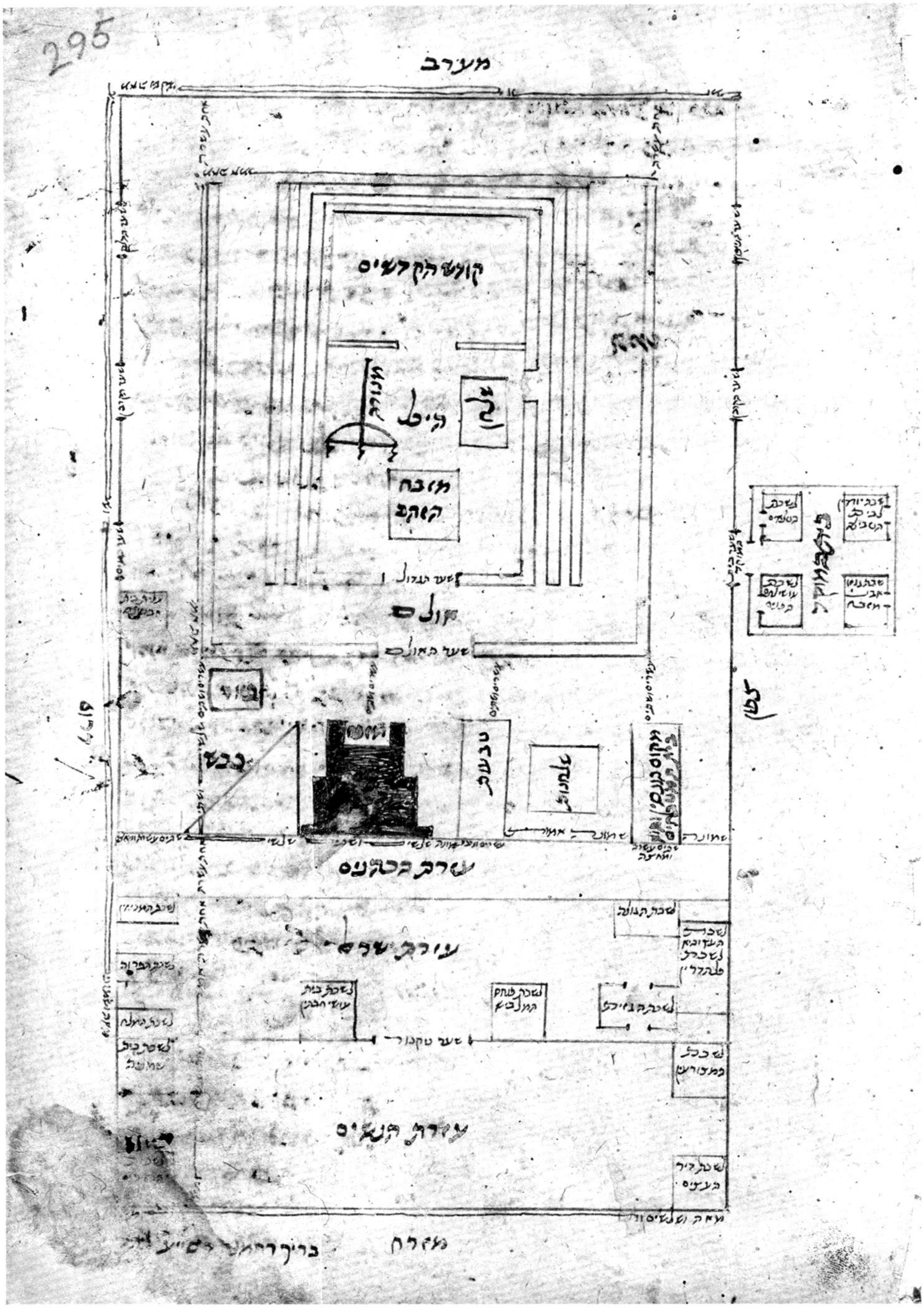

Fig. 7.5 Maimonides's plan of the temple. Oxford, Bodleian Library, MS Pococke 295, f. 295r.

within Jewish theological contexts, and Richard was aware of them. It is a testament to his utter commitment to understanding the past that he stepped over contested religious boundaries in the search for help.

In many ways, the map is where the journey into Ezekiel's vision ends, with the entire land seen as if from the heavens and spread out before the viewer. The journey into Ezekiel's world is made complete with a full acknowledgment of the diverse sources for that vision, one that remembers that the Old Testament does not belong just to twelfth-century Christians like Richard, but has a longer legacy within the religious and cultural lives of Jewish communities spread throughout Europe and whose knowledge of Ezekiel's world resonates much more acutely than it ever could for Richard or any Christian. Ezekiel, after all, describes the coming of a new Jerusalem which would arrive when the Jews returned to their homeland, an idea that must have seemed more remote than ever when Richard set about writing *In visionem Ezechielis*. In the midst of anti-Semitic violence, however, the commentary is a witness to the importance of cross-cultural and interreligious communication and to what such discussions can yield. Perhaps more important for us, and for the early history of architectural drawing more widely, is the remarkable diversity of Richard's sources. Up to now, that history has been largely dominated by Latin literature or Villard de Honnecourt's French portfolio. By simply acknowledging Richard's presence, a wide new world of drawing opens up, a diversity of sources set within theological works of not just Latin authors but Jewish as well. The earliest drawings were partly a result of interreligious communication at a time when anti-Semitic violence largely defined Jewish-Christian relations.

Afterword

In visionem Ezechielis tapers off at the end, leaving only Richard's notes attached to a transcription of the biblical text. It is an anticlimactic end to an extraordinary work. The reader is left wondering about Richard's own thoughts about the way in which he worked, his unique application of geometry to architectural problems, and even the hybridity of his plans and elevations. Despite the disappointing ending, it is possible to draw some conclusions about the commentary and its drawings.

For a start, Alberti's definition of architectural drawing bears little resemblance to Richard's aims, even if certain formal aspects of his plans and elevations overlap with Alberti's drawing types. Where Alberti sees architectural drawing as the product of an architect illustrating a building along very certain lines, for Richard such drawings are a much richer endpoint of an imaginative journey. The drawings represent one way in which architectural representation lay at the center of intellectual life at Saint Victor in the twelfth century. The visualization of the past in the manuscripts marks the end of an entire sequence of ideas and actions in which architecture dominated how the canons understood the world around them, but also, and more importantly, it illustrates to us their rich inner lives. There is a modern tendency to downplay the importance of the "imagination," as it is a synonym for the fictional or unserious, but it would be wrong to strike the same attitude with regard to *In visionem Ezechielis* or even to Hugh's ark, since the imagination was inhabited by architectural forms which were built from two-dimensional grids, forming the very fabric of an architectural language. From Richard's and Hugh's perspective, these forms came from the mind of God and bore the imprint of his creative and omnipotent powers, and so it was important to get them right. Yet the correctness of their respective solutions does not matter; instead, though Richard's architectural drawings give a sense of being correct, they overwhelm the faculty of sight to the point where it is difficult to see right from wrong. Their presence, however, is not a rhetorical flourish on Richard's part, since they are deeply embedded within contemporary practices in geometry, and are built on its solid foundations. That is what makes the drawings in *In visionem Ezechielis* unique: the fact that they are saturated with the same learning that would underpin the practice of architecture in the early modern period, and even bear witness to the application of mathematics, propels Richard's drawings into the future.

The purpose of this book, however, has been not merely to argue for the importance of Richard's drawings, but to show them for what they are: creative representations of the built environment that share more than a passing resemblance to later practices in the discipline. While histories of architectural drawing usually skip over the twelfth century, this study of *In visionem Ezechielis* shows that such an approach is no longer feasible. Previously, the century represented a series of unknown unknowns, hints that some form of architectural representation took place within places such as Saint-Denis, but now the century is open to, at the very least, some known unknowns. As pointed out throughout this book, Richard clearly had confidence that his readers understood what the drawings represented, and the careful way in which the drawings were copied, except for the final elevation of the altar, indicates his trust was well placed. As a result, we are left to wonder what other architectural drawings his readers knew if they were so proficient in interpreting those in the commentary. Certainly, as shown in the first half of this book, there were plenty of earlier plans and some elevations, but these are so temporally and geographically spread out that it is difficult to think that many people had seen these specific examples. There must, therefore, have been a language of architectural representation in the twelfth century, one that encompassed plans, elevations, and even sectional elevations, of which *In visionem Ezechielis* is only a single part.

It is tempting to think that the drawings were a result of Richard's discussions with masons working in Saint Victor throughout the century, where he was perhaps shown plans for the abbey's buildings and even sectional elevations. Seeing their potential, Richard made use of them within an exegetical context, laying out the truth of Ezekiel's vision for all to see. This may indeed be the case, but we have seen that such drawings were part of visual exegetical practices for centuries before Richard set out to write *In visionem Ezechielis*. Even if he did borrow certain representative techniques from nearby masons, he could not guarantee that his readers would know the same techniques, rendering them almost useless to nearly all of his readers. The presence of Rashi's map of the Promised Land, which is certainly derived from a theological context, suggests that the other drawings shared the same common sources, those of the monastic cloister and the many different books they knew.

What Richard does change, as demonstrated in the largest chapter of this book, is the language invoked for architecture and the visual language in the drawings. Richard could have used Vitruvian terminology, since at least some of his readers would have recognized the strange Greek words for plans and elevations, but he did not. By using the words *planum* and *superficies*, Richard was tapping into the language of twelfth-century geometry, but this sort of language may have been more recognizable as a translation of vernacular building terminology. *Superficies* makes little sense in the way Richard uses it—as a measurement that takes the slope of the mountain into account—and it may be that it refers to contemporary practice in the making of three-dimensional structures, but rendered in the Latin that Richard's clerical and monastic readers would have expected. It is difficult to be certain of this interpretation until more work is done on building terminology used in the central Middle Ages, including both the Latin terms of architectural description used in documents such as charters, and vernacular words appearing in contemporary dictionaries or descriptive texts such as the *Dictionarius*, the account of Paris for students by John de Garland (d. c. 1270).[1]

If Richard's connections to architecture are unclear, his influence on subsequent exegetical practices is a little more concrete. Indeed, the legacy of *In visionem Ezechielis* lies largely within the realms of medieval exegetical works. The reason it has remained bounded within the highly intellectual space of the cloister is likely that anyone outside of that group of people had no access to the text, and even if they did, it is unlikely they would have understood it without significant help. Even its intended readers were primarily interested in how Richard could help with their understanding of the biblical text rather than how the drawings functioned. Yet there is one exception: Nicholas of Lyra (d. 1349), whose *Postilla litteralis super totam Bibliam*, known as the *Postilla*, was a particularly popular work of the late Middle Ages. Its combination of diagrams and biblical commentary is directly related to *In visionem Ezechielis*. The *Postilla* is a literal commentary on the entire Bible, not just the book of Ezekiel; like Richard, Nicholas included a large number of diagrams including architectural images, such as those illustrating Solomon's temple. The *Postilla* is an astonishing achievement, written over nine years and disseminated throughout Europe very soon after Nicholas completed it, appearing in hundreds of manuscripts in the fourteenth and fifteenth centuries and becoming the first biblical commentary to appear in print.

The similarities between Richard's and Nicholas's commentaries have been highlighted in the past, but most have dismissed the idea that there was a strong connection between *In visionem Ezechielis* and the *Postilla*.[2] Instead, most scholarship focuses on the influence of Jewish drawings on Nicholas's work, comparing his drawings with Rashi's and Maimonides's architectural drawings. Indeed, some scholars dismiss outright any possible influence from Richard, going so far as to say that the Jewish influence on Nicholas makes it obvious that Richard "was less interested in scriptural correctness, and gave his fantasy a freer range."[3] This is an astonishing misreading of *In visionem Ezechielis* and the lengths to which Richard went to align Ezekiel's vision with his historical commentary, and an equally extraordinary dismissal of Christian influences on the *Postilla*. Hebraic and rabbinic exegesis of the Old Testament was vitally important to Nicholas, not least because he read Hebrew quite fluently and leveraged his knowledge of the language to interrogate the Hebraic Bible from a Christian point of view. But, as others rightly point out, there is clearly a Victorine quality to the combination of text and image as they appear in the *Postilla*, and the immense popularity of Nicholas's work makes it one of the most important legacies of *In visionem Ezechielis*. Even within the historical niche of biblical exegesis, *In visionem Ezechielis* has few admirers, and is largely seen as a precursor to Nicholas's more elaborate schemes.

At the very least, Nicholas certainly knew of *In visionem Ezechielis* and indeed admired it, but he suggested that Richard "pays insufficient attention to the Hebrew text" and that Richard did not elaborate on the spiritual senses in any significant way.[4] These two observations are, of course, perfectly accurate. As already shown, Rashi was an important influence on Richard, but Richard knew no Hebrew and thus could not engage with the Old Testament with the same level of detail as Nicholas. And, as discussed in the first chapter, Richard simply was not interested in offering an allegorical or tropological treatment of Ezekiel's vision, not least because Gregory the Great had already done so. Nicholas's admiration for Richard's commentary seems to have embraced the inclusion of images as well; indeed, some of his images appear quite similar to those in *In visionem Ezechielis*. In his own time, Richard's aims were misunderstood to some extent, his historical focus seen as a weakness rather than as part of Saint Victor's systematic approach to the past in the twelfth century. Such misunderstanding goes some way to explaining why *In visionem Ezechielis* made such a small impact in his own time and even today.

While Richard's legacy within the rather niche realm of biblical exegesis was small, what about his legacy for architectural drawing more widely? In this case, Alberti presents a problem when placing Richard within the history of architectural drawing. It has been pointed out that to call the twelfth century a "renaissance" risks "underestimating and even distorting the real character" of Richard's time.[5] These words are true, and especially so in the case of *In visionem Ezechielis*. Richard was not Alberti; architecture and geometry were different tools wielded for different ends; and even the drawings themselves only hint at the sophistication of the early modern period. To make the comparison is to underestimate just how original Richard was in how he visualized the past, and the theological context makes it difficult to map connections between the twelfth and fifteenth centuries. Despite this, writing on architecture since the fifteenth century uses the language of Alberti, of architects working and drawing what they see, all pointed toward material ends. As a result, it is necessary to make Richard speak that language in order to be heard; he must be translated for the modern reader. But I hope that by reading this book, seeing what I have seen every day for the last decade, the modern reader can recognize the present in the past and can identify Richard's place in history, realizing that while Richard needs some translating into the architectural language of Alberti, it is a simple task, something more like a change of dialect rather than an utterly different language.

At the beginning of this book, I stated that *In visionem Ezechielis* represents the tip of an iceberg, insofar as there must have been similar drawings made in the twelfth century, and such a depth of understanding within clerical audiences in Europe feeds into the development of architectural drawing as it appeared a century later. But it would be more accurate to see the tip of that iceberg as indicative of how rooted Richard's drawings were in the Victorine practices and as illustrating the catalyst of an imagination inhabited by scores of buildings expertly constructed and conceived to organize—to quote Dante's words—a mind beyond the human.

Acknowledgments

When I was a student, I read acknowledgments but never really understood why people had to thank so many people for one single book. I now see that books are a product of a community, but only one person has the fortune to be called the author. I owe a profound debt to that community.

Richard of Saint Victor was a large part of my life as a student at Oxford. As my supervisor during my MSt and PhD, Lesley Smith was a vital shepherd for my thoughts and ideas. She is the kindest and most generous teacher and colleague one could ask for. I first saw Richard's drawing during the final year of my undergraduate degree; during that time Roger Stalley was a great teacher and now a good friend. Sandy Heslop and Hannah Skodah read and reread my DPhil thesis with kindness, generosity, and patience, and I thank them for it. Laura Cleaver and Katherine Weikert read various portions of this book and always gave wonderful advice; they are both brilliant and kind. They and the many people I've met make being a medieval historian in the UK a great pleasure.

The book was written in three different places, all of which were important. At York University I found an extraordinary community of scholars in the History of Art department, but in particular I would like to thank Tim Ayers, Anthony Geraghty, Michael White, Hannah Vorholt, Teresa Kittler, and Cadence Kinsey. As Shuffrey Junior Research Fellow in Lincoln College, Oxford, I was lucky to be a member of a kind group of people who have always stressed the human in the humanities. I thank the Rector Henry Woodhuysen, and the fellows of the college, including Louise Durning, Perry Gauci, Mark Kirby, Melanie Marshall, Peter McCullough, and Lucy Wooding. Keble College funded much of my studies and I thank the Warden and Fellows there, especially Ian Archer. As I write this, I am about to embark on a new adventure at the University of Aberdeen, where I have been welcomed wonderfully by Joanne Anderson, Hans Hones, and Helen Pierce.

Many people helped me along the way, but I never kept a list. In its absence, I will do my best. Jennifer and Kevin Depold, along with Pippa and Ari, are family, and I would be lost without them. With Charlotte Cooper-Davis I had important chats and cups of coffee, which were a pleasure and important in keeping morale up. Geraldine Cirot and Josh Doble have been constant friends and companions for the last decade. The many more people include Hannah Bailey, Daniel Thomas, Liv Robinson, David Rundle, Emily Guerry, Helen Smith, Mary Carruthers, Martin Kauffman, Anne McLoughlin, Anna Boeles Rowland, Erin Maqlaque, Tom Johnson, Laura Carroll, Ciarán Molumby, Cillian O'Donnchadha, Fran and Linda Carroll, Daniel Anderson, Stephen

Finn, Eamon Dolan, Robert Keran, Robert Brown, Terri Levine, Henrike Lähnemann, and Cat, Ben, Lindsay, and Tom in Winchester, as well as no doubt many others I've forgotten; you are given full permission to make me feel guilty for doing so.

Sincerest thanks go to Thomas Weaver at the MIT Press, whose patience and guidance in the making of this book led to something much better than I thought possible, and for being a great teacher in the process. Tom's role in the MIT Press could be the best thing that has happened for architectural historians in the recent past. I would also like to thank Matthew Abbate and Paula Woolley for their careful editing of the manuscript.

There are some who will never read this book because they were taken away from us. Michael Clanchy was one of the kindest scholars with whom I shared a cup of coffee in Blackwell's and was never short on excellent advice. Marian Gowan taught me to look up from my book occasionally, and Terri Bellew was a second mother.

Thanks to my sister, Gemma Lyons, and the family, Emmet, Rebecca, and Hayley, for good advice when I needed it. My parents, Pat and Elaine, taught me that kindness and hard work are the most important things. I now know they were, of course, correct.

My wife, Jane Carroll, will always be the brains, and if I have done anything good it is only because she lit the way. I am lucky to have her sound sense, intelligence, and sense of fun in my life. Finally, my daughter, Beatrix, to whom I dedicate this book because while the past is interesting, the future is bright and filled with hope because she is there with us.

Manuscripts

Arras, Bibliothèque municipale, MS 703 (622).
Cambrai, Médiathèque Muncipale, MS 305.
Cambridge, Corpus Christi College, MS 315.
Cambridge, Trinity College, MS R. 17.1.
Dublin, Trinity College Library, MS 52.
Karlsruhe, Badische Landesbibliothek, Cod. Aug. perg. 214.
London, BL, MS Harley 2767.
London, Cotton MS Claudius B IV.
Oxford, Bodleian Library, MS Bodl. 459.
Oxford, Bodleian Library, MS Bodl. 494.
Oxford, Bodleian Library, MS e Mus. 62.
Paris, Bibliothèque nationale de France (BnF), MS Lat. 2165.
Paris, BnF, MS Lat. 3438.
Paris, BnF, MS Lat. 3848.
Paris, BnF, MS Lat. 7185.
Paris, BnF, MS Lat. 14516.
Paris, BnF, MS Lat. 15009.
Paris, BnF, MS Lat. 16702.
Paris, BnF, MS Nouv. Acq. Lat. 1791.
Prague, Nàrodni Knihovna České Republiky (National Library of the Czech Republic), MS XIV.D.20.
St. Gallen, Stiftsbibliothek St. Gallen, Cod. 830.
Toulouse, Bibliothèque de Toulouse, MS 206.
Troyes, Médiathèque de l'Aggolomération Troyenne, MS 544.
Vatican City, Biblioteca Apostolica Vaticana (BAV), MS Chigi B.VII.106.
Vatican City, BAV, MS Reg. Lat. 277.
Vatican City, BAV, MS Vat. Lat. 1053.
Vatican City, BAV, MS Vat. Lat. 13014.
Vienna, Nationalbibliothek, MS. 458.
Wrocław, Biblioteka Uniwersytecka, MS IF 232 (259).
Zwickau, Ratsschulbibliothek, MS IV.1.

Notes

The abbreviation PL refers to the *Patrologia Latina*, ed. J.-P. Migne, 221 vols. (Paris: Garnier Frères, 1844–1864).

Chapter 1

1. Hugh questions the seaworthiness of a hull-less ship based on his own experience. See *De arche Noe morali*, PL 176.626D–627A. For a fuller discussion, see Grover Zinn Jr., "Hugh of St. Victor and the Ark of Noah: A New Look," *Church History* 40 (1971): 263–264.

2. Specifically, Hugh tackles Origen's theory of the ark's form, which, along with Augustine's work, had become authoritative. See *De arche Noe morali*, PL 176.626A–627D. Augustine's comments on the subject appear in Saint Augustine of Hippo, *City of God*, 7 vols. (Cambridge, MA: Harvard University Press, 2014), 4:567–581. Origen's comments appear in his second homily on Genesis: Origen, *Homilies on Genesis and Exodus*, trans. Ronald E. Heine (Washington, DC: Catholic University of America Press, 2002), 72–73.

3. Massimo Scolari, *Massimo Scolari: The Representation of Architecture* (Milan: Skira; London: Thames & Hudson, 2012), 125.

4. Norman Cohn, *Noah's Flood: The Genesis Story in Western Thought* (New Haven: Yale University Press, 1996), 38.

5. Cohn, *Noah's Flood*, 12.

6. London, British Library, Cotton MS Claudius B IV, f. 15r. See also David F. Johnson, "A Program of Illumination in the Old English Illustrated Hexateuch: 'Visual Typology,'" in *The Old English Hexateuch: Aspects and Approaches*, ed. Rebecca Barnhouse and Benjamin C. Withers (Kalamazoo, MI: Medieval Institute Publications, 2000), 165–199.

7. Scolari, *Massimo Scolari: The Representation of Architecture*, 125.

8. Richard suggests that the commentary considers all of the book of Ezekiel, but it is predominantly concerned with the later chapters and the architectural vision that run from Ezekiel 40 to 48.

9. A single cubit is usually taken to be the length of a person's forearm, making it approximately 18 inches.

10. Ezekiel 40:5, 8, and 11.

11. The most complete list of manuscripts follows: Arras, Bibliothèque municipale, MS 703 (622), ff. 66r–111v; Cambrai, Médiathèque Muncipale, MS 305, ff. 240r–257v; Cambridge, Corpus Christi College, MS 315, ff. 76r–113r; Karlsruhe, Badische Landesbibliothek, Cod. Aug. perg. 214, ff. 47r–85v; Oxford, Bodleian Library, MS Bodl. 459, ff. 1v–37v, MS Bodl. 494, ff. 128r–166v, and MS e Mus. 62, ff. 76r–106r; Paris, Bibliothèque nationale de France (BnF), MS Lat. 2165, ff. 40r–69r, MS Lat. 3438, ff. 37r–81r, Lat. 3848, ff. 73r–92v, Lat. 14516, ff. 207r–252r, Lat. 16702, ff. 63r–84r and MS Nouv. Acq. Lat. 1791, ff. 1r–39r; Prague, Národní Knihovna České Republiky (National Library of the Czech Republic), MS XIV.D.20, ff. 196r–221r; Toulouse, Bibliothèque de Toulouse, MS 206, ff. 108r–199r; Troyes, Médiathèque de l'Aggolomération Troyenne (MAT), MS 544, ff. 1r–30r; Vatican City, Biblioteca Apostolica Vaticana (BAV), MS Chigi B.VII.106, ff. 253r–217v, MS Vat. Lat. 1053, ff. 152r–186r, MS Vat. Lat. 13014, ff. 52v–71v, MS Reg. Lat. 277, ff. 1r–34; Wrocław, Biblioteka Uniwersytecka, MS IF 232 (259), ff. 23v–50r; Zwickau, Ratsschulbibliothek, MS IV.1, ff. 27r–46r.

12. See Mary Carruthers, *The Craft of Thought: Meditation, Rhetoric, and the Making of Images, 400–1200* (Cambridge: Cambridge University Press, 1998), 350; Henri de Lubac, *Exégèse médiévale: Les quatres sens de l'Écriture*, 4 vols. (Paris: Auber, 1959–1964), 3:404. Peter's words are as follows: "dispositiones maecanicas in aedificiis et in dispositione templi imaginarii." The rendering of "dispositions" as "blueprint" by Carruthers is unhelpfully anachronistic here, since the term is too specific for the period; "figure" or even "diagram" would be more accurate.

13. As we will see, there are more drawings toward the beginning of the text compared to the end, which suggests that Richard tired of creating drawings for each of the buildings.

14. Jane Turner, ed., *The Dictionary of Art*, 34 vols. (New York: Grove, 1996), 2:325.

15. Oleg Grabar, *The Mediation of Ornament* (Princeton: Princeton University Press, 1992).

16. "In omni aedificatione tria sunt praecipue consideranda, ordo, dispositio et definita dimensio, habens principium et finem determinatum." Conrad Rudolph, *The Mystic Ark: Hugh of Saint Victor, Art, and Thought in the Twelfth Century* (Cambridge:

Cambridge University Press, 2014), 245.

17. Leon Battista Alberti, *On the Art of Building in Ten Books*, trans. Joseph Rykwert, Neil Leach, and Robert Tavernor (Cambridge, MA: MIT Press, 1988), 34.

18. Nikolaus Pevsner, "The Term 'Architect' in the Middle Ages," *Speculum* 17 (1942): 549–562; Nikolaus Pevsner, "Terms of Architectural Planning in the Middle Ages," *Journal of the Warburg and Courtauld Institutes* 5 (1942): 232–237.

19. Robert Branner, "Villard de Honnecourt, Reims and the Origin of Gothic Architectural Drawing," *Gazette des Beaux-Arts* 61 (1961): 129–146.

20. Pari Riahi, "Expanding the Boundaries of Architectural Representation," *Journal of Architecture* 22, no. 5 (2017): 815.

21. Peter Eisenman, *Written into the Void: Selected Writings, 1990–2004* (New Haven: Yale University Press, 2007), 88.

22. Robin Evans, *Translations from Drawing to Building and Other Essays* (London: Architectural Association Publications, 1997), 154.

23. Eisenman, *Written into the Void*, 88.

24. There are rarely any references to medieval theories of art or architecture in collections of primary sources. For example, Harry Francis Mallgrave, ed., *Architectural Theory* (Oxford: Blackwell, 2006), contains only two entries for the Middle Ages, including Abbot Suger's description of his renovations of Saint-Denis.

25. Vitruvius, *Ten Books on Architecture*, ed. and trans. Ingrid D. Rowland and Thomas Noble Howe (Cambridge: Cambridge University Press, 1999), 24–25.

26. For a discussion of Vitruvius's terms, see Rabun Taylor, *Roman Builders: A Study in Architectural Process* (Cambridge: Cambridge University Press, 2003), 21–35.

27. Christoph Luitpold Frommel, "Reflections on the Early Architectural Drawings," in *The Renaissance from Brunelleschi to Michelangelo: The Representation of Architecture*, ed. Henry A. Millon and Vittorio Magnago Lampugnani (London: Thames and Hudson, 1994), 101.

28. Collections of drawings such Bernardo della Volpaia's Codex Coner in the Soane Museum tend to use Vitruvian language.

29. Kenneth J. Conant, "The After-life of Vitruvius in the Middle Ages," *Journal of the Society of Architectural Historians* 27 (1968): 33–38; John Onians, *Bearers of Meaning: The Classical Orders in Antiquity, the Middle Ages, and the Renaissance* (Princeton: Princeton University Press, 1988), 91–94; Anat Tcherikover, "A Carolingian Lesson in Vitruvius," in *Medieval Architecture and Its Intellectual Context: Studies in Honour of Peter Kidson*, ed. Eric Fernie and Paul Crossley (London: Hambledon, 1990), 259–267; Tessa Morrison, "Architectural Planning in the Early Medieval Era," *Journal of the Australian Early Medieval Association* 5 (2009): 147–163. See also Hugh Plommer, ed. and trans., *Vitruvius and Later Roman Building Manuals* (Cambridge: Cambridge University Press, 1973).

30. Robert Ousterhout, *Master Builders of Byzantium* (Princeton: Princeton University Press, 1999), 58.

31. Ousterhout, *Master Builders*, 69.

32. Carol Herselle Krinsky, "Seventy-Eight Vitruvius Manuscripts," *Journal of the Warburg and Courtauld Institutes* 30 (1967): 36–70.

33. Faventius's text and other abridged versions of Vitruvius's *De architectura* can be found in Plommer, *Vitruvius*.

34. See Caecilla Davis-Weyer, *Early Medieval Art, 300–1150: Sources and Documents* (Toronto: University of Toronto Press, 1986), 107–108.

35. Onians, *Bearers of Meaning*.

36. Hugh of Saint Victor, *The "Didascalicon" of Hugh of St. Victor: A Medieval Guide to the Arts*, trans. Jerome Taylor (New York: Columbia University Press, 1961), 75.

37. During the twelfth century, a Benedictine monk in Germany wrote a treatise called *De diversis artibus* that describes painting, metalwork, and glass making in immense detail. See Theophilus, *The Various Arts: "De diversis artibus"* (Oxford: Oxford University Press, 1986).

38. Erwin Panofsky, *Gothic Architecture and Scholasticism* (Latrobe, PA: Archabbey Press, 1951).

39. For more on Panofsky's theory of iconology, see Erwin Panofsky, *Studies in Iconology: Humanistic Themes in the Art of the Renaissance* (New York: Harper & Row, 1972). For criticism of Panofsky's theory of Gothic architecture, see Peter Kidson, "Panofsky, Suger and St Denis," *Journal of the Warburg and Courtauld*

Institutes 50 (1987): 1–17, especially 2.

40. Charles Radding and William Clark, *Medieval Architecture, Medieval Learning: Builders and Masters in the Age of Romanesque and Gothic* (New Haven: Yale University Press, 1992), 4.

41. Erwin Panofsky, *Renaissance and Renascences in Western Art* (New York: Harper & Row, 1960), 55–113; C. H. Haskins, *The Renaissance of the Twelfth Century* (Cambridge, MA: Harvard University Press, 1927).

42. Ousterhout, *Master Builders*.

43. On the inadequacy of "reading" architecture, see William Whyte, "Do Buildings Mean? Some Issues of Interpretation in the History of Architecture," *History and Theory* 45, no. 2 (2006): 153–177.

44. Robert Bork, *The Geometry of Creation: Architectural Drawing and the Dynamics of Gothic Design* (Farnham, UK: Ashgate, 2011); Arnold Pacey, *Medieval Architectural Drawing: English Craftsmen's Methods and Their Later Persistence, 1200–1700* (Stroud: Tempus, 2007); Roland Bechmann, *Villard de Honnecourt: la pensée technique au xiiie siècle et sa communication* (Paris: Picard, 1993); François Bucher, *Architector: The Lodge Books and Sketchbooks of Medieval Architects* (New York: Abaris Books, 1979).

45. Recent work has brought back the possibility that Villard was an architect; see Jean Wirth, *Villard de Honnecourt: architecte du XIIIe siècle* (Geneva: Droz, 2015).

46. The most important work on Villard's portfolio is Villard de Honnecourt and Carl Barnes Jr., *The Portfolio of Villard de Honnecourt: A New Critical Edition and Color Facsimile* (Farnham, UK: Ashgate, 2009).

47. In reality, abbeys such as Saint Victor were frequently being built or renovated. The constant work meant masons were a constant presence in many places, although the cloister was an important space devoted to the private space of monks and canons. See Laura Varnam, *The Church as Sacred Space in Middle English Literature and Culture* (Manchester: Manchester University Press, 2018), 5.

48. Most notably, Bork, *Geometry of Creation*. Recently, many of these later drawings have been collected and discussed; see for example Johann Josef Böker et al., *Architektur der Gotik. Ulm und Donauraum: ein Bestandskatalog der mittelalterlichen Architekturzeichnungen aus Ulm, Schwaben und dem Donaugebiet* (Salzburg: Müry Salzmann, 2011); Begoña Alonso Ruiz and Alfonso Jiménez Martín, *La traça de la iglesia de Sevilla* (Seville: Cabildo Metropolitano, 2009); Valerio Ascani, *Il Trecento disegnato: Le basi progettuali dell'architettura gotica in Italia* (Rome: Viella, 1997). A more recent source is Costanza Beltrami, *Building a Crossing Tower: A Design for Rouen Cathedral of 1516* (London: Paul Holberton Publishing, 2016).

Chapter 2

1. Dante Alighieri, *The Divine Comedy of Dante Alighieri*, trans. Robert M. Durling, Ronald L. Martinez, and Robert Turner, 3 vols. (Oxford: Oxford University Press, 2011), 3:213, *Paradiso*, canto X, lines 131–132.

2. Jean Châtillon, "Richard de Saint-Victor," in *Dictionnaire de spiritualité: Ascétique et mystique: Doctrine et histoire*, ed. Marcel Viller (Paris: G. Beauchesne, 1937), 594–654. A thirteenth-century manuscript containing *In visionem Ezechielis* (Oxford, Bodleian Library, MS e Mus. 62) refers to Richard as "Scotti" or "Scottish."

3. Châtillon, "Richard de Saint-Victor," 654.

4. Gervais Dumeige, *Richard de Saint-Victor et l'idée chrétienne de l'amour* (Paris: Presses Universitaires de France, 1952), 167.

5. Contemporary authors referred to Hugh as the most important theologian of their time and as a "second Augustine." Quotations in Richard of Saint Victor, *On the Trinity: English Translation and Commentary*, trans. and with commentary by Ruben Angelici (Cambridge, UK: James Clarke, 2012), 4.

6. Significantly, Dale Coulter does not accept that Richard knew Hugh personally, writing that Richard did not arrive at St. Victor until after Hugh's death. See Dale Coulter, *Per visibilia ad invisibilia: Theological Method in Richard of St. Victor (d. 1173)* (Turnhout: Brepols, 2006), 20. Most other scholars state that Richard knew Hugh in person; for example, see Ruben Angelici's introduction to Richard of Saint Victor, *On the Trinity*, 5.

7. For example, the majority of the chapters in Hugh Feiss and Juliet Mousseau, eds., *A Companion to the Abbey*

of Saint Victor in Paris (Leiden: Brill, 2017), either focus on Hugh's work or make reference to it.

8. Dumeige, *Richard de Saint-Victor*, 166. Also, Rodney M. Thomson, "Monastic and Cathedral Book Production," in *The Cambridge History of the Book in Britain*, 6 vols., ed. Nigel J. Morgan and Rodney M. Thomson (Cambridge: Cambridge University Press, 1999), 1:136–167, especially 156.

9. The earliest copy is in Paris, BnF, MS lat 14516. For a discussion of the stylistic evidence, see Walter Cahn, "Architecture and Exegesis: Richard of St.-Victor's Ezekiel Commentary and Its Illustrations," *Art Bulletin* 76, no. 1 (1994): 54–55.

10. MS e Mus. 62 contains an extra chapter attached to the final part of *In visionem Ezechielis*. This is from a different historical commentary, although one possibly authored by Richard.

11. The Patrologia Latina Database lists thirty-one works attributed to Richard.

12. Kent Emery Jr., "Richard of St. Victor," in *A Companion to Philosophy in the Middle Ages*, ed. Jorge J. E. Gracia and Timothy Noone (Oxford: Blackwell, 2003), 588. Despite mentioning the historical focus of some of Richard's works, Emery does not reference or discuss them further.

13. Hugh of Saint Victor, *The "Didascalicon" of Hugh of St. Victor: A Medieval Guide to the Arts*, trans. Jerome Taylor (New York: Columbia University Press, 1961), 138.

14. Michael A. Signer, "Vision and History: Nicholas of Lyra on the Prophet Ezechiel," in *Nicholas of Lyra: The Senses of Scripture*, ed. Philip D. W. Krey and Lesley Smith (Leiden: Brill, 2000), 169.

15. *The Letters of Abelard and Heloise*, trans. Betty Radice (London: Penguin Book, 2003), 3–8. For more information on William's appearance in Abelard's autobiography, see John Marenbon, *The Philosophy of Peter Abelard* (Cambridge: Cambridge University Press, 1997), 9–12, and Michael Clanchy, *Abelard: A Medieval Life* (Oxford: Blackwell, 1997).

16. Parts of Saint Victor's liturgy were used in abbeys associated with it. See Lucas Jocqué and Ludovicus Milis, *Liber Ordinis Sancti Victoris Parisiensis* (Turnhout: Brepols, 1984).

17. Reimbaldus, *Libellus de diversis ordinibus et professionibus qui sunt in aecclesia*, trans. Giles Constable and Bernard Smith (Oxford: Clarendon Press, 2003), ch. 6.

18. Oxford, Bodleian Library, MS Lyell 84. See L. Cleaver and A. Worm, "The Septenarium Pictum or Rota Dominice Orationis Diagram: Combatting Vice through Prayer in the High Middle Ages," in *Ordinare il mondo: Diagrammi e simboli nelle pergamene di Vercelli*, ed. T. Leonardi and M. Rainini (Milan: Vita e Pensiero, 2019), 265–288.

19. John E. Murdoch, *Albums of Science: Antiquity and the Middle Ages* (New York: Scribner, 1984), 52.

20. Conrad Rudolph, *The Mystic Ark: Hugh of Saint Victor, Art, and Thought in the Twelfth Century* (Cambridge: Cambridge University Press, 2014), 397.

21. "Volo prius universa summatim perstringere, ut postmodum liceat in singularum partium descriptione quanto liberius." Richard of Saint Victor, *In visionem Ezechielis*, in *Patrologia Latina*, ed. Jacques-Paul Migne (Paris: 1855), 196.534B. All following quotations from *In visionem Ezechielis* use this edition (abbreviated PL); all translations are mine.

22. The drawings appear in Paris, BnF, MS Lat. 2165, f. 56r, and Durham, Cathedral and Chapter Library, MS A.III.22 (a fragment).

23. "Horum omnium quae diximus in novissima, et magna figura, sicut ibi videri potest, formam et exemplar latius expressimus." Richard of Saint Victor, *In visionem Ezechielis*, PL 196.566C.

24. Oxford, Bodleian Library, MS Bodl. 494.

25. Troyes, Médiathèque de l'Aggolomération Troyenne, MS 544.

26. The most complete list may be found in Catherine Delano-Smith, "The Exegetical Jerusalem: Maps and Plans for Ezekiel Chapters 40–48," in *Imagining Jerusalem in the Medieval West*, ed. Lucy Donkin and Hanna Vorholt (Oxford: Oxford University Press, 2012), n.13.

27. The Cistercian copy is Oxford, Bodleian Library, e Mus. 62. Alexander VII's library copy is Vatican City, Biblioteca Apostolica Vaticana, MS Chigi B.VII.106.

28. Delano-Smith, "Exegetical Jerusalem," 45.

29. Cahn, "Architecture and Exegesis," 54–55.

Chapter 3

1. PL 196.533B.

2. Since it is the earliest example of the manuscript, unless stated, the descriptions that follow are taken from the manuscript Paris, BnF, MS Lat. 14516.

3. "Habebat itaque hoc aedificium triplicem murum. Primum sexcentorum cubitorum, secundum quingentorum cubitorum, tertium vero in medio horum, et omnium minimum." PL 196.533B.

4. "Et erit ex omni parte sanctificatum quingentos per quingentos quadrifariam per circuitum" (read clockwise from top). "Murus quingentorum cubitorum dividens inter sanctuarium et vulgus locum" (read clockwise from the left side to the bottom).

5. "Suburbana" appears in Scripture—for example, in Ez 45:2, 48:15, and 48:17—referring to the area surrounding a city. The term is used in that way during the Middle Ages as well, for example in relation to the ecclesiastical settlement of Kildare and its surrounding areas. See Howard B. Clarke and Angret Simms, eds., *The Comparative History of Urban Origins in Non-Roman Europe: Ireland, Wales, Denmark, Germany, Poland, and Russia from the Ninth to the Thirteenth Century* (Oxford: B.A.R., 1985), 57.

6. "In hunc modum."

7. "Horum igitur quae jam descripsimus formam taliter repraesentamus."

8. These are shown in more detail in the plan for chapter twelve, which is discussed in detail below.

9. Later in the text, Richard states that he draws the plans "in proportion."

10. Catherine Delano-Smith and Roger J. P. Kain, *English Maps: A History* (London: British Library, 1999).

11. "Horum itaque jam descripsimus formam hujusmodi repraesentamus," PL 196.538A.

12. Discussion of the chapter twelve drawing is largely absent from the scholarship because there are so few examples of it. Catherine Delano-Smith was the first to highlight its importance; see Delano-Smith, "The Exegetical Jerusalem: Maps and Plans for Ezekiel Chapters 40–48," in *Imagining Jerusalem in the Medieval West*, ed. Lucy Donkin and Hanna Vorholt (Oxford: Oxford University Press, 2012), 41–76.

13. The drawing appears in Paris, BnF, MS Lat. 2165; Durham, Cathedral Library, MS A.III.22; Oxford, Brasenose College, MS 5. (The latter two manuscripts include fragments of *In visionem Ezechielis*, not full copies.)

14. The plan does not appear in Oxford, Bodleian Library, MS e Mus. 62, which used two different exemplars. Its absence suggests that the drawing was likely not well circulated in twelfth- and thirteenth-century manuscripts.

15. Ez 46.

16. This is the same altar as discussed in the previous section, which Richard states he will "artfully explain" further on in the text.

17. For example, Arnold Pacey, *Medieval Architectural Drawing* (Stroud: Tempus, 2007), only considers English examples from approximately 1300 to 1700.

18. The recipient is known by a transmittal note which appears in the upper margin of the plan. Walter Horn and Ernest Born, *The Plan of St. Gall*, vol. 1 (Berkeley: University of California Press, 1979), 9.

19. The date is discussed in Horn and Born, *Plan of St. Gall*, 25.

20. The dormitory appears above the cloister (i.e., to the east), where the authors indicated that the place for the monks to warm themselves is below and the dormitory is on the first floor above, "subtis calefactoria domus supra dormitorium."

21. Horn and Born, *Plan of St. Gall*, 52.

22. Horn and Born, *Plan of St. Gall*, 24.

23. Lawrence Nees, "The Colophon Drawing in the Book of Mulling: A Supposed Irish Monastery Plan and the Tradition of Terminal Illustration in Early Medieval Manuscripts," *Cambridge Medieval Celtic Studies* 5 (1983): 68. In this work, Nees likens the Saint Gall plan to a roughly contemporary but badly faded drawing on the flyleaf of the Book of Mulling. However, it is not clear if the drawing does represent a building, and for that reason it is not discussed here.

24. Lawrence Nees, "The Plan of St. Gall and the Theory of the Program of Carolingian Art," *Gesta* 25 (1986): 5.

25. Kleinbauer also highlights the combination of "vertical line projection and outline elevation" in the plan, which I have termed above as a hybrid of plan and elevation modes of architectural drawing. See Eugene W.

Kleinbauer, "Pre-Carolingian Concepts of Architectural Planning," in *The Medieval Mediterranean: Cross-Cultural Contacts*, ed. Marilyn J. Chiat and Kathryn L. Reyerson (St. Cloud, MN: North Star Press of St. Cloud, 1988), 67–79.

26. W. Braunfels, *Monasteries of Western Europe: The Architecture of the Order* (London: Thames and Hudson, 1993), 37–44.

27. Stanford Anderson, "Erinnerung in der Architektor—Memory in Architecture," *Daidalos* 58 (1995): 28–30.

28. The use of an architectural drawing as a meditative tool such as a mandala is made explicit in Grover Zinn Jr., "Mandala Symbolism and Use in Mysticism of Hugh of St. Victor," *History of Religions* 12 (1973): 317–341. The concept was taken up later by Mary Carruthers, whose work is discussed in detail in chapter 4.

29. Allegorical and typological plans did exist, for example in the ninth-century Book of Armagh (Dublin, Trinity College Library, MS 52), which depicts a plan of the celestial Jerusalem, but the Saint Gall plan is exponentially more complicated.

30. The Saint Gall plan includes *tituli* stating what each space represents.

31. Thomas O'Loughlin, "The Plan of the New Jerusalem in the Book of Armagh," *Cambrian Medieval Celtic Studies* 39 (2000): 28–29.

32. O'Loughlin, "Plan of the New Jerusalem," 37.

Chapter 4

1. The brazen man uses a reed to measure the different parts. The reed is six cubits in length, and some measurements are in "reeds" and not cubits. See Ez 40:5.

2. Sixty cubits results from the two walls on either side of the vestibule that are twenty-five cubits each and the vestibule width, which is ten cubits.

3. Cambridge, Corpus Christi College, MS 315, f.87r.

4. Dominque Barbet-Massin, "The Rite of Church Dedication in Early Medieval Ireland and the Dedication Scheme in the Angers Manuscript 477," *Peritia* 27 (2016): 11–30.

5. Hugh's work and that of the canon house of Saint Victor will be discussed in detail in the following chapter. For a brief outline of the treatise's context, see Mary Carruthers, *The Book of Memory: A Study of Memory in Medieval Culture*, 2nd ed. (Cambridge: Cambridge University Press, 2008), 100–101.

6. William M. Green, "Hugo of St. Victor: *De tribus maximus circumstantiis gestorum*," *Speculum* 18 (1943): 484–493.

7. Hugh outlines history's importance in Saint Victor's education system in his curriculum for wisdom. Hugh of Saint Victor, *The "Didascalicon" of Hugh of St. Victor: A Medieval Guide to the Arts*, trans. Jerome Taylor (New York: Columbia University Press, 1961), 135–139.

8. Mary Carruthers and Jan M. Ziolkowski, *The Medieval Craft of Memory: An Anthology of Texts and Pictures* (Philadelphia: University of Pennsylvania Press, 2004), 33.

9. Carruthers and Ziolkowski, *The Medieval Craft*, 36. Carruthers briefly discusses these methods on p. 32.

10. Carruthers and Ziolkowski, *The Medieval Craft*, 36.

11. Carruthers and Ziolkowski, *The Medieval Craft*, 37.

12. Carruthers and Ziolkowski, *The Medieval Craft*, 36–37.

13. Paris, BnF, MS Lat. 15009, ff. 3v–17v. A facsimile with translation appears in Carruthers and Ziolkowski, *The Medieval Craft*, figs. 1.1 and 1.2.

14. Those in the first column are given as participles, in order from the top: "created," "ordained," and "decorated." Those in the fourth column are "void" and "matter"; four appear in the final arch: "sky, water, air, land." Carruthers and Ziolkowski, *The Medieval Craft*, fig. 1.2.

15. "Verumptamen hoc ita memoriter retinere oportet et assidua re-tractatione domesticum et notum habere, ut promptus sit ad omnia audita cor suum aptare, et ea quae hic didiscerit ad omnia quae postmodum audierit secundum locum et tempus et personam congrua distributione assignare." Carruthers and Ziolkowski, *The Medieval Craft*, 39.

16. Carruthers and Ziolkowski, *The Medieval Craft*; Mary Carruthers, *The Craft of Thought: Meditation, Rhetoric, and the Making of Images, 400–1200* (Cambridge: Cambridge University Press, 1998); Carruthers, *Book of Memory*; Mary Carruthers, ed., *Rhetoric Beyond Words: Delight and Persuasion in the Arts of the Middle Ages* (Cambridge: Cambridge University Press, 2010).

17. Pseudo-Cicero, *Ad C. Herennium: De rationi dicendi,*

trans. Harry Caplan (Cambridge, MA: Harvard University Press, 1954).

18. Pseudo-Cicero, *Ad C. Herennium*, 209.

19. Carruthers, *Craft of Thought*, 239.

20. Carruthers, *Craft of Thought*, 238.

21. Adrian Forty, *Words and Buildings: A Vocabulary of Modern Architecture* (London: Thames and Hudson, 2004), 207.

22. "Memoria enim semper gaudet et brevitate in spatio et paucitate in numero ... ut quod animus spatio comprehendere non potest saltem numero comprehendat." Quoted in Carruthers and Ziolkowski, *Medieval Craft*, 37–38.

23. "Representatio porticus quasi a fronte vidietur."

24. Walter Cahn, "Architecture and Exegesis: Richard of St.-Victor's Ezekiel Commentary and Its Illustrations," *Art Bulletin* 76, no. 1 (1994): 63.

25. For example, Cambridge, Corpus Christi College, MS 315.

26. Markus Späth, "Architectural Representation and Monastic Identity: The Medieval Seal Images of Christchurch, Canterbury," in *Image, Memory and Devotion: Liber Amicorum Paul Crossley* (Turnhout: Brepols, 2011), 255–263.

27. This *titulus* does not appear in all copies.

28. "Laterale vestibuleum xxv cubitos."

29. "Situs thalami."

30. "Edificium vergens ad aquilonem."

31. This status was first discussed in Karl Kinsella, "Richard of St Victor's Solutions to Problems of Architectural Representation in the Twelfth Century," *Architectural History* 59 (2016): 1–22.

32. The inner atrium wall should align with the gatehouse's inner (i.e., shorter) side, as indicated in the large plan for chapter twelve, discussed at the end of this chapter.

33. "Vestibulum 8 cubitis," "situs primi thalami," and "5 cubiti inter thalamus."

34. The height of each riser must be approximately six cubits in order for the structure to make sense.

35. On the Holy Sepulchre, see Virgilio C. Corbo, *Il Santo Sepolcro di Gerusalemme: Aspetti archeologici dalle origini al periodo crociato* (Jerusalem: Franciscan Printing Press, 1981–1982); Charles Coüasnon, *The Church of the Holy Sepulchre in Jerusalem* (London: Oxford University Press for the British Academy, 1974); and Kenneth John Conant, "The Original Buildings at the Holy Sepulchre in Jerusalem," *Speculum* 31 (1956): 1–48.

36. A pandect is a complete copy of all the books of the Bible in a single volume. Due to the size of the manuscript needed to include both Old and New Testaments, pandects were rare until the thirteenth century.

37. Paul Meyvaert, "Bede, Cassiodorus, and the Codex Amiatinus," *Speculum* 71 (1996): 827–883.

38. *The Life of Ceolfrid*, ed. Douglas Samuel Boutflower (Sunderland: Hill & Company, 1991), 69. See also Francis Wormald, "Bible Illustration in Medieval Manuscripts," in *The Cambridge History of the Bible*, vol. 3, ed. G. W. H. Lampe (Cambridge: Cambridge University Press, 1969), 309–337.

39. Meyvaert's "Bede, Cassiodorus, and the Codex Amiatinus" provides a discussion of the chronology of Bede's realization that the Codex Grandior was in fact the same one mentioned in Cassiodorus's writings.

40. Bede, *On the Tabernacle*, trans. Arthur G. Holder (Liverpool: Liverpool University Press, 1994), 92; Bede, *On the Temple*, trans. Sean Connolly, introduction by Faith Wallis (Liverpool: Liverpool University Press, 1995), 66.

41. There is a debate as to whether there were two pictures originally, or if only the Tabernacle was mentioned; see, for example, Meyvaert, "Bede," 845. It does seem odd that both Cassiodorus and Bede would conflate two different structures, especially since Bede wrote a separate treatise on each building.

42. Catherine Delano-Smith states that the image represents the temple, "within which is set the Tabernacle," but it is unclear how or why she identifies it in this manner. See Catherine Delano-Smith and Roger J. P. Kain, *English Maps: A History* (London: British Library, 1999), 9.

43. Adomnán (d. 704) was the abbot of Iona abbey off the west coast of Scotland. His work *De locis sanctis* (On the Holy Land) contains four architectural drawings of buildings in and near Jerusalem, including the Holy Sepulchre.

44. Bianca Kühnel, "Jewish Symbolism of the Temple and the Tabernacle and Christian Symbolism of the Holy

Sepulchre and the Heavenly Jerusalem: A Study of Their Relationship in Late Antique and Early Medieval Art and Thought," *Jewish Art* 12–13 (1987): 151. See also Conor O'Brien, "Tabernacle, Temple or Something in Between? Architectural Representation in Codex Amiatinus, fols. IIv–IIIv," *Leeds Studies in English* 48 (2017), 7–20.

45. The curtain is described as passing on the outside of the columns. Kühnel, "Jewish Symbolism," 166.

46. Compare Bucher's statements that Villard was "a lively, versatile mason-contractor, and ... may have occasionally worked as a sculptor and furniture designer," with Bechmann's hesitation to assign a particular role for Villard. See François Bucher, *Architector: The Lodge Books and Sketchbooks of Medieval Architects* (New York: Abaris Books, 1979), 15; and Roland Bechmann, *Villard de Honnecourt: La pensée technique au xiiie siècle et sa communication* (Paris: Picard, 1993), 13.

47. James S. Ackerman, "Villard de Honnecourt's Drawing of Reims Cathedral: A Study in Architectural Representation," *Artibus et Historiae* 18 (1997): 41–49.

48. For a discussion of the term "architect" and its meaning in the Middle Ages, see Nikolaus Pevsner, "The Term 'Architect' in the Middle Ages," *Speculum* 17 (1942): 549–562.

49. Bechmann, *Villard de Honnecourt*, 85. Bechmann discusses another set of elevations which appear on page 60 of the portfolio, but which also depict Reims cathedral. While the drawing is consistent, it does not perfectly represent the finished bay or external appearance of the cathedral.

50. Robert Branner, "Villard de Honnecourt, Reims and the Origin of Gothic Architectural Drawing," *Gazette des Beaux-Arts* 61 (1963): 129–146.

51. Saint Augustine, *On Christian Teaching*, trans. R. P. H. Green (Oxford: Oxford University Press, 2008), 68.

52. Celia M. Chazelle, "Pictures, Books, and the Illiterate: Pope Gregory I's Letters to Serenus of Marseilles," *Word and Image* 6, no. 2 (1990): 139.

53. Chazelle, "Pictures," 138.

54. For example, in his liturgical commentary known as the *Gemma animae*, Honorius repeats much of Gregory's ideas. Honorius Augustodunensis, *Gemma animae*, PL 172:586B.

55. Lawrence G. Duggan, "Was Art Really the 'Book of the Illiterate'?," in *Reading Images and Texts*, ed. Marielle Hageman and Marco Mostert (Turnhout: Brepols, 2005), 63–107.

56. Quoted in Gillian Evans, "Hugh of St. Victor on History and the Meaning of Things," *Studia Monastica* 25, no. 2 (1983): 224–225.

57. Marie-Dominique Chenu, *Nature, Man, and Society in the Twelfth Century: Essays on New Theological Perspectives in the Latin West*, ed. and trans. Jerome Taylor and Lester K. Little (Toronto: University of Toronto Press, 1997), 62.

58. Fortunato Iozzelli, "Francesco d'Assisi 'Buon Samaritano' nella predicazione di Odo da Chateauroux," in *Litterae ex quibus nomen Dei componitur. Studi per l'ottantesimo compleanno di Giuseppe Avarucci*, ed. Alexander Horowski (Rome: Istituto Storico dei Cappuccini, 2016), 269–290.

59. Saint Augustine, *On Christian Teaching*, trans. R. P. H. Green (Oxford: Oxford University Press, 2008), 33.

60. Augustine, *St. Augustine on Genesis: Two Books on Genesis against the Manichees; And, On the Literal Interpretation of Genesis, an Unfinished Book*, trans. Roland J. Teske, S.J., Fathers of the Church 84 (Washington, DC: Catholic University of America Press, 1991), 146.

61. Augustine, *On Christian Teaching*, 33.

62. PL 196.575A–B.

63. I would like to thank the late Jennifer O'Reilly for pointing this out.

Chapter 5

1. Dante Alighieri, *De vulgari eloquentia*, trans. Steven Botterill (Cambridge: Cambridge University Press, 1996), 15.

2. Sean Connolly, translator's note to Bede, *On the Temple* (Liverpool: Liverpool University Press, 1995), xiv–xv.

3. For example, Paris, BnF, MS Lat. 7185.

4. Hugh of Saint-Victor, *Practical Geometry, Practica geometriae*, trans. Frederick A. Homann (Milwaukee: Marquette University Press, 1991).

5. "Qui instar calami, in Ezechiele templum mensurantis, ad votum geometricorum in coeli terraque dimensione modo inclinatur modo erigitur." Gerbert of Aurillac, *Gerberti opera mathematica (972–1003)*, ed. Nikolaï Bubnov (Hildesheim: G. Olms, 1963), 250.

6. Gerbert, *Gerberti opera mathematica*, 48–49.

7. Benjamin Wardhaugh, *The Book of Wonders: The Many Lives of Euclid's Elements* (London: William Collins, 2020).

8. Marshall Clagett, "King Alfred and the Elements of Euclid," *Isis* 45 (1954): 269–277.

9. Evgeny A. Zaitsev, "The Meaning of Early Medieval Geometry: From Euclid and Surveyors' Manuals to Christian Philosophy," *Isis* 90 (1999): 524. Cf. *Corpus agrimensorum romanorum*, ed. Carl Thulin (Leipzig: B. G. Teubner, 1913).

10. Zaitsev, "Meaning of Early Medieval Geometry," 524–555. *Geometria I* and *Geometria II* were produced in the eighth and eleventh centuries, respectively, and may synthesize some of Boethius's original texts for his work on geometry. Mario Geymonat, "Arithmetic and Geometry in Ancient Rome: Surveyors, Intellectuals, and Poets," *Nuncius* 24 (2009): 21.

11. "Utilitas geometriae triplex est, ad facultatem, ad sanitatem, ad animam. Ad facultatem, ut mechanici et architecti." The meaning of *architectus* is unclear. It may be that the author is considering Vitruvius and the broad concerns of *De architectura*. For a discussion on this subject, see Nikolaus Pevsner, "The Term 'Architect' in the Middle Ages," *Speculum* 17 (1942): 549–562. The term *mechanici* is also problematic. Isidore refers to the *machina* which he describes as the scaffolding on which the masons stand, "due to the height of the walls." See Isidore of Seville, *The Etymologies of Isidore of Seville*, trans. Stephen A. Barney et al. (Cambridge: Cambridge University Press, 2006), 377. Boethius may also have machines of some sort in mind. However, if this were the case, machines were of concern to the architect from antiquity. For example, see Vitruvius, *Ten Books on Architecture*, ed. and trans. Ingrid D. Rowland and Thomas Noble Howe (Cambridge: Cambridge University Press, 1999), 119–132.

12. There are hints in *Geometry II* that there was some confusion over the names of some of the shapes, at least one of which became associated with a building type. For example, in the chapter on the names of stone boundary shapes, one shape reads as *Sepulturam cum ossibus finale. Mauspleus*. However, in the eleventh-century manuscript (St. Gall, Cod. 830, f. 239r), the final word becomes *mausoleus*. A diagram which is tower-shaped cuts the word between the *u* and the *s*, and the diagram bears some similarity with a tower shape that is associated with Roman mausoleums.

13. Hugh, *Practical Geometry*, 18.

14. Abbot Suger, *Abbot Suger on the Abbey Church of St.-Denis and Its Art Treasures*, trans. Erwin Panofsky (Princeton: Princeton University Press), 101.

15. It has been suggested that Saint-Denis's fabric supports Suger's claim that the builders used geometrical instruments during construction. Hugh, *Practical Geometry*, 18.

16. Conrad Rudolph, *First, I Find the Center Point: Reading the Text of Hugh of Saint Victor's "The Mystic Ark"* (Philadelphia: American Philosophical Society, 2004), 17.

17. Lon R. Shelby, "The Geometrical Knowledge of Mediaeval Master Masons," *Speculum* 47 (1972): 395–421.

18. Christopher Wilson, *The Gothic Cathedral: The Architecture of the Great Church* (London: Thames & Hudson, 2000), 142–143.

19. Carl Barnes Jr., *Portfolio of Villard de Honnecourt: A New Critical Edition and Color Facsimile* (Farnham, UK: Ashgate, 2009), 24.

20. Arnold Pacey, *Medieval Architectural Drawing* (Stroud: Tempus, 2007), 42.

21. Anthony Gerbino and Stephen Johnston, eds., *Compass and Rule: Architecture as Mathematical Practice in England, 1500–1750* (Oxford: Oxford University Press, 2009), 18.

22. The only medieval example of a diagram in a copy of *De architectura* shows the direction and names of the eight winds in London; see BL, MS Harley 2767, f. 16v. See also Barbara Obrist, "Wind Diagrams and Medieval Cosmology," *Speculum* 72 (1997): 43.

23. "Dispositio autem est rerum apta conlocatio elegansque compositionibus effectus operis cum qualitate. species dispositionis, quae graece dicuntur ἰδέαι, sunt hae: ichnographia, orthographia, scaenographia. ichnographia est circini regulaeque modice continens usus, e qua capiuntur formarum in solis arearum descriptiones. orthographia autem est erecta frontis imago modiceque picta

rationibus operis futuri figura. item scaenographia est frontis et laterum abscedentium adumbratio ad circinique centrum omnium linearum responsus. hae nascuntur ex cogitatione et inventio." Vitruvius, *On Architecture*, 2 vols., ed. and trans. Frank Granger (Cambridge: Harvard University Press, 1998), 1:24–27.

24. For indications of *De architectura*'s relatively large dispersal in the Middle Ages, see Carol Herselle Krinsky, "Seventy-Eight Vitruvius Manuscripts," *Journal of the Warburg and Courtauld Institutes* 30 (1967): 36–70. Also, one Carolingian author was aware enough of this paragraph to question the meaning of *scaenographia*; see Caecilla Davis-Weyer, *Early Medieval Art, 300–1150: Sources and Documents* (Toronto: University of Toronto Press, 1986), 107–108.

25. Paris, BnF, MS Lat. 15119, f. 102r.

26. PL 196.549B. This quotation will be explored in much more detail below.

27. The abridgement was, for example, used by Isidore of Seville in his *Etymologies*, 16.

28. "Haec sunt ergo tres figurae, ichnographia, orthographia, scaenographia. Ichnographia est areae vel soli et fundamentorum description. Orthographia est laterum et altitudinis extructio. Scenographia est frontis et totius operis per picturam ostensio." Hugh Plommer, ed. and trans., *Vitruvius and Later Roman Building Manuals* (Cambridge: Cambridge University Press, 1973), 40. The Latin sentence that describes the plan was left out of the facing translation for some reason.

29. Erich Auerbach and Ralph Manheim, "Figura," in *Scenes from the Drama of European Literature*, ed. Paolo Valesio (Manchester: Manchester University Press, 1984), 11–76.

30. Herbert Bloch, "A New Edition of the Marble Plan of Ancient Rome," *Journal of Roman Studies* 51 (1961): 146.

31. The vocabulary associated with the plan is discussed in David West Reynolds, "Forma Urbis Romae: The Severan Marble Plan and the Urban Form of Ancient Rome" (PhD diss., University of Michigan, 1996), 135–186.

32. Liba Taub, "The Historical Function of the 'Forma Urbis Romae,'" *Imago Mundi* 45 (1993): 9–19.

33. Taub, "Historical Function," 17.

34. Robert Ousterhout, *Master Builders of Byzantium* (Princeton: Princeton University Press, 1999). Ousterhout discusses the decline of the Roman architect's education, contrasting it with its continuation in parts of the Eastern Empire.

35. Thomas O'Loughlin, *Adomnán and the Holy Places: The Perceptions of an Insular Monk on the Locations of the Biblical Drama* (London: T & T Clark, 2007), 62–63; also Thomas O'Loughlin, "Adomnán and Arculf: The Case of the Expert Witness," *Journal of Medieval Latin* 7 (1997): 127–146.

36. Thomas O'Loughlin, "Adomnan's Plans in the Context of His Imagining 'the Most Famous City,'" in *Imagining Jerusalem in the Medieval West*, ed. Lucy Donkin and Hanna Vorholt (Oxford: Oxford University Press, 2012), 39.

37. Charlotte Cooper has argued for the importance and centrality of paratextual material in literary works; see Charlotte Cooper, "What Is Medieval Paratext?," *Marginalia* 19 (2015): 37–50.

38. O'Loughlin, "Adomnan's Plans," 39.

39. Vitruvius, *On Architecture*, trans. Rowland and Howe, 22–25.

40. Stephen Murray, *Plotting Gothic* (Chicago: University of Chicago Press, 2014), 18.

41. Adomnán, *Adamnán's "De locis sanctis,"* trans. and ed. Denis Meehan (Dublin: Dublin Institute for Advanced Studies, 1983), 46 and 68.

42. There is an immense amount of literature on the Saint Gall plan, and it would be impossible to include everything of significance here. Particularly important works in English include: Walter Horn and Ernest Born, *The Plan of St. Gall: A Study of the Architecture and Economy of, and Life in, a Paradigmatic Carolingian Monastery* (Berkeley: University of California Press, 1979); Mary Carruthers, "The Poet as Master Builder: Composition and Locational Memory in the Middle Ages," *New Literary History* 24 (1993): 881–904; Eric Fernie, "The Proportions of the St. Gall Plan," *Art Bulletin* 60 (1978): 583–589; Warren Sanderson, "The Plan of St. Gall Reconsidered," *Speculum* 60 (1985): 615–632; Lawrence Nees, "The Plan of St. Gall and the Theory of the Program of Carolingian Art," *Gesta* 25 (1986): 1–8.

43. The full note reads: "Haec tibi dulcissime fili

cozb[er]te de posicione officinarum paucis exemplata direxi. quibus sollertiam exerceas tua[m]. meamq[ue]. devotione[m] utcumq[ue]. cognoscas. qua tuae bonae voluntati satisfacere me segnem non inveniri confido. Ne suspiceris autem me haec ideo elaborasse. quod vos putemus n[ost]ris indigere magisteriis. sed potius ob amore[m] dei tibi soli p[er]scrutinanda pinxisse amicabili fr[ater] natatis intuitu crede. Vale in xpo semp[er] memor n[ost] ri am[en]." "For thee, my sweetest son Gozbertus, have I drawn this briefly annotated copy of the layout of the monastic buildings, with which you may exercise your ingenuity and recognize my devotion, whereby I trust you do not find me slow to satisfy your wishes. Do not imagine that I have undertaken this task supposing you to stand in need of our instruction, but rather believe that out of love of God and in the friendly zeal of brotherhood I have depicted this for you alone to scrutinize. Farewell in Christ, always mindful of us, Amen." Horn and Born, *Plan of St. Gall*, 9.

44. There has been disagreement about this point; see Eric Fernie, *Romanesque Architecture: The First Style of the European Age* (New Haven: Yale University Press, 2014), 35–36.

45. Adalbert de Vogüé, "Le plan de Saint-Gall, copie d'un document officiel," *Revue Bénédictine* 94 (1984): 295–314.

46. "Quod ut facile clarescat; exempli causa linea vice pedis linearis in longum ducatur, eaque in quatuor lineares palmos hoc modo secetur." Gerbert, *Gerberti opera mathematica*, 57. Gerbert's life and work are discussed in more detail below.

47. Barnes, *Portfolio of Villard de Honnecourt*, 16–18.

48. The exegetical potential of architecture was recognized during the twelfth century and became a popular part of liturgical commentaries, for example in William Durand's work; see Guillaume Durand, *The* rationale divinorum officiorum *of William Durand of Mende: A New Translation of the Prologue and Book One*, trans. Timothy M. Thibodeau (New York: Columbia University Press, 2007). These liturgical commentaries provided historical and allegorical readings of the medieval church building as it appears in sermon literature; see Karl Kinsella, "Teaching through Architecture: Honorius Augustodunensis and the Medieval Church," in *Horizontal Learning in the High Middle Ages: Peer-to-Peer Knowledge Transfer in Religious Communities*, ed. Micol Long, Tjamke Snijders, and Steven Vanderputten (Amsterdam: Amsterdam University Press, 2019), 141–162.

49. R. W. Southern, *Platonism, Scholastic Method and the School of Chartres*, Stenton Lecture (Reading, UK: University of Reading, 1979), 7; Edward Grant, *Science and Religion, 400 B.C. to A.D. 1550: From Aristotle to Copernicus* (Westport, CT: Greenwood Press, 2004), 93–94.

50. "Sed quoniam facilius oculis subjecta retinentur, supradictarum formarum numerositas in subteriore descriptione ponatur." Boethius, *Anicii Manlii Severini Boethii: De Arithmetica*, ed. Heinrich Oosthout and Johann Schilling (Turnhout: Brepols, 1999), book 2, section 17. Boethius does not use *figura* in this example, but does so elsewhere; in fact, the power of the *descriptione* lies in its mnemonic ability, implied by the use of *retinentur*.

51. Even Saint Augustine, somewhat suspicious of pictures' pedagogical potential, recognized that sometimes it is simply easier to learn by looking at shapes: Augustine, *St. Augustine on Genesis: Two Books on Genesis against the Manichees; And, On the Literal Interpretation of Genesis, an Unfinished Book*, trans. Roland J. Teske, S.J., Fathers of the Church 84 (Washington, DC: Catholic University of America Press, 1991), 175.

52. "In hoc porro libro cum de statu agatur universae rei omniumque eorum quae mundus complectitur causa et ratio praestetur, necesse fuit multas et varias existere quaestiones: de planis figuris, de solidis corporibus, de incorporatione animae vivificantis sensibilem mundum, de motu eius et agitatione perpetua, de stellarium discursibus ratis et errantibus." Calcidius, *On Plato's Timaeus*, trans. John Magee (Cambridge, MA: Harvard University Press, 2016), 124–127.

53. "Perfecta porro corpora sunt solida quae ex tribus constant, longitudine latitudine crassitudine—prius epipedas, hoc est planas figuras, quae longititudine modo latitudine, nullam vero profunditatem habent." Calcidius, *On Plato's Timaeus*, 132–133.

54. Marco Zuccato, "Gerbert of Aurillac and a Tenth-Century Jewish Channel for the Transmission of Arabic Science to the West," *Speculum* 80 (2005): 745.

55. E. R. Truitt, "Celestial Divination and Arabic Science in Twelfth-Century England: The History of Gerbert of Aurillac's Talking Head," *Journal of the History of Ideas* 73 (2012): 201.

56. Gerbert, *Gerberti opera mathematica*, 56.

57. Gerbert, *Gerberti opera mathematica*, 64.

58. Saint Augustine of Hippo, *The Greatness of the Soul; The Teacher*, trans. J. M. Colleran (Westminster, MD: Newman Press; London: Longmans Green, 1950).

59. John North, "Diagram and Thought in Medieval Science," in *Villard's Legacy: Studies in Medieval Technology, Science, and Art in Memory of Jean Gimpel*, ed. Marie-Thérèse Zenner (Farnham, UK: Ashgate, 2004), 271.

60. Augustine, *Greatness of the Soul*, 26.

61. Augustine, *Greatness of the Soul*, 26.

62. *Spatio* is most commonly associated with geometry in the Middle Ages. See Edith Dudley Sylla, "Physics," in *Medieval Latin: An Introduction and Bibliographical Guide*, ed. F. A. C. Mantello and A. C. Rigg (Washington, DC: Catholic University of America Press, 1996), 358.

63. Colleran's edition of Augustine's *The Greatness of the Soul* includes diagrams of triangles, circles, etc., although these do not appear in all manuscripts that contain the text.

64. Gerbert, *Gerberti opera mathematica*, tables I–IV.

65. "Figurae planae dicuntur, quae profunditate, id est altitudine, carentes in longitudine tantum latitudineque considerantur. Hae vero, si rationabiliter proponuntur, aut rectis lineis, quae Graece euthyae dicuntur, determinantur et angulatae sunt, appellanturque euthygrammae; aut curvis seu circumferentibus lineis, quas Graeci cyclicas sive elycoydas sive campellas vocant, includuntur, et rotundae sive oblongae sunt, et campylogrammae nominantur, vel certe utrisque, id est rectis et curvatis, componuntur, et partim angulatae, partim lunatae seu rotundae sunt, quod genus micton a Graecis dicitur." Gerbert, *Gerberti opera mathematica*, 64.

66. The concept of solid forms and their relationship with the formation of the world, as described in Calcidius's commentary, were discussed by Isidore of Seville. See John E. Murdoch, *Albums of Science: Antiquity and the Middle Ages* (New York: Scribner, 1984), 280–281, illustration 247.

67. "Quod a quolibet facilius poterit intelligi, quam in plano de[s]cribi." Gerbert, *Gerberti opera mathematica*, 57.

68. Samuel Y. Edgerton, *The Renaissance Rediscovery of Linear Perspective* (New York: Basic Books, 1975).

69. Megan C. McNamee, "Imaging and Imagining Solidity," in *After the Carolingians: Re-defining Manuscript Illumination in the 10th and 11th Centuries*, ed. Beatrice Kitzinger and Joshua O'Driscoll (Berlin: de Gruyter, 2019), 86–117.

70. Quoted in McNamee, "Imaging and Imagining Solidity," 104. The matter is also touched upon in Megan C. McNamee, "Picturing as Practice: Placing a Square above a Square in the Central Middle Ages," in *Canonical Texts and Scholarly Practices: A Global Comparative Approach*, ed. Anthony Grafton and Glenn W. Most (Cambridge: Cambridge University Press, 2016), 200–223.

71. Murdoch, *Albums of Science*, 280.

72. I have argued this elsewhere; see Karl Kinsella, "Richard of St. Victor's Solutions to Problems of Architectural Representation in the Twelfth Century," *Architectural History* 59 (2016): 3–20.

73. Lewis Carroll, *Sylvie and Bruno Concluded* (London: Macmillan, 1893), 168–169.

74. "Tamen vel quantum de illo medio centenario ab Occidente secundum rationem plani tumor montis detraxerit," and "Sed plane quod secundum planum locus non habuit, ei ex tumore montis accrevit." PL 196.587B.

75. "Sed quia difficile, seu etiam impossibile est longitudinem, et latitudinem, et altitudinem aedificiorum in plano sub eadem figura repraesentare, sufficere arbitror omnium horum quae diximus, situm, locumque conformasse, et lineis proportionalibus ductis omnium eorum quasi quoddam fundamentum jecisse." PL 196.549B.

76. This problem would be overcome at the beginning of the thirteenth century when Villard de Honnecourt's

portfolio illustrates details from the vaulting of a space, such as the bosses and arches.

77. “Primo itaque consideremus, quot cubitos interius atrium ab Oriente in Occidentem secundum considerationem plani habeat, quod superficietenus in omnem partem absque omni ambiguo centum cubitorum erat.” PL 196.573D.

78. “Hoc tamen secundum plane superficiei considerationem dictum sit, nam ad hanc mensuram tumor montis nonnihil adjecit, de quibus in loco suo diligentius considerare oportebit.” PL 196.39B. In this instance, *plane superficiei* is a genitive construction where *plane* acts as an adjective modifying *superficiei.* The only other occurrence of *planum* acting in this manner is Richard’s description of a flat roof.

79. “Plana superficies dicitur quae aequaliter in rectis suis lineis continetur.” PL 63.1307B.

80. Euclid and Adelard of Bath, *The First Latin Translation of Euclid’s Elements Commonly Ascribed to Adelard of Bath: Books I–VIII and Books X.36–XV.2*, ed. H. L. L. Busard (Toronto: Pontifical Institute of Mediaeval Studies, 1983).

81. “Superficies plana est ab una linea ad aliam extensio, in extremitates suas eas recipiens.” Euclid and Adelard of Bath, *First Latin Translation of Euclid’s Elements*, 32.

82. Dale Coulter, *Per visibilia ad invisibilia: Theological Method in Richard of St. Victor (d. 1173)* (Turnhout: Brepols, 2006), 70.

83. Walter Cahn, “Architecture and Exegesis: Richard of St.-Victor’s Ezekiel Commentary and Its Illustrations,” *Art Bulletin* 76, no. 1 (1994): 59; Catherine Delano-Smith, “The Exegetical Jerusalem: Maps and Plans for Ezekiel Chapters 40–48,” in *Imagining Jerusalem in the Medieval West*, ed. Lucy Donkin and Hanna Vorholt (Oxford: Oxford University Press, 2012), 48–49.

84. Because Richard’s description of this section is so precise, I quote the entire original text: “Protrahatur cujuslibet magnitudinis linea in quinque aequas sectiones divisa, et ad singulas sectiones singulis litteris insignita. Sitque linea jacens A B C D E F. Supra hanc ad quartam sectionem, id est, super E alia linea erigatur, ita ut in nullam partem pronior inclinetur, sed hinc inde rectos, et adinvicem pares angulos efficiat, et tres mensuras praedictis sectionibus singulas singulis aequales contineat. Sitque linea super E erecta E G H K. Protrahatur adhuc tertia linea de A in K oblique elevata. Hoc itaque facto accepto circino, si primam et tertiam lineam, id est, A F et A K aequales inveneris, assertionis nostrae fidem proprio experimento tenebis. Ponatur itaque ut unaquaeque sectio sit viginti cubitorum. Erit ergo A F, id est, prima linea cubitorum centum, et A K ejus videlicet aequalis, id est, tertia linea erit totidem cubitorum. Linea vero erecta, id est, E K, habebit cubitos sexaginta. Atrium igitur, quemadmodum dictum est, quod octoginta cubitos habuit in base, et centum cubitos in superficie absque dubio sexaginta cubitis elevatior fuit in eminentiori parte, cujus rei formam manifeste habes in triangulo A K E. Hujus autem trianguli basim, id est, lineam jacentem, ejus quae hypotemisam, id est, lineam inclinatam si quantumlibet protraxeris, et eis cathetum, id est, lineam orthogonaliter erectam applicaveris, cujuscunque magnitudinis triangulos effeceris, tres ejus lineas eadem sibi semper proportione respondere videbis. Nam semper erit hypotemisa ad basim sexquiquarta, et basis ad cathetum sexquitertia.” PL 196.575C–D.

85. Vitruvius, *On Architecture*, trans. Rowland and Howe, 24–27.

86. Pacey, *Medieval Architectural Drawing*, 161.

87. Hugh, *Practical Geometry*, 34. Underlining this conformity is the presence of pin holes at the center of the circles in the Bodleian manuscripts of the text, implying that compasses were used to create the circles.

88. Hugh, *Practical Geometry*, 34.

89. Hugh, *Practical Geometry*, 35. Hugh also states that there is much more to be said on the subject of triangles, but suggests he would write about it elsewhere. No further work exists on the topic, however.

90. Paris, BnF, MS lat. 7185.

91. Euclid, prop. 47, *The Thirteen Books of Euclid’s Elements*, trans. Thomas L. Heath (New York: Dover, 1956), 349. In algebraic terms: $a^2+b^2=c^2$.

92. Following the above equation, we see that $80^2 + 60^2 = 100^2$.

93. Hugh uses the same phrase, *secundum planam*, in his discussion of the triangle; cf. Hugh of Saint Victor,

Opera propaedeutica: Practica geometriae, De grammatica, Epitome Dindimi in philosophicum, ed. Roger Baron (Notre Dame: University of Notre Dame Press, 1966), 32.

94. CCCC MS 315 uses the term "presentio" and not "representatio" for the two gatehouse elevations, suggesting the copyist had a deficient version of the drawings.

95. Barnes, *Portfolio of Villard de Honnecourt*, 17.

96. Barnes, *Portfolio of Villard de Honnecourt*, 19.

97. For example, in Bodl. 494, the last plan of the gatehouse appears on folio 139v, but the front and lateral elevations do not appear until folios 155v and 156r.

98. The enumeration of the northern gatehouse's measurements appears in the previous chapter.

99. The "outer part" refers to the side not facing the inner courtyards, and appears on the left side of the lateral elevation; the inner part appears on the right.

100. "A tecto autem thalami, id est, a pavimento coenaculi usque ad tectum portae fuerunt, ut legitur, cubiti viginti quinque. Jungantur isti viginti quinque superioribus, et quadraginta habemus. His omnibus et adhuc supra tectum ipsius portae quasi ad propugnacula facienda quinque cubitos adjicimus, et sic quadraginta quinque cubitos altitudinis ab interiori parte implemus. Erat autem, ut superius dictum est, quadraginta quinque cubitis demissior in exteriori latere, et secundum hoc tota ejus altitudo ab exteriori parte videtur in nonaginta cubitos consurgere." PL 196.576C–D.

101. The *titulus* reads "devexitas montis in ea parte in qua habet porticum triplicem" (The slope of the mountain in each part on which it has a triple gateway).

102. Walter Cahn, "Architectural Draftsmanship in Twelfth-Century Paris: The Illustration of Richard of Saint-Victor's Commentary on Ezekiel's Temple Vision," *Gesta* 15, nos. 1–2 (1976): 250. Cahn seems to misunderstand this section, as he does not understand why Richard has placed the steps inside the building, although Richard clearly states that there are two sets of steps. The more pertinent question is why Richard omits the exterior steps from his frontal elevation. "Hinc est, quod de australi portico exterior legitur: Et in gradibus septem ascendebatur ad eam; et item australi interior: Et octo gradus errant quibus ascendebatur per eam. [Here is what is read about the southern exterior gate: There were seven steps ascending to it; and likewise to the southern interior side: and there were eight steps through which they ascended through it.]" PL 196.535B.

103. Starting from the outer side (i.e., the left) and moving upward toward the inner side (i.e., moving right), these tituli read: *vestibulum. viii. cub*; *sicut primi thalami*; *v. cubita inter thalami*; *situs secundi thalami*; *v. cubiti inter thalami*; *situs tertii thalami*; *vestibulum. viii. cubitorum*. These *tituli* are consistently represented across the Oxford manuscripts, and appear in Paris, BnF, MS lat. 14519.

104. "Ab hinc sursum cenaculum primum ab exteriori latere."

105. "Tabulatum cenaculi et erat pro recto thalami," and "mensus est porta ab tecto thalami usque ad tectum eius xxv. Cubitorum."

106. "Tectum totius porticus."

107. "Representatio porticus quasi a latere videretur." The scribe of this *titulus* seems to have slightly confused the matter: there is no space between the *a* and *l* of *a latere*, and it was originally rendered *altere*, but a corrector added the necessary *a* at a later stage.

Chapter 6

1. Ez 40:48–49, 41:1–5.

2. Ez 41:1–2.

3. "Trabes itaque de parietibus proeminebat, et latera supportabant; sed idcirco tabulata quae super ipsas fundata erant non usquequaque usque ad parietem pertingebant." PL 196.584A.

4. "Et introduxit me in vestibulum templi et mensus est vestibulum quinque cubitis hinc et quinque cubitis inde." PL 196.579D. The sentence overlaps with Ez 41:1–2.

5. Ez 42:2.

6. "Quibusdam gradibus ejus ostia descenderetur." PL 196.592D.

7. Richard's discussion of the door and its placement is in chapter two of *In visionem Ezechielis*.

8. "Quod igitur superius legimus, quia terra usque ad fenestras erat: de fenestris primi coenaculi intelligere debemus," PL 196.592D.

9. "Videtur itaque mihi longitudo ejus ab anteriori parte sub basi altaris incipere, et

usque post tergum altaris se extendere, ita ut sanguinem qui ad basim fundebatur, excipere posset, et post tergum altaris quasi ad extrahendos influentes cineres pateret." PL 196.598B.

10. "In Scriptura sacra primum locum tenet historia." PL 196.199D.

11. "Et tunc, ut eis videtur, spiritualis intelligentiae structura firmius statuitur quando in historici sensus solido apte fundatur." PL 196.527B.

12. The use of this architectural metaphor is common for authors influenced by twelfth-century Victorine exegesis; see Henri de Lubac, *Medieval Exegesis: The Four Senses of Scripture*, trans. E. M. Macierowski, 3 vols. (Edinburgh: T & T Clark, 1998), 2:49.

13. Hugh of Saint-Victor, *The "Didascalicon" of Hugh of St. Victor: A Medieval Guide to the Arts*, trans. Jerome Taylor (New York: Columbia University Press, 1961), 135.

14. John Onians, "Architecture, Metaphor and the Mind," *Architectural History* 35 (1992): 192–207.

15. Stephen Murray, *Plotting Gothic* (Chicago: University of Chicago Press, 2014), 48.

16. Valerie Flint, "Heinricus of Augsburg and Honorius Augustodunensis: Are They the Same Person?," *Revue Bénédictine* 92, nos. 1–2 (1982): 151. Honorius is known for his use of visual exegesis in one of his commentaries on the Song of Songs; see Michael Curschmann, "Imagined Exegesis: Text and Picture in the Exegetical Works of Rupert of Deutz, Honorius Augustodunensis, and Gerhoch of Reichensberg," *Traditio* 44 (1988): 145–169. *In visionem Ezechielis* and Honorius's second commentary on the Song of Songs are bound together in one instance; see Troyes, Médiathèque de l'Aggolomération Troyenne, MS 544.

17. "Scandalizantur itaque saepe potius quam aedificentur, qui ejusmodi sunt, cum hujusmodi Scripturarum loca incurrunt." PL 196.527B.

18. For a broader discussion on the subject, see de Lubac, *Medieval Exegesis*, 2:49.

19. "Sed inertiae suae ejusmodi velamen habentes, otio torpent et aliorum industriam in veritatis investigatione et inventione derident, subsannant, exsufflant. Sed qui habitat in coelis irridebit eos, et Dominus subsannabit eos." PL 196.527C–D.

20. "Et hoc quidem verum, sed secundum eam acceptionem, quam ipse ibi assignavit; nam si eamdem de qua hoc dicit litteram velimus secundum aliam acceptionem discutere, fortassis, etiam juxta historicum sensum, ex ipsa poterimus congruum intellectum eruere." PL 196.527D–528A.

21. "Quibus uerbis quid aperte indicat, nisi quia nihil de ciuitate quam uiderat iuxta litteram dicat? Nam spiritaliter de ea loquitur quam spiritaliter contemplator." Gregory the Great, *Homiliae in Hiezechihelem prophetam* (Turnhout: Brepols, 1971), 209.

22. Beryl Smalley, *The Study of the Bible in the Middle Ages* (Oxford: Blackwell, 1983), 92–95.

23. Underlining the lack of commentaries up to the twelfth century, at that time a compendium of glosses applied to every part of the Bible was published in sections. Called the *Glossa ordinaria*, it contains a very narrow range of authors for the commentaries on the book of Ezekiel. For a modern facsimile of the *Glossa ordinaria*, see *Biblia latina cum Glossa ordinaria: Facsimile Reprint of the Editio Princeps*, ed. Karlfried Froehlich, Margaret Gibson, and Adolph Rusch (Turnhout: Brepols, 1992). For a discussion of the Gloss's history, see Lesley Smith, *The Glossa Ordinaria: The Making of a Medieval Bible Commentary* (Leiden: Brill, 2009).

24. Hugh of Saint Victor, *Didascalicon*, 136.

25. For a broad discussion of Lubac's theories on this issue, see Duncan Robertson, *Lectio Divina: The Medieval Experience of Reading* (Collegeville, MN: Cistercian Publications, 2011), 19–20.

26. Isidore of Seville, *The Etymologies of Isidore of Seville*, trans. Stephen A. Barney et al. (Cambridge: Cambridge University Press, 2006), 67.

27. Suzanne Fleischman, "On the Representation of History and Fiction in the Middle Ages," *History and Theory* 22 (1983): 278–310.

28. Jan van Zwieten, "The Place and Significance of Literal Exegesis in Hugh of St. Victor: An Analysis of His Notes on the Pentateuch, the Book of Judges and the Four Books of Kings" (PhD diss., Universiteit van Amsterdam, 1992), 10. The liberal arts, trivium, and quadrivium are discussed in the introduction.

29. Michael A. Signer, "*Peshat*, *Sensus Litteralis*, and Sequential Narrative: Jewish Exegesis and the School of

St. Victor in the Twelfth Century," in *The Frank Talmage Memorial Volume*, ed. Barry Walfish (Haifa: Haifa University Press, 1993), 208.

30. Dale Coulter, *Per visibilia ad invisibilia: Theological Method in Richard of St. Victor (d. 1173)* (Turnhout: Brepols, 2006), 69.

31. Coulter, *Per visibilia*, 107.

32. "Nomine enim portae aliquando designamus ipsum ostium quod aperitur et clauditur. Aliquando ipsum hiatum seu aditum per quem transitur. Aliquando ipsum ambitum quo hiatus ipse cingitur, ea videlicet pars muri quae ostium amplectitur, et reliquo parieti in materia vel forma ornatus causa dissimilis et supereminens cernitur." PL 196.580D–581A.

33. Richard of Saint Victor, *Liber exceptionum: Texte critique avec introduction, notes et tables*, edited by Jean Châtillon (Paris: J. Vrin, 1958), 103.

34. Richard, *Liber exceptionum*, 103.

35. Richard, *Liber exceptionum*, 103.

36. Richard, *Liber exceptionum*, 114.

37. Richard, *Liber exceptionum*, 116.

38. Richard, *Liber exceptionum*, 116.

39. Richard, *Liber exceptionum*, 129.

40. Signer, "*Peshat*," 205.

41. "Hujusmodi viam gradibus ascendentem, et se in gyrum flectentem videmus quotidie in ascensionibus turrium, vel ejusmodi sublimium aedificiorum." PL 196.584B.

42. "De fenestris primi coenaculi intelligere debemus, ita ut quibusdam gradibus ejus ostia descenderetur, quemadmodum in cellariis videmus." PL 196.592D.

43. Murray, *Plotting Gothic*, 48.

44. Mary Carruthers, *The Craft of Thought: Meditation, Rhetoric, and the Making of Images, 400–1200* (Cambridge: Cambridge University Press, 1998), 239.

45. Alexander Nagel and Christopher S. Wood, "Toward a New Model of Renaissance Anachronism," *Art Bulletin* 87 (2005): 403–415. See also Nagel and Wood, *Anachronic Renaissance* (New York: Zone Books, 2010), as well as a special issue of the *Art Bulletin* in response to Nagel and Wood's 2005 essay: Charles Dempsey, "Response: Historia and Anachronism in Renaissance Art," *Art Bulletin* 87 (2005): 416–421.

Chapter 7

1. The map appears in Cambridge, Corpus Christi College, MS 315, f. 113r; Oxford, Bodleian Library, MS Bodl. 459 and MS Bodl. 494; Paris, BnF, MS Lat. 2165, MS Lat. 3438, MS Lat. 3848, and MS Lat. 16702; MS Nouv. Acq. Lat. 1791; Troyes, Médiathèque de l'Aggolomération Troyenne, MS 544; Vatican City, Biblioteca Apostolica Vaticana, MS Vat. Lat. 1053 and MS Vat. Lat. 13014.

2. Cubits are not given in either the map or by Ezekiel in his description of the Promised Land. I am writing the measurements as cubits to keep them consistent with the measurements in the architectural drawings.

3. Guibert of Nogent, *A Monk's Confession: The Memoirs of Guibert of Nogent*, trans. Paul Archambault (Toronto: Toronto University Press, 1996), 111. Robert Chazan, *God, Humanity, and History: The Hebrew First Crusade Narratives* (Berkeley: University of California Press, 2000), 84–85. See also H. H. Ben-Sasson, *A History of the Jewish People* (London: Kegan Paul, 1976), 462.

4. William C. Jordan, *The French Monarchy and the Jews: From Philip Augustus to the Last Capetians* (Philadelphia: University of Pennsylvania Press, 1989), 9.

5. Robert Chazan, *European Jewry and the First Crusade* (Berkeley: University of California Press, 1987), 202.

6. Beryl Smalley, *Hebrew Scholarship among the Christians in Thirteenth Century England: As Illustrated by Some Hebrew-Latin Psalters* (London: Shapiro, Vallentine, 1939), 1.

7. Beryl Smalley, *Study of the Bible in the Middle Ages* (Oxford: Blackwell, 1983), 102.

8. Jan van Zwieten, "The Place and Significance of Literal Exegesis in Hugh of St. Victor: An Analysis of His Notes on the Pentateuch, the Book of Judges and the Four Books of Kings" (PhD diss., Universiteit van Amsterdam, 1992), 11.

9. Mayer I. Gruber, *Rashi's Commentary on the Psalms 1–89 (Books I–III)* (Atlanta: Scholars Press, 1998), 11.

10. Herman Hailperin, *Rashi and the Christian Scholars* (Pittsburgh: University of Pittsburgh Press, 1963), 31.

11. Michael A. Signer, "*Peshat*, *Sensus Litteralis*, and Sequential Narrative: Jewish Exegesis and the School of St. Victor in the Twelfth Century," in *The Frank Talmage*

Memorial Volume, ed. Barry Walfish (Haifa: Haifa University Press, 1993), 203.

12. Avraham Grossman, "The School of Literal Jewish Exegesis in Northern France," in *Hebrew Bible / Old Testament: The History of Its Interpretation*, vol. 1, ed. Magne Sæbø et al. (Göttingen: Vandenhoeck & Ruprecht, 1996), 321.

13. G. Hadfield, "Andrew of St. Victor, a Twelfth Century Hebraist: An Investigation of His Works and Sources" (DPhil thesis, University of Oxford, 1971).

14. Grossman, "The School of Literal Jewish Exegesis," 346.

15. Richard of Saint Victor, *De Emmanuele*, PL 196.601.

16. See J. W. M. van Zwieten, "Jewish Exegesis within Christian Bounds: Richard of St. Victor's *De Emmanuele* and Victorine Hermeneutics," *Bijdragen* 48 (1987): 326–352.

17. Van Zwieten, "Jewish Exegesis," 326–335.

18. J. Greenberg, *Foreign Words in the Bible Commentary of Rashi* (Jerusalem: J. Greenberg, 1988).

19. "I would say that it was a circular platform 'like the one about which we taught: it was smooth at first and they surrounded it with a gallery; And on that platform were the chambers. And from what is said about the pavement 'by the side of the gates' and that its lowest part was facing the height of the gates we can deduce that this pavement was a platform." Rashi, *Rashi's Commentary on Ezekiel 40–48*, ed. A. F. Levy (Philadelphia: Dropsie College for Hebrew and Cognate Learning, 1931), 71. Thanks are due to Dr. Joanna Weinberg for her translation.

20. Rashi, *Rashi's Commentary*.

21. Hailperin, *Rashi and the Christian Scholars*, 37.

22. Hailperin, *Rashi and the Christian Scholars*, 38.

23. The representation of the southern city in the Berlin manuscript is unclear, because the city is represented as proportionally much larger than it is in the other copies, and there is no boundary line to the west.

24. Ez 48:30–35.

Afterword

1. John de Garlande, *The Dictionary of John de Garlande*, trans. B. B. Rubin (Lawrence, KS: Coronado Press, 1981). Useful dictionaries include Judith Olszowy-Schlanger, ed., *Dictionnaire hébreu-latin-français de la Bible hébraïque de l'abbaye de Ramsey* (Turnhout: Brepols, 2008).

2. Krey and Smith draw attention to Nicholas indebtedness to "Victorine authors," and highlight the need for a full study of the subject. Philip D. W. Krey and Lesley Smith, introduction to *Nicholas of Lyra: The Senses of Scripture*, ed. Krey and Smith (Leiden: Brill, 2000), 11.

3. Helen Rosenau, "The Architecture of Nicolaus de Lyra's Temple Illustrations and the Jewish Tradition," *Journal of Jewish Studies* 25 (1974): 301.

4. Michael A. Signer, "Vision and History: Nicholas of Lyra on the Prophet Ezechiel," in *Nicholas of Lyra: The Senses of Scripture*, ed. Philip D. W. Krey and Lesley Smith (Leiden: Brill, 2000), 169.

5. E. Sanford, "The Twelfth Century—Renaissance or Proto-Renaissance?," *Speculum* 26, no. 4 (1951): 643.

Bibliography

Primary Sources

Adomnán. *Adamnán's "De locis sanctis."* Translated by Denis Meehan. Dublin: Dublin Institute for Advanced Studies, 1983.

Alberti, Leon Battista. *On the Art of Building in Ten Books.* Translated by Joseph Rykwert, Neil Leach, and Robert Tavernor. Cambridge, MA: MIT Press, 1988.

Augustine, Saint. *City of God.* 7 vols. Cambridge, MA: Harvard University Press, 2014.

Augustine, Saint. *The Greatness of the Soul; The Teacher.* Translated by J. M. Colleran. Westminster, MD: Newman Press; London: Longmans Green, 1950.

Augustine, Saint. *On Christian Teaching.* Translated by R. P. H. Green. Oxford: Oxford University Press, 2008.

Augustine, Saint. *St. Augustine on Genesis: Two Books on Genesis against the Manichees; And, On the Literal Interpretation of Genesis, an Unfinished Book.* Translated by Roland J. Teske, S.J. Fathers of the Church 84. Washington, DC: Catholic University of America Press, 1991.

Bede. *On the Tabernacle.* Translated by Arthur G. Holder. Liverpool: Liverpool University Press, 1994.

Bede. *On the Temple.* Translated by Sean Connolly, introduction by Faith Wallis. Liverpool: Liverpool University Press, 1995.

Biblia latina cum glossa ordinaria: Facsimile Reprint of the Editio Princeps. Edited by Karlfried Froehlich, Margaret Gibson, and Adolph Rusch. Turnhout: Brepols, 1992.

Boethius. *Anicii Manlii Severini Boethii: De arithmetica.* Edited by Heinrich Oosthout and Johann Schilling. Turnhout: Brepols, 1999.

Boethius. *De institutione arithmetica libri duo, De institutione musica libri quinque, accedit Geometria quae fertur Boetii.* Edited by Godofredus Friedlein. Leipzig: B. G. Teubner, 1867.

Calcidius. *On Plato's Timaeus.* Translated by John Magee. Cambridge, MA: Harvard University Press, 2016.

Corpus agrimensorum romanorum. Edited by Carl Thulin. Leipzig: B. G. Teubner, 1913.

Dante Alighieri. *De vulgari eloquentia.* Translated by Steven Botterill. Cambridge: Cambridge University Press, 1996.

Dante Alighieri. *The Divine Comedy of Dante Alighieri.* Translated by Robert M. Durling, Ronald L. Martinez, and Robert Turner. 3 vols. Oxford: Oxford University Press, 2011.

Dictionnaire hébreu-latin-français de la Bible hébraïque de l'abbaye de Ramsey. Edited by Judith Olszowy-Schlanger. Turnhout: Brepols, 2008.
Durand, Guillaume. *The* rationale divinorum officiorum *of William Durand of Mende: A New Translation of the Prologue and Book One*. Translated by Timothy M. Thibodeau. New York: Columbia University Press, 2007.

Euclid. *The Thirteen Books of Euclid's Elements*. Translated by Thomas L. Heath. New York: Dover, 1956.
Euclid and Adelard of Bath. *The First Latin Translation of Euclid's Elements Commonly Ascribed to Adelard of Bath: Books I–VIII and Books X.36–XV.2*. Edited by H. L. L. Busard. Toronto: Pontifical Institute of Mediaeval Studies, 1983.

Garlande, John de. *The Dictionary of John de Garlande*. Translated by B. B. Rubin. Lawrence, KS: Coronado Press, 1981.
Gerbert of Aurillac. *Gerberti opera mathematica (972–1003)*. Edited by Nikolaï Bubnov. Hildesheim: G. Olms, 1963.
Gregory the Great. *Homiliae in Hiezechihelem prophetam*. Corpus Christianorum Series Latina 142. Turnhout: Brepols, 1971.
Guibert of Nogent. *A Monk's Confession: The Memoirs of Guibert of Nogent*. Translated by Paul Archambault. Toronto: Toronto University Press, 1996.

Honorius Augustodunensis. *Gemma animae*. In *Patrologia Latina*, edited by J.-P. Migne, 172:0541A–0738B. Paris: Garnier Frères, 1864.
Hugh of Saint Victor. *De arche Noe morali*. In *Patrologia Latina*, edited by J.-P. Migne, 176:626D–627A. Paris: Garnier Frères, 1864.
Hugh of Saint-Victor. *Didascalicon de studio legendi*, edited by Ch. H. Buttimer. Turnhout: Brepols, 2010.
Hugh of Saint Victor. *The "Didascalicon" of Hugo of St. Victor: A Medieval Guide to the Arts*. Translated by Jerome Taylor. New York: Columbia University Press, 1961.
Hugh of Saint-Victor. *Practical Geometry, Practica geometriae*. Translated by Frederick A. Homann. Milwaukee: Marquette University Press, 1991.
Hugh of Saint Victor. *Selected Spiritual Writings*. Translated by a Religious of C.S.M.V. London: Faber and Faber, 1962.

Isidore of Seville. *The Etymologies of Isidore of Seville*. Translated by Stephen A. Barney et al. Cambridge: Cambridge University Press, 2006.

Letters of Abelard and Heloise, The. Translated by Betty Radice. London: Penguin Books, 2003.
Life of Ceolfrid, The. Edited by Douglas Samuel Boutflower. Sunderland: Hill & Company, 1991.

Origen. *Homilies on Genesis and Exodus*. Translated by Ronald E. Heine. Washington, DC: Catholic University of America Press, 2002.

Patrologia Latina (PL). Edited by J.-P. Migne. 221 vols. Paris: Garnier Frères, 1844–1864.

Plommer, Hugh, ed. and trans. *Vitruvius and Later Roman Building Manuals*. Cambridge: Cambridge University Press, 1973.

Pseudo-Cicero. *Ad C. Herennium: De rationi dicendi*. Translated by Harry Caplan. Cambridge, MA: Harvard University Press, 1954.

Rashi. *Rashi's Commentary on Ezekiel 40–48*. Edited by A. F. Levy. Philadelphia: Dropsie College for Hebrew and Cognate Learning, 1931.

Reimbaldus. *Libellus de diversis ordinibus et professionibus qui sunt in aecclesia*. Translated by Giles Constable and Bernard Smith. Oxford: Clarendon Press, 2003.

Richard of Saint Victor. *De Emmanuele*. In *Patrologia Latina*, edited by J.-P. Migne, 196:601–666A. Paris: Garnier Frères, 1855.

Richard of Saint Victor. *In visionem Ezechielis*. In *Patrologia Latina*, edited by J.-P. Migne, 196:527A–600C. Paris: Garnier Frères, 1855.

Richard of Saint Victor. *Liber exceptionum: Texte critique avec introduction; notes et tables*. Edited by Jean Châtillon. Paris: J. Vrin, 1958.

Richard of Saint Victor. *On the Trinity*. Translated and commentary by Ruben Angelici. Cambridge: James Clarke, 2012.

Suger, Abbot. *Abbot Suger on the Abbey Church of St.-Denis and Its Art Treasures*. Translated by Erwin Panofsky. Princeton: Princeton University Press, 1979.

Theophilus. *The Various Arts: "De diversis artibus."* Oxford: Oxford University Press, 1986.

Vitruvius. *Ten Books on Architecture*. Edited and translated by Ingrid D. Rowland and Thomas Noble Howe. Cambridge: Cambridge University Press, 1999.

Secondary Sources

Ackerman, James S. "Villard de Honnecourt's Drawing of Reims Cathedral: A Study in Architectural Representation." *Artibus et Historiae* 18 (1997): 41–49.

Alonso Ruiz, Begoña, and Alfonso Jiménez Martín. *La traça de la iglesia de Sevilla*. Seville, Cabildo Metropolitano, 2009.

Anderson, Stanford. "Erinnerung in der Architektor—Memory in Architecture." *Daidalos* 58 (1995): 28–30.

Ascani, Valerio. *Il Trecento disegnato: Le basi progettuali dell'architettura gotica in Italia*. Rome: Viella, 1997.
Auerbach, Erich, and Ralph Manheim. "Figura." In *Scenes from the Drama of European Literature*, edited by Paolo Valesio, 11–76. Manchester: Manchester University Press, 1984.

Barbet-Massin, Dominque. "The Rite of Church Dedication in Early Medieval Ireland and the Dedication Scheme in the Angers Manuscript 477." *Peritia* 27 (2016): 11–30.
Barnes, Carl, Jr. *The Portfolio of Villard de Honnecourt: A New Critical Edition and Color Facsimile*. Farnham, UK: Ashgate, 2009.
Bechmann, Roland. *Villard de Honnecourt: La pensée technique au xiiie siècle et sa communication*. Paris: Picard, 1993.
Beltrami, Constanza. *Building a Crossing Tower: A Design for Rouen Cathedral of 1516*. London: Paul Holberton Publishing, 2016.
Ben-Sasson, H. H. *A History of the Jewish People*. London: Kegan Paul, 1976.
Bloch, Herbert. "A New Edition of the Marble Plan of Ancient Rome." *Journal of Roman Studies* 51 (1961): 143–152.
Böker, Johann Josef, et al. *Architektur der Gotik. Ulm und Donauraum: ein Bestandskatalog der mittelalterlichen Architekturzeichnungen aus Ulm, Schwaben und dem Donaugebiet*. Salzburg: Müry Salzmann, 2011.
Bork, Robert. *The Geometry of Creation: Architectural Drawing and the Dynamics of Gothic Design*. Farnham, UK: Ashgate, 2011.
Branner, Robert. "Villard de Honnecourt, Reims and the Origin of Gothic Architectural Drawing." *Gazette des Beaux-Arts* 61 (1961): 129–146.
Braunfels, W. *Monasteries of Western Europe: The Architecture of the Order*. London: Thames and Hudson, 1993.
Bucher, François. *Architector: The Lodge Books and Sketchbooks of Medieval Architects*. New York: Abaris Books, 1979.

Cahn, Walter. "Architectural Draftsmanship in Twelfth-Century Paris: The Illustration of Richard of Saint-Victor's Commentary on Ezekiel's Temple Vision." *Gesta* 15, nos. 1–2 (1976): 247–254.
Cahn, Walter. "Architecture and Exegesis: Richard of St.-Victor's Ezekiel Commentary and Its Illustrations." *Art Bulletin* 76, no. 1 (1994): 53–68.
Carpo, Mario. *Architecture in the Age of Printing: Orality, Writing, Typography, and Printed Images in the History of Architectural Theory*. Cambridge, MA: MIT Press, 2001.
Carroll, Lewis. *Lewis Carroll: Complete Illustrated Works*. London: CRW Publishing, 2010.
Carruthers, Mary. *The Book of Memory: A Study of Memory in Medieval Culture*. 2nd ed. Cambridge: Cambridge University Press, 2008.
Carruthers, Mary. *The Craft of Thought: Meditation, Rhetoric, and the Making of Images, 400–1200*. Cambridge: Cambridge University Press, 1998.

Carruthers, Mary. "The Poet as Master Builder: Composition and Locational Memory in the Middle Ages." *New Literary History* 24 (1993): 881–904.
Carruthers, Mary. *Rhetoric Beyond Words: Delight and Persuasion in the Arts of the Middle Ages*. Cambridge: Cambridge University Press, 2013.
Carruthers, Mary, and Jan M. Ziolkowski, editors. *The Medieval Craft of Memory: An Anthology of Texts and Pictures*. Philadelphia: University of Pennsylvania Press, 2004.
Châtillon, Jean. "Richard de Saint-Victor." In *Dictionnaire de spiritualité: Ascétique et mystique: Doctrine et histoire*, edited by Marcel Viller, 594–654. Paris: G. Beauchesne, 1937.
Chazan, Robert. *European Jewry and the First Crusade*. Berkeley: University of California Press, 1987.
Chazan, Robert. *God, Humanity, and History: The Hebrew First Crusade Narratives*. Berkeley: University of California Press, 2000.
Chazelle, Celia M. "Pictures, Books, and the Illiterate: Pope Gregory I's Letters to Serenus of Marseilles." *Word and Image* 6, no. 2 (1990): 138–153.
Chenu, Marie-Dominique. *Nature, Man, and Society in the Twelfth Century: Essays on New Theological Perspectives in the Latin West*. Edited and translated by Jerome Taylor and Lester K. Little. Toronto: University of Toronto Press, 1997.
Clagett, Marshall. "King Alfred and the Elements of Euclid." *Isis* 45 (1954): 269–277.
Clanchy, Michael. *Abelard: A Medieval Life*. Oxford: Blackwell, 1997.
Clarke, Howard B., and Angret Simms, eds. *The Comparative History of Urban Origins in Non-Roman Europe: Ireland, Wales, Denmark, Germany, Poland, and Russia from the Ninth to the Thirteenth Century*. BAR International Series 255. Oxford: B.A.R. Publishing, 1985.
Cleaver, L., and A. Worm. "The Septenarium Pictum or Rota Dominice Orationis Diagram: Combatting Vice through Prayer in the High Middle Ages." In *Ordinare il mondo: Diagrammi e simboli nelle pergamene di Vercelli*, edited by T. Leonardi and M. Rainini, 265–288. Milan: Vita e Pensiero, 2019.
Cohn, Norman. *Noah's Flood: The Genesis Story in Western Thought*. New Haven: Yale University Press, 1996.
Conant, Kenneth J. "The After-life of Vitruvius in the Middle Ages." *Journal of the Society of Architectural Historians* 27 (1968): 33–38.
Conant, Kenneth J. "The Original Buildings at the Holy Sepulchre in Jerusalem." *Speculum* 31 (1956): 1–48.
Cooper, Charlotte. "What Is Medieval Paratext?" *Marginalia* 19 (2015): 37–50.
Corbo, Virgilio C. *Il Santo Sepolcro di Gerusalemme: Aspetti archeologici dalle origini al periodo crociato*. Jerusalem: Franciscan Printing Press, 1981–1982.

Coüasnon, Charles. *The Church of the Holy Sepulchre in Jerusalem*. London: Oxford University Press for the British Academy, 1974.

Coulter, Dale. *Per visibilia ad invisibilia: Theological Method in Richard of St. Victor (d. 1173)*. Turnhout: Brepols, 2006.

Curschmann, Michael. "Imagined Exegesis: Text and Picture in the Exegetical Works of Rupert of Deutz, Honorius Augustodunensis, and Gerhoch of Reichensberg." *Traditio* 44 (1988): 145–169.

Davis-Weyer, Caecilia. *Early Medieval Art, 300–1150: Sources and Documents*. Toronto: University of Toronto Press, 1986.

Delano-Smith, Catherine. "The Exegetical Jerusalem: Maps and Plans for Ezekiel Chapters 40–48." In *Imagining Jerusalem in the Medieval West*, edited by Lucy Donkin and Hanna Vorholt, 41–75. Oxford: Oxford University Press, 2012.

Delano-Smith, Catherine, and Roger J. P. Kain. *English Maps: A History*. London: British Library, 1999.

Dempsey, Charles. "Response: Historia and Anachronism in Renaissance Art." *Art Bulletin* 87 (2005): 416–421.

Duggan, Lawrence G. "Was Art Really the 'Book of the Illiterate'?" In *Reading Images and Texts*, edited by Marielle Hageman and Marco Mostert, 63–107. Turnhout: Brepols, 2005.

Dumeige, Gervais, *Richard de Saint-Victor et l'idée chrétienne de l'amour*. Paris: Presses Universitaires de France, 1952.

Edgerton, Samuel Y. *The Renaissance Rediscovery of Linear Perspective*. New York: Basic Books, 1975.

Eisenman, Peter. *Written into the Void: Selected Writings, 1990–2004*. New Haven: Yale University Press, 2007.

Emery, Kent, Jr. "Richard of St. Victor." In *A Companion to Philosophy in the Middle Ages*, edited by Jorge J. E. Gracia and Timothy Noone, 588–594. Oxford: Blackwell, 2003.

Evans, Gillian. "Hugh of St. Victor on History and the Meaning of Things." *Studia Monastica* 25, no. 2 (1983): 223–234.

Evans, Robin. *Translations from Drawing to Building and Other Essays*. London: Architectural Association Publications, 1997.

Feiss, Hugh, and Juliet Mousseau, eds. *A Companion to the Abbey of Saint Victor in Paris*. Leiden: Brill, 2017.

Fernie, Eric. "The Proportions of the St. Gall Plan." *Art Bulletin* 60 (1978): 583–589.

Fernie, Eric. *Romanesque Architecture: The First Style of the European Age*. New Haven: Yale University Press, 2014.

Fleischman, Suzanne. "On the Representation of History and Fiction in the Middle Ages." *History and Theory* 22 (1983): 278–310.

Flint, Valerie. "Heinricus of Augsburg and Honorius Augustodunensis: Are They the Same Person?" *Revue Bénédictine* 92, nos. 1–2 (1982): 148–158.
Forty, Adrian. *Words and Buildings: A Vocabulary of Modern Architecture*. London: Thames and Hudson, 2004.
Frommel, Christoph Luitpold. "Reflections on the Early Architectural Drawings." In *The Renaissance from Brunelleschi to Michelangelo: The Representation of Architecture*, edited by Henry A. Millon and Vittorio Magnago Lampugnani, 101–120. London: Thames and Hudson, 1994.

Gerbino, Anthony, and Stephen Johnston, eds. *Compass and Rule: Architecture as Mathematical Practice in England, 1500–1750*. Oxford: Oxford University Press, 2009.
Geymonat, Mario. "Arithmetic and Geometry in Ancient Rome: Surveyors, Intellectuals, and Poets." *Nuncius* 24 (2009): 11–34.
Grabar, Oleg. *The Mediation of Ornament*. Princeton: Princeton University Press, 1992.
Grant, Edward. *Science and Religion, 400 B.C. to A.D. 1550: From Aristotle to Copernicus*. Westport, CT: Greenwood Press, 2004.
Green, William M. "Hugo of St. Victor: *De tribus maximus circumstantiis gestorum*." *Speculum* 18 (1943): 484–493.
Greenberg, J. *Foreign Words in the Bible Commentary of Rashi*. Jerusalem: J. Greenberg, 1988.
Grossman, Avraham. "The School of Literal Jewish Exegesis in Northern France." In *Hebrew Bible / Old Testament: The History of Its Interpretation*, vol. 1, edited by Magne Sæbø et al., 321–371. Göttingen: Vandenhoeck & Ruprecht, 1996.
Gruber, Mayer I. *Rashi's Commentary on the Psalms 1–89 (Books I–III)*. Atlanta: Scholars Press, 1998.

Hadfield, G. "Andrew of St. Victor, a Twelfth Century Hebraist: An Investigation of His Works and Sources." DPhil thesis, University of Oxford, 1971.
Hailperin, Herman. *Rashi and the Christian Scholars*. Pittsburgh: University of Pittsburgh Press, 1963.
Horn, Walter, and Ernest Born. *The Plan of St. Gall*. 3 vols. Berkeley: University of California Press, 1979.

Iozzelli, Fortunato. "Francesco d'Assisi 'Buon Samaritano' nella predicazione di Odo da Chateauroux." In *Litterae ex quibus nomen Dei componitur. Studi per l'ottantesimo compleanno di Giuseppe Avarucci*, edited by Alexander Horowski, 269–290. Rome: Istituto Storico dei Cappuccini, 2016.

Jocqué, Lucas, and Ludovicus Milis. *Liber Ordinis Sancti Victoris Parisiensis*. Turnhout: Brepols, 1984.

Johnson, David F. "A Program of Illumination in the Old English Illustrated Hexateuch: 'Visual Typology.'" In *The Old English Hexateuch: Aspects and Approaches*, edited by Rebecca Barnhouse and Benjamin C. Withers, 165–199. Kalamazoo, MI: Medieval Institute Publications, 2000.

Jordan, William C. *The French Monarchy and the Jews: From Philip Augustus to the Last Capetians*. Philadelphia: University of Pennsylvania Press, 1989.

Kidson, Peter. "Panofsky, Suger and St Denis." *Journal of the Warburg and Courtauld Institutes* 50 (1987): 1–17.

Kinsella, Karl. "Richard of St Victor's Solutions to Problems of Architectural Representation in the Twelfth Century." *Architectural History* 59 (2016): 1–22.

Kinsella, Karl. "Teaching through Architecture: Honorius Augustodunensis and the Medieval Church." In *Horizontal Learning in the High Middle Ages: Peer-to-Peer Knowledge Transfer in Religious Communities*, edited by Micol Long, Tjamke Snijders, and Steven Vanderputten, 141–162. Amsterdam: Amsterdam University Press, 2019.

Kleinbauer, Eugene W. "Pre-Carolingian Concepts of Architectural Planning." In *The Medieval Mediterranean: Cross-Cultural Contacts*, edited by Marilyn J. Chiat and Kathryn L. Reyerson, 67–79. St. Cloud, MN: North Star Press of St. Cloud, 1988.

Krinsky, Carol Herselle. "Seventy-Eight Vitruvius Manuscripts." *Journal of the Warburg and Courtauld Institutes* 30 (1967): 36–70.

Kühnel, Bianca. "Jewish Symbolism of the Temple and the Tabernacle and Christian Symbolism of the Holy Sepulchre and the Heavenly Jerusalem: A Study of Their Relationship in Late Antique and Early Medieval Art and Thought." *Jewish Art* 12–13 (1987): 147–168.

Lubac, Henri de. *Medieval Exegesis: The Four Senses of Scripture*. Translated by E. M. Macierowski. 3 vols. Edinburgh: T & T Clark, 1998.

Mallgrave, Harry Francis, ed. *Architectural Theory*. Oxford: Blackwell, 2006.

Marenbon, John. *The Philosophy of Peter Abelard*. Cambridge: Cambridge University Press, 1997.

McNamee, Megan C. "Imaging and Imagining Solidity." In *After the Carolingians: Re-defining Manuscript Illumination in the 10th and 11th Centuries*, edited by Beatrice Kitzinger and Joshua O'Driscoll, 86–117. Berlin: de Gruyter, 2019.

McNamee, Megan C. "Picturing as Practice: Placing a Square above a Square in the Central Middle Ages." In *Canonical Texts and Scholarly Practices: A Global Comparative Approach*, edited by Anthony Grafton and Glenn W. Most, 200–223. Cambridge: Cambridge University Press, 2016.

Meyvaert, Paul. "Bede, Cassiodorus, and the Codex Amiatinus." *Speculum* 71 (1996): 827–883.

Morris, Colin. *The Sepulchre of Christ and the Medieval West: From the Beginning to 1600*. Oxford: Oxford University Press, 2005.

Morrison, Tessa. "Architectural Planning in the Early Medieval Era." *Journal of the Australian Early Medieval Association* 5 (2009): 147–163.

Murdoch, John E. *Albums of Science: Antiquity and the Middle Ages*. New York: Scribner, 1984.

Murray, Stephen. *Plotting Gothic*. Chicago: University of Chicago Press, 2014.

Nagel, Alexander, and Christopher S. Wood. *Anachronic Renaissance*. New York: Zone Books, 2010.

Nagel, Alexander, and Christopher S. Wood. "Toward a New Model of Renaissance Anachronism." *Art Bulletin* 87 (2005): 403–415.

Nees, Lawrence. "The Colophon Drawing in the Book of Mulling: A Supposed Irish Monastery Plan and the Tradition of Terminal Illustration in Early Medieval Manuscripts." *Cambridge Medieval Celtic Studies* 5 (1983): 67–91.

Nees, Lawrence. "The Plan of St. Gall and the Theory of the Program of Carolingian Art." *Gesta* 25 (1986): 1–8.

O'Brien, Conor. "Tabernacle, Temple or Something in Between? Architectural Representation in Codex Amiatinus, fols. II^{v}–III^{v}." *Leeds Studies in English* 48 (2017): 7–20.

Obrist, Barbara. "Wind Diagrams and Medieval Cosmology." *Speculum* 72 (1997): 33–84.

O'Loughlin, Thomas. "Adomnan's Plans in the Context of His Imagining 'the Most Famous City.'" In *Imagining Jerusalem in the Medieval West*, edited by Lucy Donkin and Hanna Vorholt, 15–40. Oxford: Oxford University Press, 2012.

O'Loughlin, Thomas. "The Plan of the New Jerusalem in the Book of Armagh." *Cambrian Medieval Celtic Studies* 39 (2000): 23–38.

Onians, John. "Architecture, Metaphor and the Mind." *Architectural History* 35 (1992): 192–207.

Onians, John. *Bearers of Meaning: The Classical Orders in Antiquity, the Middle Ages, and the Renaissance*. Princeton: Princeton University Press, 1988.

Ousterhout, Robert. *Master Builders of Byzantium*. Princeton: Princeton University Press, 1999.

Pacey, Arnold. *Medieval Architectural Drawing: English Craftsmen's Methods and Their Later Persistence, 1200–1700*. Stroud: Tempus, 2007.

Panofsky, Erwin. *Gothic Architecture and Scholasticism*. Latrobe, PA: Archabbey Press, 1951.
Panofsky, Erwin. *Studies in Iconology: Humanistic Themes in the Art of the Renaissance*. New York: Harper & Row, 1972.
Pevsner, Nikolaus. "The Term 'Architect' in the Middle Ages." *Speculum* 17 (1942): 549–562.
Pevsner, Nikolaus. "Terms of Architectural Planning in the Middle Ages." *Journal of the Warburg and Courtauld Institutes* 5 (1942): 232–237.

Radding, Charles, and William Clark. *Medieval Architecture, Medieval Learning: Builders and Masters in the Age of Romanesque and Gothic*. New Haven: Yale University Press, 1992.
Reynolds, David West. "Forma Urbis Romae: The Severan Marble Plan and the Urban Form of Ancient Rome." PhD diss., University of Michigan, 1996.
Riahi, Pari. "Expanding the Boundaries of Architectural Representation." *Journal of Architecture* 22, no. 5 (2017): 815–824.
Robertson, Duncan. *Lectio Divina: The Medieval Experience of Reading*. Collegeville, MN: Cistercian Publications, 2011.
Rorem, Paul. *Hugh of Saint Victor*. Oxford: Oxford University Press, 2009.
Rosenau, Helen. "The Architecture of Nicolaus de Lyra's Temple Illustrations and the Jewish Tradition." *Journal of Jewish Studies* 25 (1974): 294–304.
Rosewell, Roger. *Medieval Wall Paintings in English and Welsh Churches*. Woodbridge: Boydell Press, 2008.
Rudolph, Conrad. "Bernard of Clairvaux's Apologia as a Description of Cluny, and the Controversy over Monastic Art." *Gesta* 27, nos. 1–2 (1988): 125–132.
Rudolph, Conrad. *First, I Find the Center Point: Reading the Text of Hugh of Saint Victor's "The Mystic Ark."* Philadelphia: American Philosophical Society, 2004.
Rudolph, Conrad. *The Mystic Ark: Hugh of Saint Victor, Art, and Thought in the Twelfth Century*. Cambridge: Cambridge University Press, 2014.

Sanderson, Warren. "The Plan of St. Gall Reconsidered." *Speculum* 60 (1985): 615–632.
Sanford, E. "The Twelfth Century—Renaissance or Proto-Renaissance?" *Speculum* 26, no. 4 (1951): 635–642.
Schatzberg, Eric. *Technology: Critical Reception of a Concept*. Chicago: University of Chicago Press, 2018.
Scolari, Massimo. *Massimo Scolari: The Representation of Architecture*. Milan: Skira; London: Thames & Hudson, 2012.
Shelby, Lon R. "The Geometrical Knowledge of Mediaeval Master Masons." *Speculum* 47 (1972): 395–421.

Signer, Michael A. "*Peshat, Sensus Litteralis*, and Sequential Narrative: Jewish Exegesis and the School of St. Victor in the Twelfth Century." In *The Frank Talmage Memorial Volume*, edited by Barry Walfish, 204–216. Haifa: Haifa University Press, 1993.
Signer, Michael A. "Vision and History: Nicholas of Lyra on the Prophet Ezechiel." In *Nicholas of Lyra: The Senses of Scripture*, edited by Philip D. W. Krey and Lesley Smith, 147–171. Leiden: Brill, 2000.
Smalley, Beryl. *Hebrew Scholarship among the Christians in Thirteenth Century England: As Illustrated by Some Hebrew-Latin Psalters*. London: Shapiro, Vallentine, 1939.
Smalley, Beryl. *The Study of the Bible in the Middle Ages*. Oxford: Blackwell, 1983.
Smith, Lesley. *The Glossa Ordinaria: The Making of a Medieval Bible Commentary*. Leiden: Brill, 2009.
Southern, R. W. *Platonism, Scholastic Method and the School of Chartres*. Reading, UK: University of Reading, 1979.
Späth, Markus. "Architectural Representation and Monastic Identity: The Medieval Seal Images of Christchurch, Canterbury." In *Image, Memory and Devotion: Liber Amicorum Paul Crossley*, edited by Zoë Opačić and Achim Timmerman, 255–263. Turnhout: Brepols, 2011.
Sylla, Edith Dudley. "Physics." In *Medieval Latin: An Introduction and Bibliographical Guide*, edited by F. A. C. Mantello and A. C. Rigg, 355–362. Washington, DC: Catholic University of America Press, 1996.

Taub, Liba. "The Historical Function of the 'Forma Urbis Romae.'" *Imago Mundi* 45 (1993): 9–19.
Taylor, Rabun. *Roman Builders: A Study in Architectural Process*. Cambridge: Cambridge University Press, 2003.
Tcherikover, Anat. "A Carolingian Lesson in Vitruvius." In *Medieval Architecture and Its Intellectual Context: Studies in Honour of Peter Kidson*, edited by Eric Fernie and Paul Crossley, 259–267. London: Hambledon, 1990.
Thomson, Rodney M. "Monastic and Cathedral Book Production." In *The Cambridge History of the Book in Britain*, edited by Nigel J. Morgan and Rodney M. Thomson, vol. 1. Cambridge: Cambridge University Press, 1999.
Truitt, E. R. "Celestial Divination and Arabic Science in Twelfth-Century England: The History of Gerbert of Aurillac's Talking Head." *Journal of the History of Ideas* 73 (2012): 201–222.
Turner, Jane, ed. *The Dictionary of Art*. New York: Oxford University Press, 1996.

Varnam, Laura. *The Church as Sacred Space in Middle English Literature and Culture*. Manchester: Manchester University Press, 2018.

Varnam, Laura. "'Synne to shewe, vs to frame': Representing the Church in Robert Mannyng's *Handlyng Synne*." *Leeds Studies in English* 48 (2017): 89–104.
Vogüé, Adalbert de. "Le plan de Saint-Gall, copie d'un document officiel." *Revue Bénédictine* 94 (1984): 295–314.

Wardhaugh, Benjamin. *The Book of Wonders: The Many Lives of Euclid's Elements*. London: William Collins, 2020.
Whyte, William. "Do Buildings Mean? Some Issues of Interpretation in the History of Architecture." *History and Theory* 45, no. 2 (2006): 153–177.
Wilkinson, John. *Jerusalem Pilgrims before the Crusades*. Oxford: Oxbow Books, 2002.
Wilson, Christopher. *The Gothic Cathedral: The Architecture of the Great Church*. London: Thames & Hudson, 2000.
Wirth, Jean. *Villard de Honnecourt: architecte du XIIIe siècle*. Geneva: Droz, 2015.
Wormald, Francis. "Bible Illustration in Medieval Manuscripts." In *The Cambridge History of the Bible*, edited by G. W. H. Lampe, 3:309–337. Cambridge: Cambridge University Press, 1969.

Zaitsev, Evgeny A. "The Meaning of Early Medieval Geometry: From Euclid and Surveyors' Manuals to Christian Philosophy." *Isis* 90 (1999): 522–553.
Zinn, Grover, Jr. "Hugh of St. Victor and the Ark of Noah: A New Look." *Church History* 40 (1971): 261–272.
Zinn, Grover, Jr. "Mandala Symbolism and Use in Mysticism of Hugh of St. Victor." *History of Religions* 12 (1973): 317–341.
Zuccato, Marco. "Gerbert of Aurillac and a Tenth-Century Jewish Channel for the Transmission of Arabic Science to the West." *Speculum* 80 (2005): 742–763.
Zwieten, Jan van. "Jewish Exegesis within Christian Bounds: Richard of St. Victor's *De Emmanuele* and Victorine Hermeneutics." *Bijdragen* 48 (1987): 326–352.
Zwieten, Jan van. "The Place and Significance of Literal Exegesis in Hugh of St. Victor: An Analysis of His Notes on the Pentateuch, the Book of Judges and the Four Books of Kings." PhD diss., Universiteit van Amsterdam, 1992.

Index

The MIT Press would like to thank the anonymous peer reviewers who provided comments on drafts of this book. The generous work of academic experts is essential for establishing the authority and quality of our publications. We acknowledge with gratitude the contributions of these otherwise uncredited readers.

This book was set in Haultin Normal by New Best-set Typesetters Ltd.
Printed and bound in Canada

Library of Congress Cataloging-in-Publication Data

Names: Kinsella, Karl, 1982- author.
Title: God's own language : architectural drawing in the twelfth century / Karl Kinsella.
Description: Cambridge : The MIT Press, [2023] | Includes bibliographical references and index.
Identifiers: LCCN 2022022397 | ISBN 9780262047746 (hardcover)
Subjects: LCSH: Richard, of St. Victor, -1173. In visionem Ezechielis. | Architectural drawing—History—To 1500. | Architecture and religion. | Symbolism in architecture.
Classification: LCC NA2707.R525 K56 2023 | DDC 720.28/40902—dc23/eng/20221011
LC record available at https://lccn.loc.gov/2022022397

10 9 8 7 6 5 4 3 2 1

Quinquaginta cubiti in suburbana.
Vulgi locus. quinquaginta cubitorum latitudinis
Murus exterior habens portam cum edificio supposito
unius cubiti latitudinis et altitudinis.